Understanding the Sacraments of Initiation

A Rite-Based Approach

RANDY STICE

Nihil Obstat
Reverend Daniel J. Smilanic, JCD
Vicar for Canonical Services
Archdiocese of Chicago
January 9, 2017

Imprimatur
Very Reverend Ronald A. Hicks
Vicar General
Archdiocese of Chicago
January 9, 2017

This book was edited by Kevin Thornton. Christian Rocha was the production editor, Anna Manhart was the designer, and Luis Leal was the production artist.

21 20 19 18 17 1 2 3 4 5

Printed in the United States of America.

Library of Congress Control Number: 2017930851

ISBN 978-1-61671-313-3

USI

Contents

FOREWORD

Perhaps your experience of preparing to receive the sacraments was different from mine. I hope it was. When it was all over, due to the folly of youth and poor catechesis, I was left thinking of the sacraments as quasimaterialistic "packages" of grace that I, the recipient, "get" when I go to Church.

While I didn't remember receiving grace (along with forgiveness of sin) at my Baptism as an infant, by the time I was in second grade, grace became tangible—even tasteable—in the Eucharist. More grace came my way at Confirmation, grace that "made me an adult" in the faith.

The inheritance of sacramental theology bequeathed by my after-school CCD program, while not untrue, lacks the richness and depth it ought to have had. "Sacraments," the *Catechism* says, "are 'powers that comes forth' from the Body of Christ, which is ever-living and life-giving" (1116). Far from being a kind of "supernatural vitamin," as my adolescent theology saw it, each sacrament's reality is Jesus himself—the key to life to the full, both here and hereafter.

Who knew? Not I.

As I say, your sacramental formation may have been different from the experience I describe here. If not—or even if so—Father Randy Stice's *Understanding the Sacraments of Initiation: A Rite-Based Approach* will aid you as a catechist—and those in your care—to see the brilliant truth and life-changing potential that the sacraments hold out for every member of the Body of Christ.

Sacraments are not abstractions; they are not lifeless; they are not impersonal forces; they are not irrelevant for everyday life. Nor are they some sort of inexplicable magic spell or conjuration that only the initiated could comprehend. On the contrary, sacraments are accessible and brim with life—with Christ—and make us sharers in the very divine life of the Trinity itself. They are "masterworks of God" (CCC, 1116) and meant to make those who receive them as alive and radiant as God himself.

Father Stice examines sacraments according to their foundations —which are also pastoral in their application. Three truths in particular help the sacraments come alive in *Understanding the Sacraments of*

Initiation: their Trinitarian source and goal, their ritual clothing, and their required catechesis of "mystagogy."

The Trinity, called the "most fundamental and essential teaching in the 'hierarchy of the truths of faith,'" is the beginning and end of history—that is, of world history or my own personal history. Sacraments are contextualized within this history, which is known as the Economy of Salvation, the story of the Trinity's work of creation and redemption. As the driving force of the Ark of the Church, the sacraments lead Peter's Barque safely back to its heavenly port. Should it not stand to reason, then, that the sacraments—and in particular those initiation sacraments of Baptism, Confirmation, and the Eucharist—can only be understood through the portal of the Trinity?

The point of access to this Trinitarian "portal" is the sacramental rite. A ritual is a tapestry of signs and symbols, words and actions, as well as images, music, and art. These tangible, sensible elements which comprise the rite are the privileged means by which we encounter Jesus today. And the beauty of this ritual approach to the sacraments is that the rite and its constituent parts are on display for all to see—they are not the sole possession of professional theologians, academics, or clergy.

Nonetheless, the sacraments do require—and reward—study. Each of the baptized needs a particular formation to see Christ in the rite, to access Trinitarian life through the sacraments. There is what Father Stice calls a "language of the sacraments"—much like there is a language of any other reality, such as medicine, parenting, or auto mechanics. Here is where "mystagogy," a third key concept, comes into play. For any attentive onlooker, the sacraments can be at least sensed: cool water is poured over the head, fragrant chrism is applied to the forehead, and Precious Blood is tasted under the form of wine. But there is more than meets the eye—or skin or tongue. With the help of Old Testament figures and events, "mystagogy" leads one from what one initially senses to the otherwise undetectable Christ.

Such a sacramental understanding as Father Stice presents here is securely focused on the Trinity, the rite, and mystagogy. For this reason, the book goes far in making sacraments more fruitful to those who receive them: our children, our Catholic school or CCD students, and ourselves. Lives can then be transformed—another emphasis of Father Stice's book—into masterpieces of holiness, as we are initiated into the company of the joyful saints. *Understanding the Sacraments of Initiation* will help you clarify for others and yourself that the Catholic sacraments are encounters between God the Father and his children in Christ through an unmerited and loving outpouring of the Holy Spirit.

Christopher Carstens
Director, Office of Sacred Worship
Diocese of Lacrosse, WI
Adjunct Faculty, University of St. Mary of the Lake,
Mundelein Seminary

Abbreviations

CB *Ceremonial of Bishops*

CCC *Catechism of the Catholic Church*

CIC *Code of Canon Law* (*Codex Iuris Canonici*) (Canon Law Society of America, 1998)

DC *Dominicae Cenae (The Mystery and Worship of the Eucharist),* St. John Paul II, 1980

DCA *Dedication of a Church and an Altar*

DCE *Deus Caritas Est (God Is Love),* Benedict XVI, 2005

DCN *Divinae Consortium Naturae (Apostolic Constitution on Confirmation),* Paul VI

DD *Dies Domini (On Keeping the Lord's Day Holy),* St. John Paul II, 1998

DiM *Dives in Misericordia (The Mercy of God),* St. John Paul II, 1980

EE *Ecclesia de Eucaristia (On the Eucharist in Its Relationship to the Church),* St. John Paul II, 2003

EG *Evangelii Gaudium (The Joy of the Gospel),* Pope Francis, 2013

EM *Eucharisticum Mysterium (Instruction on the Worship of the Eucharistic Mystery),* Vatican Council II

GICI *Christian Initiation,* General Introduction

GIRM *General Instruction of the Roman Missal*

IOM *Introduction to the Order of Mass,* USCCB

LF *Lumen Fidei (The Light of Faith),* Pope Francis, 2013

LG *Lumen Gentium (Dogmatic Constitution on the Church)* Vatican Council II

LM *Lectionary for Mass*

MC *Mystici Corporis (Mystical Body),* Pius XII, 1943

MND *Mane Nobiscum Domine (Stay with Us Lord),* St. John Paul II

MS *Musicam Sacram (Instruction on Music in the Liturgy),* Vatican Council II

NABRE *New American Bible, Revised Edition,* St. Joseph medium size ed. (New Jersey: Catholic Book Publishing, 2011)

NJB *New Jerusalem Bible* (New York: Doubleday, 1985)

NJBC *New Jerome Biblical Commentary,* ed. Raymond E. Brown, Joseph A. Fitzmyer, and Roland E. Murphy (Upper Saddle River, NJ: Prentice Hall, 1990)

OC *Order of Confirmation*

PO *Presbyterorum Ordinis (Decree on the Ministry and Life of Priests),* Vatican Council II

RaP *Reconciliation and Penance* St. John Paul II

RBC *Rite of Baptism for Children*

RM *The Roman Missal,* 3rd ed.

RO *Rite of Ordination*

RP *Rite of Penance*

RPont *The Roman Pontifical*

SacCar *Sacramentum Caritatis (The Sacrament of Charity),* Benedict XVI, 2007

SC *Sacrosanctum Concilium* (*Constitution on the Sacred Liturgy*), Vatican Council II

SL *Sing to the Lord,* USCCB

UR *Unitatis Redintegratio (Decree on Ecumenism),* Vatican Council II

VD *Verbum Domini (The Word of the Lord),* Benedict XVI, 2010

VL *Varietates Legitimae* (*Inculturation and the Roman Liturgy*)

VQA *Vicesimus Quintus Annus (Twenty-fifth Anniversary of the Second Vatican Council),* St. John Paul II

General Introduction

> "Behold, I am with you always, until the end of the age."
> Matthew 28:20

Before Jesus ascended to the Father, he promised the apostles that he would remain with them always. The seven sacraments of the Church—Baptism, Confirmation, the Eucharist, Penance and Reconciliation, Anointing of the Sick, Holy Orders, Matrimony—are the primary ways that Jesus continues to fulfill the promise of his abiding presence. An encounter with the Trinity is the way the *Catechism of the Catholic Church* describes the sacraments: "a sacramental celebration is a meeting of God's children with their Father, in Christ and the Holy Spirit" (CCC, 1153). While various approaches and disciplines such as history, sociology, anthropology, psychology, semiotics, and ritual can deepen our understanding and experience of the sacraments, these approaches are secondary and build on what is primary—the personal encounter with the Trinity.

This Trinitarian sacramental encounter is a "dialogue" that uses both "actions and words" that together constitute "a language" (CCC, 1153). Like any language, this sacramental language has its own vocabulary, grammar, and syntax that must be learned if one is to enter into the sacramental dialogue with the Father in Christ and the Holy Spirit. The aim of this book is to explore and master the language of the sacraments, looking in detail at the sacraments of initiation—Baptism, Confirmation, and the Eucharist—so that we can participate fully, consciously, and actively in this dialogue with the Trinity through the words and actions of the sacramental celebration.

Trinitarian

While Christ's institution of and action through the sacraments is rightly stressed, it is important to always remember and explore the Trinitarian dimension of the sacraments. "We are called to be a dwelling for the Most Holy Trinity: 'If a man loves me,' says the Lord, 'he will keep my word, and my Father will love him, and we will come to him, and make our home with him' [Jn 14:23]" (CCC, 260). The work of the Trinity in creation and salvation, what is known as "the divine economy," is performed jointly by the Three Divine Persons, although each Divine Person contributes to the common work "according to his unique personal property" (CCC, 258). If we don't affirm the distinction of the Persons we deny that God is a Trinity of Persons, and if we don't affirm the unity and commonality of the Three Persons' work, we profess three gods, not One. Throughout this volume I will delineate the activity of each Divine Person in the common work of the sacraments so that we can experience in our lives what the *Catechism* affirms, that "the whole Christian life is a communion with each of the divine persons, without in any way separating them" (CCC, 259).

Terminology

Throughout this work you will encounter references not only to the sacraments but also to the liturgy, to liturgical celebrations as well as sacramental celebrations. The terms *liturgy* and *sacrament* are overlapping but not synonymous. *Liturgy* as it is used in this book is the more inclusive term, referring to the official public worship of the Church for which there are official ritual books. It includes the seven sacraments, but also such celebrations as the blessings found in the *Book of Blessings*, the *Liturgy of the Hours*, and the *Rite of Christian Initiation for Adults*. *Sacrament* is a narrower term that refers just to the seven sacraments of the Church. Everything said of the liturgy or liturgical celebrations is true of the sacraments, but references to the sacraments or sacramental celebrations are not necessarily true of non-sacramental liturgical celebrations such as those taken from the *Book of Blessings* or the *Liturgy of the Hours*. The *Catechism*'s summary concisely characterizes the relationship between the liturgy and the sacraments: "The whole liturgical life of the Church revolves around the Eucharistic sacrifice and the sacraments" (CCC, 1113).

Rite-Based

As the title indicates, my approach in this volume is rite-based. The rite itself is always the best starting point, for these are the words we hear and say, the gestures and postures we adopt, and the signs and symbols that engage us. In addition, the liturgy is one of the primary ways that the Church has passed on the faith entrusted to her by the Lord. Christ has entrusted to the Church the responsibility of passing on "the faith in its integrity so that the 'rule of prayer' (*lex orandi*) of the church may correspond to the 'rule of faith' (*lex credendi*)" (VL, 27). In other words, "The law of prayer is the law of faith: the Church believes as she prays. Liturgy is a constitutive element of the holy and living Tradition" (CCC, 1124). The Church has always understood the inseparable relationship between her worship and her faith, and for this reason the sacramental rite is always the best starting point for understanding the meaning of the sacrament itself.

Sources

Since our approach is rite-based, our most important source will be the rite itself, which includes not only the words and actions of the rite but also the biblical readings for each of the sacraments. In addition, *The Roman Missal* contains ritual masses for the celebration of the sacraments within the Mass (with the exception of the Sacrament of Penance and Reconciliation), and these texts (e.g., prayers, prefaces, and solemn blessings) are also part of the sacramental rite. We will supplement the words and actions of the rite with selected other sources. The most frequently cited source is the *Catechism of the Catholic Church*, which St. John Paul II called "a sure and authentic reference text for teaching Catholic doctrine" and which he offered "to all the faithful who wish to deepen their knowledge of the unfathomable riches of salvation (cf. Eph 3:8)" (*Fidei Depositum*). Its presentation of the Catholic faith, illumined by Sacred Scripture, the writings of the saints, and the teaching of councils and popes, makes it a rich and invaluable source of information on the sacraments. Readers of this book are encouraged to have a copy of the *Catechism of the Catholic Church* at hand. It is also available online at the Vatican website. We will also make reference to the documents of the Second Vatican Council (1962–1965), which made the reform and restoration of the liturgy its first priority in the *Constitution on the Sacred Liturgy* (*Sacrosanctum Concilium*). These foundational documents will be supplemented by papal writings, including St. John Paul II's *On the Eucharist in Its Relationship to the Church (Ecclesia de Eucaristia)* and *Stay with Us, Lord* (*Mane Nobiscum Domine*) as well as Pope Benedict

XVI's apostolic exhortations *The Sacrament of Charity (Sacramentum Caritatis)* and *The Word of the Lord* (*Verbum Domini*). We will also have occasion to cite documents produced by Vatican congregations. Finally, we will also listen to the saints, especially the Church Fathers from the early centuries of the Church. We will also refer to works by contemporary theologians, liturgists, and historians.

As these sources suggest, we are not engaged in a speculative work of theology. We are not proposing a new theory of the sacraments. Rather, our goal is to listen—attentively and prayerfully—to the voice of Christ and his Church in order to deepen our sacramental encounter with the Trinity.

Methodology

In this book we are using a method of sacramental catechesis described by Pope Benedict XVI in his apostolic exhortation *The Sacrament of Charity* (*Sacramentum Caritatis*). This type of catechesis is called mystagogy, from the Greek word for the person who led the initiate into a mystery. Its goal is to lead people from the signs of the sacrament to the spiritual realities they signify. Pope Benedict XVI proposes looking at three aspects of a sacrament:

1. Old Testament origins of the sacrament
2. The meaning of the signs and symbols which comprise the sacrament
3. The meaning of the sacrament for the whole of one's life (living the sacrament)

We will examine in detail each of these three aspects of the Sacraments of Baptism, Confirmation, and the Eucharist by looking closely at the various elements of the rite and the different sources described above.

Organization

The book is divided into three parts. In part 1, we will briefly delve into an introduction to sacramental theology, consisting of chapters 1–3. Chapter 1 examines the different ways in which the Trinity is present in a sacramental celebration. Chapter 2 looks at the different sacramental signs that comprise the celebration. Chapter 3 introduces the method of mystagogical catechesis using examples from different sacraments to illustrate first the Old Testament roots, then the meaning of the sacramental signs and symbols, and finally the comprehensive transformative power of the sacraments as we live sacramental lives. While the focus of this book is on the sacraments of initiation, part 1 includes examples from the sacraments of vocation and healing as well as initiation in order to provide the reader with some catechesis on all seven sacraments, not just the Sacraments of Baptism, Confirmation, and the Eucharist.

Part 2 is a presentation of the Sacrament of Baptism. Chapter 4 traces the Old Testament origins of this sacrament, chapter 5 analyzes the signs and symbols of the sacrament, and chapter 6 explores the meaning of Baptism as a lived experience. Part 3 looks at the Sacrament of Confirmation, following the same structure as part 2: chapter 7 treats the Old Testament roots, chapter 8 examines the meaning of the constituent elements of the sacrament, and chapter 9 looks at the lived experience of the sacramental life. Part 4 examines the Sacrament of the Eucharist, following the same structure as parts 2 and 3: Old Testament roots (chapter 10), the meaning of the signs that comprise the sacrament (chapter 11), and the transforming power of the sacrament for the whole of life (chapter 12). Chapter 13 summarizes the unity of the sacraments of initiation.

Audience and Use / Activities

This book can be used by individuals as well as groups. It is primarily intended as a resource for those who are involved in preparing others for reception of the sacraments of initiation. It is also appropriate for some religious education classes, adult faith formation, diaconate programs, undergraduate sacraments classes, and even high school sacraments classes. To facilitate its use in class or group settings, this volume includes a number of activities that are intended to help the reader review and synthesize the material, explore a given topic in more detail (in some cases using the *Catechism of the Catholic Church*), and aid the reader in deepening his or her experience of the liturgy.

The Privileged Place for Encounter

Although we encounter God in many different ways, "the Liturgy is the privileged place for the encounter of Christians with God and the one whom he has sent, Jesus Christ" (cf. Jn 17:3)" (in VQA, 7). It is there that "all Christian prayer finds its source and goal. Through the liturgy the inner man is rooted and grounded in 'the great love with which [the Father] loved us' in his beloved Son. It is the same 'marvelous work of God' that is lived and internalized by all prayer,' at all times in the Spirit" (CCC, 1073). It is our hope that this work will assist the reader in participating in the celebration of the Sacraments of Baptism, Confirmation, and the Eucharist as privileged places of encounter with the Blessed Trinity, experiencing there the Father's love for us in Christ, poured into our hearts through the Holy Spirit.

PART I

Introduction to Sacramental Theology

This book is an introduction to the sacraments of initiation: Baptism, Confirmation, and Eucharist. However, before looking in detail at these three sacraments, we will first consider the nature and power of the sacraments in general. The first three chapters of this volume present a concise introduction to sacramental theology—What is a sacrament? How does God act through the sacraments? How do the sacraments affect our lives? How can we enter more fully into each sacramental celebration?

The Catechism of the Catholic Church describes a sacramental celebration as "a meeting of God's children with their Father, in Christ and the Holy Spirit" (CCC, 1153). This is the fundamental conviction of this book: the sacraments are encounters with the Father in Christ and the Holy Spirit—the Trinity. We will begin by examining in chapter 1 how the sacraments fulfill Christ's promise to his apostles to be with them always. We will look particularly at how each person of the Trinity—Father, Son, and Holy Spirit—is present and active in a sacramental celebration. We will give special attention to how the sacraments make present the Passion, Death, Resurrection, and Ascension of Christ and how they dispense divine life to us (CCC, 1131).

The focus of chapter 2 is on the meeting of God with his children in a sacramental celebration that "takes the form of a dialogue, through actions and words," that is, through signs that comprise a sacramental language (CCC, 1153). Here we will look at several signs which are common to many or all of the sacraments: signs such as images, song, the Sign of the Cross, movement, incense, and color. Our discussion of these different sacramental signs will focus on how they are "bearers of the saving and sanctifying action of Christ," how the Spirit acts through these signs to impart to us the power of Christ's saving sacrifice to the praise and glory of God the Father (CCC, 1189).

In order for us to participate fully and fruitfully in sacramental celebrations, we must approach them with faith and understanding. The final chapter of this section describes an approach to liturgical catechesis that helps us do that. It has three elements. It begins by looking at the Old Testament roots of the sacrament, revealing the unity and progressive fulfillment of God's saving work that culminates in the person and work of Jesus Christ. Next, it analyzes the meaning of the different liturgical signs that comprise each sacrament. Finally, it considers the way each sacrament transforms our lives. In chapter 3 we will describe this method of catechesis and illustrate it with examples from the sacraments of vocation (Holy Orders and Marriage) and the sacraments of healing (Penance and Reconciliation and Anointing of the Sick). Taken together, these first three chapters will give us the foundation and tools for a detailed study of the sacraments of initiation.

Chapter 1

The Sacraments: An Encounter with the Blessed Trinity

As Jesus was about to ascend to the Father, he gathered his disciples on the mountain. There he commanded them to "make disciples of all nations" and promised to be with them always: "And behold, I am with you always, until the end of the age" (Mt 28:19–20). Then "he parted from them and was taken up to heaven" (Lk 24:51). Luke tells us that the disciples experienced the Ascension with joy, not sadness: "they did him homage and then returned to Jerusalem with great joy" (Lk 24:52). Why were the disciples joyful at Jesus' departure? Because they had experienced Christ's new way of being with them. Christ's sacramental presence is beautifully expressed in his encounter with the two disciples on the road to Emmaus who do not recognize him (Lk 24:13–35). After an introductory conversation (vv. 13–24), "beginning with Moses and all the prophets, [Jesus] interpreted to them what referred to him in all the scriptures" (v. 27). The two disciples then invited him to stay with them, and they shared a meal. When Jesus was at table with them, "he took bread, said the blessing, broke it, and gave it to them" (v. 30)—these are Eucharistic actions. "With that their eyes were opened and they recognized him, but he vanished from their sight" (v. 31).

This account has the same structure as the Mass. It begins with the Liturgy of the Word—Jesus explaining to them how the Scriptures speak of him—and it concludes with the Liturgy of the Eucharist, when Jesus took bread which he blessed, broke, and gave to them. At that moment he vanished from their sight, because he was now present in the Eucharist. This is Luke's way of explaining Jesus' new way of being with his disciples—his presence is now a sacramental presence, manifested through sacramental signs, preeminently through the signs of bread and wine. The *Catechism* explains the reason for Christ's new way of being with his disciples: "In this age of the Church Christ now lives and acts in and with his Church, in a new way appropriate to this new age" (CCC, 1076). Christ the Head is now present in and acts powerfully through his Body the Church, which "is like a sacrament (sign and instrument) in which the Holy Spirit dispenses the mystery of salvation" (CCC, 1111). Christ continues to proclaim the Kingdom of God through words and deeds, just as he did during his earthly ministry, only the manner is different—bodily in the Gospels, now sacramentally through signs and symbols, words and actions, through his Body, the Church, in the liturgy. The *Catechism* explains how Christ acts through the sacraments by recalling healing miracles found in the Gospels in which power came forth from Jesus to heal the sick. On one occasion, for example, a crowd was trying to touch Jesus, "because power came forth from him and healed them all" (Lk 6:19). On another occasion, a woman who had been sick for twelve years touched the fringe of his garment and was healed. Jesus instantly knew what had happened. He told Peter, "Someone has touched me; for I know that *power has gone out* from me" (8:46, italics added). These events prefigure what Christ now accomplishes through the sacraments: "Sacraments are *'powers that come forth'* from the Body of Christ, which is ever-living and life-giving" (CCC, 1116, italics added). All that Jesus did during his earthly ministry he continues to do today through the sacraments—*sacramentally*—"by means of signs perceptible to the senses" (SC, 7).

The Paschal Mystery

There is a second reason why the disciples were joyful at his Ascension. Jesus was still with them and he had introduced a new presence and power into the world through his Paschal mystery. Christ's Paschal Mystery (from the Greek noun *pascha*, which means "Passover," and the Greek verb *paschō*, which means "to suffer") refers to "his blessed passion, resurrection from the dead, and glorious ascension, whereby 'dying, he destroyed our death, and rising, restored our life'" (SC, 5). The Paschal Mystery is unique among all historical events: while all other historical events happen and then pass away, the Paschal Mystery "cannot remain only in the past, because by his death he destroyed death, and all that Christ is—all that he did and suffered for all men—participates in the divine eternity, and so transcends all times while being made present in them all. The event of the Cross and Resurrection *abides* and draws everything toward life" (CCC, 1085). It is not just an event which we reverently remember, it is an ever-present reality "that the Church proclaims and celebrates in her liturgy so that the faithful may live from it and bear witness to it in the world" (CCC, 1068). It constitutes, wrote St. John Paul II, "the content of the daily life of the Church" (VQA, 6).

There is an integral connection between Jesus' earthly ministry and his Paschal Mystery. His words and actions during his earthly ministry anticipated in different ways the saving power of the Paschal Mystery that is now communicated through the Church in the liturgy (CCC, 1085). He himself was baptized by John in the Jordan, and he commanded his disciples to baptize new believers; he commissioned and empowered his followers to continue his ministry (Mt 28:18–20). He healed the sick and sent his disciples out to do the same (Mt 10:1). He forgave sinners and imparted the Spirit to the apostles to continue this ministry (cf. Jn 20:22–23). He celebrated the Last Supper with his disciples and commanded them to celebrate it often (Mt 26:26–29). He imparted to the Twelve a special power and authority to act in his name, and the apostles continued this in the early Church (Lk 24:49). In these events Christ announced and prepared what he would give the Church when all had been accomplished (Jn 19:30). "The mysteries of Christ's life are the foundations of what he would henceforth dispense in the sacraments, through the ministers of his Church" (CCC, 1115). In the memorable formulation of Pope St. Leo the Great, "what was visible in our Savior has passed over into his mysteries [sacraments]" (CCC, 1115).

The Paschal Mystery and the Other Sacraments

All of the sacraments draw their power from the Paschal Mystery of Christ. "The Paschal Mystery is celebrated and made present in the liturgy of the Church, and its saving effects are communicated through the sacraments" (CCC, glossary). This is true in a preeminent way of the Eucharist, for "in the sacrifice of the Mass the passion of Christ is again made present" (RP, 2). However, it is also true of the other sacraments. For example, the *Rite of Baptism of Children* explains the effects of Baptism: it is "the door to life and to the kingdom of God" (*Christan Initiation,* General Introduction [GICI], 3); it incorporates recipients into the Church (GICI, 4); and it "washes away every stain of sin, original and personal, makes us sharers in God's own life and his adopted children" (GICI, 5). All of these effects are produced "by the power of the mystery of the Lord's passion and resurrection. . . . For baptism recalls and makes present the paschal mystery itself, because in baptism we pass from the death of sin into life" (GICI, 6).

The sacrament of Reconciliation also derives its power from the Paschal Mystery, for through the words of absolution, the imposition of hands, and the Sign of the Cross, "the saving power of the passion, death and resurrection of Jesus is also imparted to the penitent as the 'mercy stronger than sin and offense'" (RaP, 31.III). Indeed, the words of absolution show "the connection between the reconciliation of the sinner and the paschal mystery of Christ" (RP, 19): "God, the Father of mercies, through the death and resurrection of his Son, has reconciled the world to himself. . . . " The *Catechism* summarizes the relationship between the paschal mystery and the sacraments as follows: "The Paschal Mystery is celebrated and made present in the liturgy of the Church, and its saving effects are communicated through the sacraments, especially the Eucharist, which renews the paschal sacrifice of Christ as the sacrifice offered by the Church" (CCC, glossary).

The Sacraments: The Work of the Trinity

While Christ's role in the liturgy is rightly emphasized, it is important to remember that the Paschal Mystery is the work of the entire Trinity, as we read in the Letter to the Hebrews: "*Christ*, who through the eternal *spirit*, offered himself without blemish to *God*" (9:14, italics added). Indeed, everything accomplished by God in creation and salvation history is the joint work of the Trinity.[1] This is how St. Teresa of Avila explained it: "In all three Persons there is no more than one will, one power, and one dominion, in such a way that one cannot do anything without the others. . . . Could the Son create an ant without the Father? No, for it is all one power, and the same goes for the Holy Spirit; thus there is only one all-powerful God and all three Persons are one Majesty."[2]

1. "However, each divine person performs the common work according to his unique personal property" (CCC, 258).

2. Teresa of Avila, *The Collected Works of Teresa of Avila*, trans. Kieran Kavanaugh and Otilio Rodriguez, vol. 1, *The Book of Her Life, Spiritual Testimonies, Soliloquies* (Washington, DC: ICS Publications, 1980), 401.

The sacraments are the work of the Trinity, for "a sacramental celebration is a meeting of God's children with their Father, in Christ and the Holy Spirit" (CCC, 1153). The Father is the source of blessing, which "is a divine and life-giving action" (CCC, 1078). "From the beginning until the end of time the whole of God's work is a *blessing*" (CCC, 1079). Examples of God's blessing include creation, his covenants with Noah and Abraham, the deliverance from Egypt, the gift of the promised land, God's presence in the Temple, and Israel's purifying exile and return (CCC, 1080–1081). However, it is in the liturgy that "the divine blessing is fully revealed and communicated" (CCC, 1082). Since the liturgy is a dialogue, we respond to the revelation and communication of the Father's blessing by rendering to him blessing and adoration for "all the blessings of creation and salvation with which he has blessed us in his Son, in order to give us the Spirit of filial adoption" (CCC, 1110).

Christ's action in the liturgy is to point to and make present through perceptible signs—his new, sacramental way of being with us—his own Paschal Mystery. He accomplishes this by manifesting his sacramental presence in a number of ways. He is present in the assembly in fulfillment of his promise that "where two or three are gathered together in my name, there am I in the midst of them" (Mt 18:20). He is also present in his ordained ministers, who are "sacramental signs of Christ" (CCC, 1087). He is also present in his Word. And he is present "especially under the eucharistic elements" (SC, 7). Christ acts in the liturgy according to his new way of being with us, communicating to us the fruits of his Passion, Death, Resurrection, and Ascension.

The Holy Spirit, "teacher of the faith of the People of God and artisan of 'God's masterpieces,' the sacraments of the New Covenant" (CCC, 1091), acts in a number of ways in the liturgy. He prepares the people of God to receive Christ by awakening faith, conversion of heart, and adherence to the Father's will (CCC, 1098). He also recalls the mystery of Christ by "giving life to the Word of God," giving "a spiritual understanding of the Word of God," and giving the "grace of faith" to the listeners so that they may respond to the word in faith (CCC, 1100–1102). The Spirit also makes present the Paschal Mystery of Christ through his "transforming power in the liturgy (CCC, 1107). Finally, the Holy Spirit, "who is the Spirit of communion," brings the assembly into communion with Christ, forming them into his Body (CCC, 1108). This section of the *Catechism* on the Holy Spirit in the liturgy (CCC, 1091–1109) is worth a careful and prayerful reading, for it "makes a remarkable contribution to a new Trinitarian understanding of the liturgy."[3]

The presence and work of the Trinity is beautifully expressed in Eucharistic Prayer III: "You are indeed Holy, O *Lord* . . . for through your Son our Lord *Jesus Christ*, by the power and working of the *Holy Spirit*, you give life to all things and make them holy" (italics added). God the Father, through the Son, by the power and working of the Holy Spirit, gives life and sanctifies all things. The Sacrament of Penance is another example of a sacramental encounter with the Trinity, for the words and gestures of absolution constitute "the moment at which, in response to the penitent, the Trinity becomes present in order to blot out sin and restore innocence" (RaP, 31.III). Thus, every sacramental celebration is an action of the three Persons of the Trinity and draws us ever more deeply into the mystery of Trinitarian love.

The Nature of the Liturgy

Before considering in more detail the sacraments as works of the Trinity, we need to look briefly at the nature of the liturgy. In the *Constitution on the Sacred Liturgy* the Second Vatican Council described the liturgy in the following terms:

> Rightly, then, the liturgy is considered as an exercise of the priestly office of Jesus Christ. In the liturgy, by means of signs perceptible to the senses, human sanctification is signified and brought about in ways proper to each of these signs; in the liturgy the whole public worship is performed by the Mystical Body of Jesus Christ, that is, by the Head and his members.
>
> From this it follows that every liturgical celebration, because it is an action of Christ the Priest and of his Body which is the Church, is a sacred action surpassing all others; no other action of the Church can equal its effectiveness by the same title and to the same degree. (SC, 7)

3. Francis Eugene Cardinal George, "Sacrosanctum Concilium Anniversary Address: The Foundations of Liturgical Reform," in *Cardinal Reflections: Active Participation and the Liturgy* (Chicago: Hillenbrand Books, 2005), 47.

This description makes three important assertions.

- First, the liturgy is "an exercise of the priestly office of Jesus Christ," which means that he is the celebrant at every liturgy.
- Second, Christ is present in the liturgy through "signs perceptible to the senses" and he works "in ways proper to each of these signs." This is what we mean when we speak of Christ being present and acting *sacramentally*—he is truly present, but now through "signs perceptible to the senses."
- Third, the liturgy "is performed by the Mystical Body of Jesus Christ, that is, by the Head and his members." Christ is manifested sacramentally as Body and Head in distinct ways.

Christ Is Present, Head and Body

Christ's presence in his Mystical Body is a fulfillment of his promise to his disciples: "Where two or three are gathered together in my name, there am I in the midst of them" (Mt 18:20). Although this presence is manifested in different ways, we will look at only one example. In the Eucharist it is accomplished through the celebrant's Greeting—"The Lord be with you"—and the people's response—"And with your spirit." The celebrant's greeting "signifies the presence of the Lord to the assembled community" (GIRM, 50). Together with the people's response, "the mystery of the Church gathered together is made manifest" (GIRM, 50). In other words, through this simple dialogue, a profound change takes place—the congregation has become a new sacramental reality—it has become the Mystical Body of Christ gathered in this place, making visibly present the mystery of the Church. It is no longer just a group of people gathered in one place; now it is the Body of Christ prepared to perform the public worship of the Church.

The greeting and response also make sacramentally present Christ the Head, for according to the *Catechism of the Catholic Church*, "Through the ordained ministry, especially that of bishops and priests, the presence of Christ as head of the Church is made visible in the midst of the community" (CCC, 1549).

In the Eucharist, this visible presence of Christ as head is manifested especially through the people's response, "And with your spirit." This is more than a simple greeting along the lines of "and also with you"; it is a reference to the gift of the Spirit received at ordination. This understanding of the people's response is very ancient. In the fifth century, Narsai of Nisibis explained that "spirit" refers "not to the soul of the priest but to the Spirit he has received through the laying on of hands."[4] It is only through the gift of the Spirit received at ordination that the liturgy is able to go forward. In the words of a contemporary scholar, "The community's response could be understood as a short intercession for its president, that he may fulfill well his role as president with the help of the Lord and in the ministerial grace bestowed by his Spirit."[5] The Church also urges the priest to make this sacramental reality apparent through his celebration of the Mass: "by his bearing and by the way he pronounces the divine words he must convey to the faithful the living presence of Christ" (GIRM, 93).

The Word of God

Christ is also present in his Word. When the Holy Scriptures are proclaimed in the liturgy, it is "he himself who speaks" (SC, 7). Christ is present through his Word in multiple ways in the liturgy. First, "it is from Scripture that the readings are given and explained in the homily and that psalms are sung." Second, "the prayers, collects, and liturgical songs are *scriptural in their inspiration*" (italics added). Third, "it is from the Scriptures that actions and signs derive their meaning" (SC, 24). Christ the eternal Word proclaims his Word in the liturgical assembly, his Word gives the prayers and liturgical text their unique power, and it interprets the signs and actions that comprise the liturgy.

Indeed, there is an intrinsic unity between God's deeds and words. "In salvation history there is no separation between what God *says* and what he *does*. His word appears as alive and active (cf. Heb 4:12)" (VD, 53). God created through his word: "God said: Let there be light, and there was light" (Gn 1:3). This same power is evident in many of Jesus' miracles. Jesus said to the paralytic, "I say to you, rise, pick up your mat, and go home" (Mk 2:11). The paralytic was immediately healed. When Jesus and his disciples were engulfed in a storm at sea,

4. Robert Cabié, *The Eucharist*, trans. Matthew J. O'Connell, vol. 2 of *The Church at Prayer* (Collegeville, MN: The Liturgical Press, 1986), 51.

5. Michael Kunzler, *The Church's Liturgy*, trans. Placed Murray, Henry O'Shea, and Cilian Ó Sé (London: Continuum, 2001), 198.

Jesus rebuked the wind and said to the sea, "Quiet! Be still!" (Mk 4:39). The wind immediately ceased and a great calm prevailed. Pope Benedict XVI calls this the "performative character" of God's word, which is not confined to the past, but is a present reality. "In the liturgical action too, we encounter his word which accomplishes what it says" (VD, 53).

The performative character of the Word of Christ in the liturgy is supremely evident in the Eucharist when the priest pronounces the words of Christ over the bread and wine. This is how St. John Chrysostom explained this mystery: "The priest, in the role of Christ, pronounces these words, but their power and grace are God's. This is my body, he says. This word transforms the things offered" (CCC, 1375).[6] Sixteen hundred years later, St. John Paul II affirmed this same reality. It is the priest "who says with the power coming to him from Christ in the Upper Room: 'This is my body which will be given up for you. . . . This is the cup of my blood, poured out for you. . . .' The priest says these words, or rather *he puts his voice at the disposal of the One who spoke these words in the Upper Room*" (EE, 5). God's Word is efficacious, accomplishing what it signifies.

The Word of God proclaimed in the liturgy "is always a living and effective word through the power of the Holy Spirit. It expresses the Father's love that never fails in its effectiveness towards us" (VD, 52). The Word of the Father is made present and personal through the action of the Holy Spirit. "In the word of God proclaimed and heard, and in the sacraments, Jesus says today, here and now, to each person: 'I am yours, I give myself to you'; so that we can receive and respond, saying in return: 'I am yours'" (VD, 51). Understanding the performative character of God's Word in the liturgy can help us recognize God's activity in salvation history and in our own lives (VD, 53), acting at times in ways that surprise and amaze us, for as Pope Francis reminds us, "God's word is unpredictable in its power" (EG, 22).

---

6. It is the constant teaching of the Church that the bread and wine are transformed into the Body and Blood of Christ through the Word of Christ and the working of the Holy Spirit: "The Church Fathers strongly affirmed the faith of the Church in the efficacy of the Word of Christ and of the action of the Holy Spirit to bring about this conversion" (CCC, 1375).

> **Digging into the Catechism**
>
> The reading of the Gospel during Mass is accompanied by a rich variety of sacramental signs. What are the different signs that accompany this highpoint of the Liturgy of the Word? (Cf. CCC, 1154)

Invoking the Holy Spirit: The Epiclesis

The invocation of the Holy Spirit is one of the central elements of every sacrament. This invocation is called the *epiclesis*, from the Greek word meaning "to call upon." Every sacrament includes an epiclesis, a "prayer asking for the sanctifying power of God's Holy Spirit" (CCC, glossary). It is accompanied by the biblical gesture of blessing: extending the hands over the persons or things (bread and wine; oil; water) to be transformed by the Holy Spirit. This gesture recalls the Spirit's activity in Creation and the Incarnation: "The life-giving power of the Spirit, who moved over the waters in the first days of creation and overshadowed Mary in the moment of the incarnation, is vividly expressed by the ancient gesture of bringing together the hands with the palms downward and extended over the elements to be consecrated" (*Introduction to the Order of the Mass*, 118). The epiclesis ensures that "there is an outpouring of the Holy Spirit that makes the unique mystery present" (CCC, 1104).

Liturgical Remembering: The Anamnesis

The second element "at the heart of each sacramental celebration" (CCC, 1106) is the anamnesis. The word itself is a transliteration of a Greek word that is translated as "reminder" or "remembrance." It occurs twice in the earliest account of the Last Supper, 1 Corinthians 11:23–26, written by St. Paul in the mid-50s. Jesus' words over the bread (11:24) and the cup (11:25) conclude with the command to "do this . . . in remembrance [anamnesis] of me." The anamnesis, the "remembrance" or "memorial," is "a living re-presentation before God of the saving deeds he has accomplished in Christ, so that their fullness and power may be effective here and now."[7]

The anamnesis or remembrance "is not merely the recollection of past events but the proclamation of the mighty works wrought by God for men. In the liturgical celebration of these events, *they become in a certain way present and real.* This is how Israel understands its liberation from Egypt: every time the Passover is celebrated, the Exodus events are made present to the memory of believers so that they may conform their lives to them" (CCC, 1363, italics added). "In the New Testament, the memorial takes on new meaning. When the Church celebrates the Eucharist, she commemorates Christ's Passover, and *it is made present*: the sacrifice Christ offered once for all on the cross remains ever present. 'As often as the sacrifice of the Cross by which "Christ our Pasch has been sacrificed" is celebrated on the altar, the work of our redemption is carried out'" (CCC, 1364, italics added).

In the Sacrament of Baptism the anamnesis is found in the Prayer over the Water: "O God, whose Son, baptized by John in the waters of the Jordan, was anointed with the Holy Spirit, and, *as he hung upon the Cross, gave forth water from his side along with blood, and after his Resurrection,* commanded his disciples: 'Go forth, teach all nations, baptizing them in the name of the Father and of the Son and of the Holy Spirit'" (RM, 46, italics added). In the Sacrament of Reconciliation, the anamnesis occurs at the beginning of the formula of absolution: "God, the Father of mercies, through the death and resurrection of his Son, has reconciled the world to himself and sent the Holy Spirit among us for the forgiveness of sins" (RP, 46). Through the words of the anamnesis the events of our salvation are made present and effective for us.

The Real Presence—Par Excellence

Finally, Christ is present in the Eucharistic species in a manner that is utterly unique and "raises the Eucharist above all the sacraments as 'the perfection of the spiritual life and the end to which all the sacraments tend'" (CCC, 1374). In the Eucharistic species "the body and blood, together with the soul and divinity, of our Lord Jesus Christ and,

---

7. Bishops' Committee on the Liturgy, *Introduction to the Order of Mass*, Pastoral Liturgy Series, vol.1 (Washington, DC: United States Conference of Catholic Bishops, 2003), n. 121.

therefore, *the whole Christ is truly, really, and substantially* contained" (CCC, 1374): truly, "not simply through image or form," really, "not only subjectively through the faith of believers," and substantially, "in his profound reality, which cannot be seen by the senses, and not in the appearances which remain that of bread and wine."[8] In affirming the real presence of Christ in the Eucharistic species the Church is not denying Christ's real presence in other ways. Rather, his presence in the Eucharistic species "is presence in the fullest sense: that is to say, it is a *substantial* presence by which Christ, God and man, makes himself wholly and entirely present" (CCC, 1374). The Eucharist, therefore, contains "the entire spiritual wealth of the church, namely Christ himself our Pasch" (PO, 5).

This presence is expressed in several ways in the words of the Mass. In the Liturgy of the Eucharist, the Preface, Eucharistic Prayer, and Our Father are all addressed to God the Father. However, the prayers following the Our Father are addressed to Christ, now substantially present on the altar. Immediately following the Our Father the priest addresses Christ: "Lord Jesus Christ, who said to your apostles . . ." This is followed by the "Lamb of God," which is also addressed to Christ, now substantially present on the altar. Finally, the priest shows the consecrated host and blood and says, "Behold the Lamb of God, behold him who takes away the sins of the world."[9] We do not behold "It", a holy thing, but the person of Christ, the Son of God, under the appearance of bread. Sacramental Communion also has the character of a personal encounter. For this reason, "ordained ministers and those who . . . are authorized to exercise the ministry of distributing the Eucharist [should] make every effort to ensure that this simple act preserves its importance as a personal encounter with the Lord Jesus in the sacrament" (Benedict XVI, *Sacrament of Charity*, 50).

St. Teresa of Avila expressed the reality of Christ's presence in the Eucharist with particularly vivid and personal language: "Receiving Communion is not like picturing with the imagination. . . . In Communion the event is happening now, and it is entirely true. . . . Now, then, if when He went about in the world the mere touch of His robes cured the sick, why doubt, if we have faith, that miracles will

8. Raniero Cantalamessa, *The Eucharist: Our Sanctification*, rev. ed. (Collegeville, MN: The Liturgical Press, 1995), 81.

9. IOM, 132.

be worked while He is within us and that He will give what we ask of Him, since He is in our house? His Majesty is not accustomed to paying poorly for His lodging if the hospitality is good."[10]

Finally, the presence of Christ in the liturgy is manifested through the signs and symbols which make up the liturgical rites. Through the power of the Spirit, they "become *bearers of the saving and sanctifying action of Christ*" (CCC, 1189, italics added). They comprise the language of the liturgy, which is the subject of the next chapter.

Digging into the Rite of Reconciliation and Penance

What elements of God's presence do you find in the formula of absolution from the Rite of Penance?

Then the priest extends his hands over the head of the penitent (or at least extends his right hand):

"God, the Father of mercies,
through the death and resurrection of his Son,
has reconciled the world to himself
and sent the Holy Spirit among us for the forgiveness of sins;
through the ministry of the Church
may God give you pardon and peace,
and I absolve you from your sins
in the name of the Father,
and of the Son, + and of the Holy Spirit."
(Rite of Penance, 46)

10. Teresa of Avila, *The Collected Works of Teresa of Avila*, trans. Kieran Kavanaugh and Otilio Rodriguez, vol. 2, *The Way of Perfection, Meditations on the Song of Songs, The Interior Castle* (Washington, DC: ICS Publications, 1980), 172.

Chapter 2

The Language of the Liturgy

The liturgy is composed of signs and symbols through which God manifests his presence as well as his saving and sanctifying action. He mediates his presence through signs and symbols because this corresponds to our very nature, to the way he created us. We are both body and spirit, so we express and perceive "spiritual realities through physical signs and symbols" (CCC, 1146). In addition, because we have been created as social beings, we need "signs and symbols to communicate with others, through language, gestures, and actions" (CCC, 1146). This is equally true of our relationship with God. "For in God's design the humanity and loving kindness of our Savior have visibly appeared to us and so God uses visible signs to give salvation and to renew the broken covenant" (RP, 6d).

The signs of the liturgy confer salvation and renew the broken covenant because they are "bearers of the saving and sanctifying action of Christ" (CCC, 1189). Their power stems from their origin: "the visible signs used by the liturgy to signify invisible divine things have been chosen by Christ or the Church" (SC, 33). Examples of signs chosen by Christ include unleavened bread and wine for the Eucharist, the use of oil for the Anointing of the Sick, and the baptismal formula "in the name of the Father and of the Son and of the Holy Spirit." Signs chosen by the Church include liturgical vestments and colors, postures such as standing and kneeling, and gestures such as the sign of the cross. These signs, whether chosen by Christ or the Church, are bearers of the power of Christ's Paschal Mystery in a way that is not possible with signs chosen by us. Furthermore, they are "necessary for the mystery of salvation to be really effective in the Christian community" and to ensure "the presence of God."[1] Through signs the liturgy makes present the transforming power of Christ's Paschal Mystery, bringing us into relationship with the Trinity.

---

1. *Liturgiae Instaurationes*, Third Instruction on the Correct Implementation of the Constitution on the Sacred Liturgy (1970), 1.

When the Church speaks of liturgical signs, she uses the term in a broad and comprehensive way, including material objects, words, actions, song, and music. They are drawn from elements and actions "relating to creation (candles, water, fire), human life (washing, anointing, breaking bread) and the history of salvation (the rites of the Passover)" (CCC, 1189). All of the liturgical signs and symbols are related to Christ and find their fulfillment in him. When we talk about liturgical signs and symbols, the distinction between sign and symbol is not the important point: "what is important is that, whichever term is employed—be it 'sign' or 'symbol'—the meaning each has for the Church is one of fullness, reality, and truth. In fact, that to which signs and symbols point is *the* fullness, reality, and truth: Christ himself."[2] The whole Trinity acts through the liturgical signs: the Holy Spirit uses the words, actions, and signs that make up a liturgical celebration to put "both the faithful and the ministers into a living relationship with Christ, the Word and Image of the Father, so that they can live out the meaning of what they hear, contemplate, and do in the celebration" (CCC, 1101). Through the faith of the Church and the power of the Holy Spirit, God communicates the fruits of Christ's Paschal Mystery to us by means of this liturgical language.

There is a close relationship between the power of liturgical signs and their intelligibility. The intelligibility of the signs and symbols of the liturgy was a primary concern of the Second Vatican Council in its reform of the liturgy. "It is, therefore, of the greatest importance that the faithful should easily understand the sacramental signs" (SC, 59) so that they can "take part in them fully, actively, and as a community" (SC, 21). Intelligible signs enable the liturgy to enter "firmly and effectively . . . into the minds and lives of the faithful" (EM, 4). When misunderstood, the language of the liturgy can be confusing or meaningless, but when understood it is inexhaustibly rich, varied, and powerful.

Sacramental Signs and Symbols

Sacramental signs are different from the signs that we encounter in our daily life. For example, a hospital sign indicates the location of a hospital, but it does not contain the hospital itself. It is merely an indicator, a

2. Christopher Carstens and Douglas Martis, *Mystical Body, Mystical Voice: Encountering Christ in the Words of the Mass* (Chicago: Liturgy Training Publications, 2011), 40.

pointer. Sacramental signs also point to another reality, but unlike conventional signs, they also make present the reality they signify. "The liturgical word and action are inseparable both insofar as they are signs and instruction and insofar as *they accomplish what they signify*. When the Holy Spirit awakens faith, he not only gives an understanding of the Word of God, but *through the sacraments also makes present the 'wonders' of God* which it proclaims" (CCC, 1155, italics added). This reality is expressed in the liturgy itself. Consider, for example, the Prayer after Communion for the Thirtieth Sunday in Ordinary Time: "May your Sacraments, O Lord, we pray, perfect in us what lies within them, that what we now celebrate in signs we may one day possess in truth." God uses the signs and symbols of the liturgy to communicate the power and reality of the Paschal Mystery to us.

Through the richness and diversity of its signs, the liturgy engages the whole person: mind, body, and senses. It engages the hearing through words and song; smell through incense; sight through vestments, images, colors; feeling through posture and gesture; and taste through the Body and Blood of Christ under the appearance of bread and wine. Through these different "kinds of language" the liturgy operates "on different levels of communication" and engages the whole person (SacCar, 40) so that each participant can enter into the liturgy with his or her whole being.

Let us now consider some of the signs common to many liturgical celebrations. We looked at a few liturgical signs in the previous chapter, such as the liturgical word and the gesture that accompanies the invocation of the Holy Spirit. In this chapter we will consider additional signs and symbols that are common to many of the Church's sacramental celebrations: images, song, the sign of the cross, silence, movement, incense, and color. Finally, we will consider the importance of the harmony of the liturgical signs.

Images

An element common to all Catholic churches, and therefore a part of every liturgical celebration, is the liturgical image. Sacred art is a direct consequence of the Incarnation. No image can "represent the invisible and incomprehensible God, but the incarnation of the Son of God has ushered in a new 'economy' of images" (CCC, 1159). St. John Damascene explained this new "economy of images" in the seventh century: "Previously God, who has neither a body nor a face, absolutely could not be represented by an image. But now that he has made himself visible in the flesh and has lived with men, I can make an image of what I have seen of God . . . and contemplate the glory of the Lord, his face unveiled" (CCC, 1159). The sacred image and sacred word teach and reinforce the one Gospel message of Jesus Christ. In 787, the Second Council of Nicea affirmed this reciprocal relationship between Sacred Scripture and sacred art: "the production of representational artwork . . . accords with the history of the preaching of the Gospel. For it confirms that the incarnation of the Word of God was real and not imaginary, and to our benefit as well, for realities that illustrate each other undoubtedly reflect each other's meaning" (CCC, 1160, quoting the Council of Nicea II).

Sacred images "truly signify Christ, who is glorified in them" (CCC, 1161), and in a certain way make present an integral aspect of every sacramental celebration, the "cloud of witnesses" spoken of in Hebrews 12:1, "who continue to participate in the salvation of the world and to whom we are united, above all in sacramental celebrations" (CCC, 1161). This heavenly dimension was reaffirmed by the Second Vatican Council: "In the earthly liturgy we take part in a foretaste of that heavenly liturgy which is celebrated in the holy city of Jerusalem toward which we journey as pilgrims, where Christ is sitting at the right hand of God, a minister of the holies and of the true tabernacle; we sing a hymn to the Lord's glory with all the warriors of the heavenly army" (SC, 8). Sacramental celebrations unite heaven and earth, joining us with the entire heavenly host, as evidenced, for example, in the invocation of the Penitential Rite "therefore I ask Blessed Mary ever-Virgin, all the Angels and Saints, and you, my brothers and sisters to pray for me to the Lord our God" (*Order of Mass,* Confiteor).

This heavenly, vertical dimension of the liturgy is deeply rooted in our tradition. In the fifth century, St. John Chrysostom described the angelic presence at the Eucharist: "The angels surround the priest. The whole sanctuary and the space around the altar are filled with the heavenly powers to honor Him Who is present on the altar."[3] Three centuries later St. Bede (d. 735) exhorted the faithful in the following words:

3. Jean Daniélou, *The Angels and Their Mission,* trans. David Heimann (Westminster, MD: The Newman Press, 1956), 62.

"We are not permitted to doubt that where the mysteries of the Lord's body and blood are being enacted, a gathering of the citizens from on high is present. . . . Hence we must strive meticulously, my brothers, when we come into the church to pay the due service of divine praise or to perform the solemnity of the mass, to be always mindful of the angelic presence, and to fulfill our heavenly duty with fear and fitting veneration."[4] In a real and powerful way heaven becomes present on earth at every liturgical celebration.

Sacred images are an integral part of the liturgy, for they help us perceive the heavenly host present with us at every liturgical celebration. "Images point to a presence; they are essentially connected with what happens in the liturgy. Their whole point is to lead us beyond what can be apprehended at the merely material level, to awaken new senses in us, and to teach us *a new kind of seeing,* which perceives the Invisible in the visible."[5] In other words, sacred images help us to "look not to the things that are seen but to the things that are unseen; for the things that are seen are transient, but the things that are unseen are eternal" (2 Cor 4:18). Every liturgical celebration is a participation in the heavenly liturgy eternally celebrated in the heavenly Jerusalem. Sacred images assist us in understanding and entering into this vital aspect of the liturgy.

Song

Music, as with all liturgical signs, manifests the presence of God, for "God, the giver of song, is present whenever his people sing his praises" (SL, 1). It enriches the liturgy in a variety of ways. Prayer, when sung, "is expressed in a more attractive way" (SL, 1). Song also manifests more clearly the "hierarchical and communal nature" of "the mystery of the liturgy," since different parts of the liturgy are sung by the priest celebrant (the prayers/orations, the Preface), the cantor (the Responsorial Psalm), the schola or choir, and the entire assembly (e.g., the Kyrie, the Gloria, and the Entrance Chant) (SL, 1). The union of voices contributes to "the unity of hearts," one of the ways that we, though many, are one body in Christ. Also, through song "minds are more easily raised to

---

4. Erik M. Heen and Philip D. W. Krey, eds., *Hebrews*, vol. NT 10 of *Ancient Christian Commentary on Scripture* (Downers Grove, IL: InterVarsity Press, 2005), 30.

5. Joseph Ratzinger, *The Spirit of the Liturgy*, trans. John Saward (San Francisco: Ignatius, 2000), 133; italics added.

heavenly things by the beauty of the sacred rites (MS, 5)." St. John Chrysostom emphasized this dimension in the exhortation "Lift up your hearts": "Let no one have any thought of earthy, but let him lose himself of every earthly thing and transport himself whole and entire into heaven. Let him abide there beside the very throne of glory, hovering with the Seraphim, and singing the most holy song of the God of glory and majesty."[6]

As we noted above, the earthly liturgy is a participation in the heavenly liturgy. Music is an important aspect of that participation. In the words of the Second Vatican Council, "we sing a hymn to the Lord's glory with all the warriors of the heavenly army" (SC, 8). St. John Chrysostom described this dimension of the liturgy: "Think now of what kind of choir you are going to enter. Although vested with a body, you have been judged worthy to join the Powers of heaven in singing the praises of Him who is Lord of all."[7] Music and song, along with sacred images, manifest the heavenly dimension of the earthly liturgy. Through song, the whole liturgy "more clearly prefigures that heavenly liturgy which is enacted in the holy city of Jerusalem" (MS, 5).

Music in the liturgy is a rich and powerful bearer of the saving and sanctifying power of Christ in many ways. It enhances prayer. It manifests the mystery of the Church, which is simultaneously hierarchical and unified. It helps us set our mind on heavenly things. Through song we join the heavenly choir that never ceases to sing the praises of God (Rev 4:8). Liturgical song is "a sign of God's love for us and of our love for him" (SL, 2), one of the sacramental signs through which we are brought into unity with the Trinity and with one another, are made holy, and give glory to God.

The Sign of the Cross

Gestures are another kind of liturgical sign. Perhaps the one that is most common and familiar to every sacramental celebration is the sign of the cross. This is a very ancient Christian gesture. Tertullian (ca. 200) saw the sign of the cross prefigured in Ezekiel 9:4, in which the Lord instructed the prophet to go through Jerusalem and mark on the

---

6. Daniélou, *Angels*, 62.

7. Ibid.

forehead those "who sigh and groan over all the abominations that are committed in it." Here is Tertullian's explanation:

> [Christ] foretold that His just ones should suffer equally with Him—both the apostles and all the faithful in succession; and He signed them with that very seal of which Ezekiel spake: "The Lord said unto me, go through the gate, through the midst of Jerusalem, and set the mark Tau upon the foreheads of the men." Now the Greek letter Tau and our own letter T is the very form of the cross, which He predicted would be the sign on our foreheads in the true Catholic Jerusalem, in which, according to the twenty-first Psalm, the brethren of Christ or children of God would ascribe glory to God the Father, in the person of Christ Himself addressing His Father: "I will declare Your name unto my brethren; in the midst of the congregation will I sing praise unto Thee."[8]

He also describes how frequently it was made by the early Christians: "At every forward step and movement, at every going in and out, when we put on our clothes and shoes, when we bathe, when we sit at table, when we light the lamps, on couch, on seat, in all the ordinary actions of daily life, we trace upon the forehead the sign."[9] Through the sign of the cross, prefigured in Old Testament prophecy and fulfilled in Christ, Christians proclaim their fidelity to the thrice-holy God, symbolized by the sign of the cross.

A century and a half later, St. Cyril of Jerusalem explained the sign of the cross to the newly-baptized Christians. It is, first of all, a confession of faith: "Let us not then be ashamed to confess the Crucified. Be the Cross our seal made with boldness by our fingers on our brow, and on everything."[10] It was still used by Christians to sanctify the moments and events of daily life: "over the bread we eat, and the cups we drink; in our comings in, and goings out; before our sleep, when we lie down and when we rise up; when we are in the way, and when we are still." St. Cyril also describes the power of the sign of the cross to keep Christians safe against the wiles and attacks of the

8. Tertullian, *Against Marcion*, in *The Ante-Nicene Fathers: Translations of the Writings of the Fathers Down to A.D. 325*, vol. 3, ed. Alexander Roberts, DD, and James Donaldson, LLD (Grand Rapids, MI: Eerdmans Publishing Company, 1980), 340–341.

9. Tertullian, *De Corona*, in *The Ante-Nicene Fathers: Translations of the Writings of the Fathers Down to A.D. 325*, vol. 3, ed. Alexander Roberts, DD, and James Donaldson, LLD (Grand Rapids, MI: Eerdmans Publishing Company, 1980), 94–95.

10. Cyril of Jerusalem, "Catechetical Lectures, Lecture XIII," in *A Select Library of Nicene and Post-Nicene Fathers of the Christian Church,* Second Series, vol. 7, ed. Philip Schaff and Henry Wace (Grand Rapids, MI: Eerdman's Publishing Company, 1983), 92.

enemy: "Great is that preservative; it is without price, for the sake of the poor; without toil, for the sick; since also its grace is from God. It is the Sign of the faithful, and the dread of devils: for He triumphed over them in it, having made a show of them openly [Col 2:15]; for when they see the Cross they are reminded of the Crucified; they are afraid of Him, who bruised the heads of the dragon. Despise not the Seal, because of the freeness of the gift; out for this the rather honor your Benefactor."[11] Through this simple gesture we too can profess our faith, sanctify the events of our daily life, and invoke the power of God.

The sign of the cross, as with many liturgical signs, conveys a wealth of meaning. It is the mark of those zealous for the holiness and glory of God and a sign of the power of God displayed in the Cross of Christ. St. Cyril's description of the sign of the cross as a great preservative and weapon against the enemy is a wonderful example of how a sacramental sign makes present the reality it signifies. The sign of the cross truly enables us to "enter into the power of the blessing of Christ."[12]

Digging into the Catechism

Where, by whom, and how often is the sign of the cross made during the Mass?

What is the meaning of each of these signs of the cross?

Silence

Another, somewhat different kind of liturgical sign is silence. In its *Constitution on the Sacred Liturgy*, the Second Vatican Council listed it as one of the elements of active participation: "To promote active participation, the people should be encouraged to take part by means of acclamations, responses, psalmody, antiphons, and songs, as well as by actions, gestures, and bearing. And at the proper times all should observe a reverent silence" (SC, 30). Liturgical silence is not merely an absence of words, nor is it simply a pause or interlude. "Rather, it is a

11. Cyril of Jerusalem, *Catechetical Lectures*, Lecture XIII, in *A Select Library of Nicene and Post-Nicene Fathers of the Christian Church*, Second Series, vol. 7, ed. Philip Schaff and Henry Wace (Grand Rapids, MI: Eerdman's Publishing Company, 1983), 92.

12. Ratzinger, *Spirit*, 184.

stillness, a quieting of spirits, a taking time and leisure to hear, assimilate, and respond. . . . The dialogue between God and the community of faith taking place through the Holy Spirit requires intervals of silence, suited to the congregation, so that all can take to heart the word of God and respond to it in prayer" (IOM, 48). Note especially the language of relationship and encounter—hearing the word of God addressed to us, understanding it, and responding to the One who has addressed us. Silence, then, facilitates relationship with the Blessed Trinity and becomes a means to greater communion with the Father through the Son under the action of the Holy Spirit.

The purpose of liturgical silence varies. During the Mass, for example in the Penitential Rite and after the invitation to pray before the Collect, it provides an opportunity for personal recollection. Following the readings or the homily it creates a space for meditation on the proclaimed Word. Silence after Communion is a time for prayer and praise. "This, in all truth, is the moment for an interior conversation with the Lord who has given himself to us, for that essential 'communicating' . . . without which the external reception of the Sacrament becomes mere ritual and therefore unfruitful".[13] St. Teresa of Avila urged her nuns to spend time in prayer after receiving Communion: "Be with Him willingly; don't lose so good an occasion for conversing with Him as is the hour after having received Communion. . . . This, then, is a good time for our Master to teach us, and for us to listen to Him, kiss His feet because He wanted to teach us, and beg Him not to leave." "Why doubt," she asked, " if we have faith, that miracles will be worked while He is within us and that He will give what we ask of Him, since He is in our House? His Majesty is not accustomed to paying poorly for His lodging if the hospitality is good."[14] Silence at different moments in the liturgy develops our docility to the Holy Spirit and invites the Lord to act.

Silence during the liturgy can be challenging, even uncomfortable. "Ours is not an age which fosters recollection; at times one has the impression that people are afraid of detaching themselves, even for a moment, from the mass media" (*Verbum Domini* [VD], 66). This calls for a special catechesis on the meaning of silence in the liturgy in order to

13. Ibid., 210.

14. Teresa of Avila, *Collected Works*, vol. 2, 172.

Activity

The Church suggests silence during the Mass at seven different points:

1. Prior to the beginning of Mass (GIRM, 45)
2. Prior to the Penitential Act (GIRM, 54)
3. After the invitation to pray (before the Collect) (GIRM, 54)
4. Before the Liturgy of the Word begins (GIRM, 56)
5. After the First and Second Readings (GIRM, 56)
6. After the homily (GIRM, 56)
7. After Communion

At which of these points is silence most meaningful for you?

rediscover "a sense of recollection and inner repose. Only in silence can the word of God find a home in us, as it did in Mary, woman of the word and, inseparably, woman of silence. Our liturgies must facilitate this attitude of authentic listening" (VD, 66). In the words of the great Spanish doctor Saint John of the Cross, "The Father spoke on Word, which was his Son, and this Word he speaks always in eternal silence, and in silence must it be heard by the soul."[15]

Movement

Movement is another important liturgical sign. The prescribed movements of the ministers and people manifest important aspects of the sacramental reality that is being celebrated. A good example is the Sacrament of Baptism. One of the fruits of Baptism is that the recipient is incorporated into the Church of Christ. This sacramental reality is manifested through the movements and stations of the rite, what one might call the "geography" of the sacrament. It typically begins at the entrance of the church signifying that one is asking for membership in the Church. Here all are welcomed, the parents are questioned, the

15. John of the Cross, *Sayings of Light and Love* (London: Westminster Roman Catholic Diocesan Trust, 2011), 100.

child is signed on the forehead, the Liturgy of the Word is celebrated, followed by the prayer of exorcism and the prebaptismal anointing. At the entrance to the church these introductory rites prepare one for membership in the Church.

Following the anointing with the oil of catechumens, all go to the baptismal font for the celebration of the sacrament: the blessing of the baptismal water, renunciation of sin and profession of faith, Baptism, clothing with the white garment, presentation of the lighted candle, and the prayer over the ears and mouth. Through these rites the child's sins are forgiven, he or she is made a child of God, a temple of the Holy Spirit, and a member of Christ's Church. This sacramental reality is next signified by a procession to the altar, which also manifests the fact that Baptism is oriented to Eucharistic Communion. Here the assembly prays the Lord's Prayer, receives a blessing from the celebrant, and is dismissed. The Rite of Baptism thus takes place at three distinct stations—the entrance of the church, the baptismal font, and the altar—which physically manifest the spiritual reality being enacted.

Movement is also an important part of the Eucharist. The Mass includes four separate processions: the entrance procession, the procession with the Book of the Gospels, the procession with the gifts, and the Communion procession. With the exception of the Gospel procession, all the processions begin in the nave and move to the sanctuary. This reflects the symbolism of the church building. The sanctuary is the fulfillment of the Old Testament holy of holies as well as an image of the heavenly Jerusalem, the dwelling place of God. The nave is the dwelling of the people of God. "In this perspective, procession represents the pilgrimage of the people of God to its heavenly homeland; it represents the union of God and man, begun now in grace, and progressing toward its perfection in glory."[16]

Let's look more closely at one of these processions, the procession with the gifts of bread, wine, and money that follows the Prayers of the Faithful. It normally begins in the nave and moves to the sanctuary where the gifts are received by the priest. This procession manifests a rich symbolism. It expresses the congregation's participation in the Eucharist, an aspect that "is best expressed if the procession passes right through their midst" (IOM, 105). It also manifests "the humble and

16. John Mary Burns, "The Procession of the Ordo Missae: Liturgical Structure and Theological Meaning," *Antiphon* 13:2 (2009): 162.

contrite heart, the dispossession of self that is necessary for making the true offering, which the Lord Jesus gave his people to make for him. The procession with the gifts expresses also our eager willingness to enter into the 'holy exchange' with God: 'accept the offerings you have given us, that we in turn may receive the gift of yourself [12/19, Prayer over Offerings]'" (IOM, 105).

This procession is also a form of intercession for the world, as Pope Benedict XVI explains: "This humble and simple gesture is actually very significant: in the bread and wine that we bring to the altar, all creation is taken up by Christ the Redeemer to be transformed and presented to the Father. In this way we also bring to the altar all the pain and suffering of the world, in the certainty that everything has value in God's eyes" (SacCar, 47). So what can appear as a strictly functional action is in fact a movement of profound spiritual meaning and power. It expresses the participation of the assembly in the Mass, the humility and contrition of the people of God, their willingness to offer themselves, and their intercession for the whole world.

Movement then is one of the ways that the liturgy engages the whole person. It also reveals the sacramentality of the church building and effects its participation in the liturgy. It reminds us that here we are "aliens and sojourners" (1 Pt 2:11) whose "citizenship is in heaven" (Phil 3:20) toward which we journey as God's "pilgrim Church on earth" (Eucharistic Prayer III). Finally, liturgical movement helps form in us the proper dispositions for fruitful participation in sacramental celebrations.

Incense

The liturgy also makes use of different kinds of material signs—for example, water, oil, and bread. Incense is one of the material signs used in a number of liturgical celebrations. It is recommended for more solemn celebrations of the Eucharist, during exposition and benediction of the Blessed Sacrament, in the Rite of Dedication of a Church and an Altar, at solemn celebrations of Morning Prayer and Evening Prayer, funerals, and "in any procession of some solemnity" (CB, 88). Incense is another kind of liturgical language, another way that the liturgy engages the whole person, for it appeals to our senses of sight and smell. For this reason, the Church encourages its use "in amounts sufficient to be seen and smelled" (IOM, 58).

As a liturgical sign, incense is rich in meanings. First and foremost, it is a sign of prayer. This meaning is rooted in the Old and New Testaments. The psalmist begged God, "Let my prayer be counted as incense before you" (Ps 141:2). St. John saw it used in the heavenly liturgy: "Another angel came and stood at the altar with a golden censer; and he was given much incense to mingle with the prayers of all the saints upon the golden altar before the throne" (Rev 8:3). It also symbolizes the Church's gifts rising to the Father. During the Mass, the gifts on the altar as well as the cross and altar are incensed "so as to signify the Church's offering and prayer rising like incense in the sight of God" (GIRM, 75). In addition, incense is a sign of the dignity of the ordained ministry as well as the priesthood of the baptized: "the Priest, because of his sacred ministry, and the people, by reason of their baptismal dignity, may be incensed by the Deacon or by another minister" (GIRM, 75). Incense is also an expression of reverence, "a sign of respect and honor" before Christ (IOM, 58). In addition, it recalls the pillar of cloud (Ex 13:21) by which God led Israel in the wilderness, the cloud itself symbolizing "God's glory and presence in the midst of the Israelites" (IOM, 58). In this way it "suggests both the otherness of the transcendent God and . . . can contribute powerfully to a sense of mystery" (IOM, 58).

Incense

During the Mass, for example, incense can be used at five points: the entrance procession, the Introductory Rites, the proclamation of the Gospel, the Preparation of the Gifts, and the elevation of the sacred species following the Consecration.

What is the significance of incense at each of these points?

The use of incense in the liturgy expresses many meanings. It signifies the prayers and gifts of the assembly rising up to God. It acknowledges Christ present as Head (in the ordained minister) and Body (all the baptized). It is a sign of the dignity of the ordained ministers and the priesthood of the baptized who together celebrate the liturgy as Christ Head and Body. It engages yet another of our senses, contributing to the participation of the whole person. Finally, it conveys reverence for Christ and the transcendent otherness of God present in the midst of his people, enriching the solemnity and mystery of the liturgy.

Liturgical Colors

The last liturgical sign we will examine is color. Pope Innocent III (1198–1216) first determined specific colors for specific days, and his choices are approximately those still in force today: white, red, green, and black. However, it wasn't until the Missal of 1570 that an obligatory liturgical color scheme first appeared. The approved liturgical colors in the United States are white, red, green, violet or purple, black, and rose (GIRM, 346). Gold and silver are approved for use in the United States "on more solemn occasions" (GIRM, 346). In the liturgy, colors contribute to the expression of "the specific character of the mysteries of faith to be celebrated" (GIRM, 345), which we will now consider.

White is a symbol of God, who dwells in unapproachable light (1 Tm 6:16) and of Christ, "the light of the world" (Jn 8:12). Therefore, it is used during Christmas Time, Easter Time, the Solemnity of the Most Holy Trinity, and celebrations of the Lord (except for the Passion). It is also a sign of purity, so it is also used for celebrations of the Blessed Virgin Mary, of the Holy Angels, and of the Saints who were not martyrs. It is also used on a few other liturgical celebrations such as the Solemnity of All Saints (November 1) and the feast of the Conversion of St. Paul (January 25).[17] Finally, white is a sign of joy, and so it is used in processions with the Blessed Sacrament, and in the sacraments of Baptism, Confirmation (or red), Anointing of the Sick, and Viaticum. The joy of the angels at the birth of Christ, his resurrection victory over sin and death, the radiance of the Blessed Trinity, and the purity and innocence of the saints all find liturgical expression in the color white.

Like the color white, the color red also signifies diverse aspects of the faith. It is the color of fire, which is one of the biblical images of the Holy Spirit (Acts 2:3), so it is used on Pentecost Sunday and in the celebration of the Sacrament of Confirmation within the Mass. As the color

17. Liturgical celebrations are categorized according to their importance. First in importance are solemnities, such as the Immaculate Conception of the Blessed Virgin Mary (December 8), which begin on the evening of the preceding day. Next in importance are feasts, such as the Feast of the Transfiguration (August 6). Third in rank are memorials, which are either obligatory or optional.

of blood, it signifies the suffering of the Lord and the saints, so it is also used on Palm Sunday, Good Friday, celebrations of the Lord's Passion, on the "birthday" feast days of the Apostles and Evangelists, and on the celebrations of saints who were martyred. The color red is a sign to us of Christ's suffering with us and for us, of the faithful and courageous testimony of the martyrs, and of the Gift of God which contains all gifts, the Holy Spirit.

Green, the color of springtime, new growth, and hope, is used in Ordinary Time, especially "in the ordinary Sundays of the year, which are commemorations of the great Sunday of the Resurrection, when hope once again returned to the world."[18] The color violet or purple is a sign of sorrow, mourning, penance, and repentance. Thus, it is used in Advent and Lent, as well as in the Sacrament of Penance. Rose, a sign of subdued joy, is used during the penitential seasons of Advent (Gaudete Sunday, the Third Sunday of Advent) and Lent (Laetare Sunday, the Fourth Sunday of Lent). Although white is most commonly worn at funerals, violet and black, a symbol of mourning and death, are also permitted.

In addition to expressing the specific character of the liturgical mysteries, liturgical colors also give "a sense of Christian life's passage through the course of the liturgical year" (GIRM, 345). "In the liturgical year the various aspects of the one Paschal mystery unfold" (CCC, 1171). In the course of the liturgical year the Church recalls "the mysteries of redemption . . . [and] opens to the faithful the riches of her Lord's powers and merits, so that these are in some way made present for all time, and the faithful are enabled to lay hold upon them and become filled with saving grace" (SC, 102). However, the liturgical year, which begins with Advent, does not unfold in a strictly chronological order (if it did, Easter would be celebrated at the end of the year rather than in the middle). Rather, taking

> the Easter Triduum as its source of light, the new age of the Resurrection fills the whole liturgical year with its brilliance. Gradually, on either side of this source, the year is transfigured by the liturgy. It really is a "year of the Lord's favor" [Lk 4:19]. The economy of salvation is at work within the framework of time, but since its fulfillment in the Passover of Jesus and the outpouring of the Holy Spirit, the culmination of history is anticipated "as a foretaste," and the kingdom of God enters into our time. (CCC, 1168)

---

18. Virgil Michel, OSB, *The Liturgy of the Church* (NY: MacMillan, 1937), 77.

This unfolding of time now transfigured by the "new age of the Resurrection" finds expression in the liturgical use of color. The brilliance of the Resurrection is signified by the use of white, gold, or silver throughout the season of Easter. The use of violet or purple in the forty days leading up to the Triduum assist us in preparing for the great event through sorrow, contrition, and penance. The green of Ordinary Time that precedes Lent and follows Easter is a sign of hope and faith as the events of our Lord's life that find their definitive power and fulfillment in the age of the Resurrection and the riches of our Lord's powers and merits are made liturgically present. Finally, the overflowing radiance of the Triduum reaches back to the penitential and expectant character of Advent, expressed through the use of violet/purple vestments, while also reaching forward to the radiant culmination of the liturgical year, the Solemnity of Christ the King, symbolized by white, silver, or gold. In this way we see how the liturgical colors visually express our pilgrim journey toward our heavenly homeland.

Liturgical Color

What is the liturgical color for each of the following celebrations?

The Assumption (August 15)

Triumph of the Cross (September 14)

The Lord's Supper (Holy Thursday)

Christ the King (Last Sunday in Ordinary Time)

The Sacred Heart (Friday following the Second Sunday after Pentecost)

Liturgical colors combine with the other liturgical signs to make present the various aspects of the one Paschal Mystery. They characterize the central mystery of our faith, the Paschal Mystery. Within the major seasons of the liturgical year—Advent, Christmas, Ordinary Time, Lent, Easter—are expressed the individual events and mysteries of the life of Christ and the saints. In the liturgy, colors contribute to the expression of "the specific character of the mysteries of faith to be celebrated" (GIRM, 345), aiding us in entering into the liturgy with our whole being.

The Essential Rite

For centuries the Church, using the language of medieval Scholastic theology, has identified two elements as necessary for the celebration of each sacrament, the *matter* and the *form*. The matter is the required visible, material element, and the form is the prayer that accompanies and explains the matter. However, in the case of the Sacrament of Penance and Reconciliation the matter "is not so straightforward because there is no immediately visible element upon which the creative word [the form] can confer a salvific meaning."[19] The Church considers the acts of the penitent—confession, contrition, and satisfaction—the quasi-matter (*quasi* meaning "as it were"[20]) of the sacrament. Similarly, the Sacrament of Marriage lacks a visible element that constitutes the matter: "the matter is the mutual self-giving of the spouses, and the form is the mutual acceptance of this self-giving."[21] As these examples illustrate, the terms *matter* and *form* more clearly describe the key elements of some sacraments than of others.

The *Catechism of the Catholic Church* does not use the language of matter and form, referring instead to the "essential rite." For example, the essential rite for Baptism is the triple immersion in the baptismal water, or the triple pouring of water—the matter, along with the words, "N. I baptize you in the name of the Father, and of the Son, and of the Holy Spirit"—the form (CCC, 1239–1240). If the "essential rite" is changed or omitted, the sacrament is invalid; in other words, it did not take place. When discussing the individual sacraments, we will use the language of the *Catechism*, the essential rite, rather than the traditional language of matter and form.

Harmony of Signs

While the individual liturgical signs constitute a complex liturgical language that appeals to different senses and engages the whole person, they also combine in a harmonious way to make present in all of its richness the one Paschal Mystery of Christ. For this reason, the

---

19. Paul Haffner, *The Sacramental Mystery*, rev. ed. (Herefordshire, UK: Gracewing, 2007), 152.

20. Ibid., 153.

21. Ibid., 243–244.

Catechism speaks of "the harmony of signs" (1158), the way that words and silence, movement and gesture, song and music, sight and smell, combine to make present in its fullness the Paschal Mystery.

The *Catechism* cites the contemplation of sacred icons as an example of this harmony of signs: "the contemplation of sacred icons, united with meditation on the Word of God and the singing of liturgical hymns, enters into the harmony of the signs of the celebration so that the mystery celebrated is imprinted in the heart's memory and is then expressed in the new life of the faithful" (CCC, 1162). Here we see how three liturgical signs—sacred images, Sacred Scripture, and liturgical song—together make present a specific event ("the mystery celebrated") from the life of our Lord (e.g., the Nativity, the Transfiguration, or the Resurrection) or the Blessed Virgin Mary (e.g., the Annunciation, the Visitation, or the Crucifixion) that can transform the life of the faithful.

While we have considered examples of the different kinds of signs that comprise the language of the liturgy, these elements do not occur in isolation. Rather, they combine in distinct but complementary ways to make present the one Paschal Mystery of Christ through which the Father draws us into the Trinitarian life of love through his beloved Son in the Holy Spirit. The more we can understand and appreciate the meaning and harmony of the different signs, the more effectively are we able to participate fully, actively, and consciously in the liturgy for our sanctification and the glory of God.

Conclusion

In one of his letters on Holy Thursday, St. John Paul II encouraged pastors to instruct the faithful on the meaning of the signs and symbols of the liturgy "by which the faithful are helped to understand the meaning of the liturgy's words and actions, to pass from its signs to the mystery which they contain, and to enter into that mystery in every aspect of their lives" (MND, 17). This exhortation eloquently summarizes the dynamic nature of the language of the liturgy. The signs and symbols of the liturgy "contain" the mystery that they signify. However, it is only when we understand the liturgical signs and symbols that we are able "to pass from its signs to the mystery they contain," for "when minds are enlightened and hearts are enkindled, signs begin to 'speak'" (MND, 14). This is the essence of full, active, and conscious participation in the liturgy, passing from its visible signs to an encounter with the Blessed Trinity and the power of the Paschal Mystery which they contain and make present.

Harmony of Signs

An example of this harmony of signs that is familiar to all Catholics is the Communion Rite of the Mass. Receiving the Body and Blood of the Lord "in a paschal meal is the culmination of the Eucharist" (IOM, 125). The Communion Rite is composed of the following elements: The Lord's Prayer, the Rite of Peace, the Fraction Rite, Communion (including procession), the Communion Chant, and the Prayer after Communion. While each element is rich in meaning, "in the context of the whole celebration they constitute together a transition from one high point, the Eucharistic Prayer, to another, the sharing in Holy Communion" (IOM, 125).

1. Which of the liturgical signs and symbols discussed in chapters 1 and 2 are present in the Communion Rite? Consider such things as words, silence, movement, color, posture, images, song.
2. How do these different liturgical signs contribute to the effectiveness of this part of the Mass?
3. What might hinder or disrupt the harmony of signs?

Chapter 3

From Sign to Mystery: Mystagogical Catechesis

As we have seen in the preceding chapters, through the faith of the Church and the power of the Holy Spirit, God communicates the fruits of Christ's Paschal Mystery to us by means of a rich and varied liturgical language that engages the whole person. The challenge for us today is mastering the language of the liturgy, a task that "is particularly important in a highly technological age like our own, which risks losing the ability to appreciate signs and symbols" (SacCar, 64). It is the task of liturgical catechists to "initiate people into the mystery of Christ by proceeding from the visible to the invisible, from the sign to the thing signified, from the 'sacraments' to the 'mysteries'" (CCC, 1075). This type of catechesis is called *mystagogy*, from the Greek word for the person who led an initiate into a mystery. Its goal is to lead people from the signs to the spiritual realities they signify.

St. John Paul II encouraged this kind of catechesis. "Pastors should be committed to that *'mystagogical' catechesis* so dear to the Fathers of the Church, by which the faithful are helped to understand the meaning of the liturgy's words and actions, to pass from its signs to the mystery which they contain, and to enter into that mystery in every aspect of their lives" (MND, 17). He affirms the theme of the previous chapter: liturgical signs contain the mystery they signify. Pope Francis, speaking specifically of the sacraments of initiation, has also encouraged a mystagogical approach to catechesis that involves the whole community and opens up the meaning of liturgical signs. Such an approach, writes Pope Francis, should be part of "a broader growth process and the integration of every dimension of the person within a communal journey of hearing and response" (EG, 166). Understanding the words and actions of the liturgy enables us to pass from the outward signs and actions of the liturgy to the spiritual reality and power they contain. The sacraments have the power to utterly transform every aspect of our lives.

Mystagogical catechesis is a part of the Church's Tradition, a method of catechesis "so dear to the Fathers of the Church" (MND, 17). In the first centuries of the Church, following the reception of the sacraments of initiation—Baptism, a postbaptismal anointing which we know as Confirmation, and first Eucharist—the new Christians were given a detailed catechesis explaining the meaning of the sacraments and the significance of the words and actions of the rite they had just received. The purpose of mystagogical catechesis was not to prepare people to receive the sacraments, but rather to help them understand more deeply the sacraments they had just received. The fourth century was the golden age of mystagogical catechesis. From this period we have important mystagogical texts from such illustrious Church Fathers as St. Cyril of Jerusalem (d. 386), St. Ambrose (d. 397), Theodore of Mopsuestia (d. 428) and St. John Chrysostom (d. 407). The writings of the Church Fathers continue to instruct us about the meaning of the sacraments and constitute an important source for our exploration of the sacraments.

Pope Benedict XVI expanded St. John Paul II's emphasis on catechesis that leads people into the mystery. In *Sacrament of Charity*, he proposed a model of mystagogical catechesis consisting of three elements.

1. *"It interprets the rites in the light of the events of our salvation,* in accordance with the Church's living tradition. . . . From the beginning; the Christian community has interpreted the events of Jesus' life, and the Paschal Mystery in particular, in relation to the entire history of the Old Testament."
2. It explains *"the meaning of the signs* contained in the rites."
3. It should emphasize "the *significance of the rites for the Christian life* in all its dimensions—work and responsibility, thoughts and emotions, activity and repose." Ultimately, this kind of catechesis should lead to "an awareness that one's life is being progressively transformed by the holy mysteries being celebrated." (SacCar, 64)

Old Testament Roots

The first part of a mystagogical catechesis is to explain the sacrament in the light of its Old Testament roots. The sacraments of the Church are prefigured by the Old Testament persons (Adam, Joseph, Isaac, and

David, for example, prefigured in different ways the person and work of Christ) and events, such as anointing, the consecration of kings and priests, sacrifices, the laying on of hands, and above all the Passover. "The Church sees in these signs a prefiguring of the sacraments of the New Covenant" (CCC, 1150). The persons and events of the Old Testament point to the mysteries of Christ and reveal different aspects of his Paschal Mystery, "for he himself is the meaning of all of these signs" (CCC, 1151). There are three readily available sources that reveal the Old Testament roots of each sacrament:

- The rite itself
- The biblical readings prescribed for each sacrament
- *The Catechism of the Catholic Church*

The Rite Itself

The rite itself is always the best starting point, for these are the words we hear and say, the gestures and postures we adopt, and the signs and symbols that engage us and that lead us deeper into the mystery of the sacrament. The liturgy is one of the primary ways that the Church has passed on the faith entrusted to her by the Lord. Christ has entrusted to the Church the responsibility of passing on "the faith in its integrity so that the 'rule of prayer' (*lex orandi*) of the church may correspond to the 'rule of faith' (*lex credendi*)" (VL, 27). The terms "rule of prayer" (*lex orandi*) and "rule of faith" (*lex credendi*) refer to a principle that dates back to Prosper of Aquitaine (fifth century). The *Catechism of the Catholic Church* explains this principle: "The law of prayer is the law of faith: the Church believes as she prays. Liturgy is a constitutive element of the holy and living Tradition" (1124). Another Church Father, St. Irenaeus (late second century), expressed this principle with respect to the Mass: "Our way of thinking is attuned to the Eucharist, and the Eucharist in turn confirms our way of thinking" (CCC, 1327). From the earliest days the Church has understood the inseparable relationship between her worship and her faith, and for this reason the sacramental rite is always the best starting point for understanding the meaning of the sacrament itself.

An excellent example of this is the Prayer of Ordination for deacons from the Sacrament of Holy Orders. This prayer cites the Lord's choice of the sons of Levi as prefiguring the three degrees of ministers in the new covenant:

> as once you chose the sons of Levi
> to minister in the former tabernacle,
> so now you establish three ranks of ministers
> in their sacred offikto serve in your name.

God's choice of the sons of Levi is recorded in Numbers 1:48–53. God tells Moses not include the Levites "in the census along with the other Israelites" (49). Rather, they are to have "charge of the tabernacle of the covenant with all its equipment and all that belongs to it" and "shall be its ministers" (50). The Levites' ministry is also one of the Old Testament readings for the ordination of deacons as recorded in Numbers 3:5–9. In this passage the Lord tells Moses to station the Levites "before Aaron the priest to serve him" (5). They are responsible for all of the furnishings of the tent of meeting and for maintaining the tabernacle. They are "assigned unconditionally" to Aaron and his sons (9).

This passage prefigures an important aspect of the diaconate, the liturgical ministry of deacons. Just as the Levites were assigned to assist Aaron and his sons, so men are ordained to the diaconate "so as to serve as a vested minister in the sanctification of the Christian community, in hierarchical communion with the bishop and priests. They provide a sacramental assistance to the ministry of the bishop and, subordinately, to that of the priests which is intrinsic, fundamental and distinct."[1] Their ministry at the altar is distinct both from the liturgical ministry of the lay faithful and from that of the ministerial priesthood.[2] So, for example, "in the Eucharistic Sacrifice, the deacon does not celebrate the mystery: rather, he effectively represents on the one hand, the people of God and, specifically, helps them to unite their lives to the offering of Christ; while on the other, in the name of Christ himself, he helps the Church to participate in the fruits of that sacrifice."[3]

---

1. Congregation for the Clergy, *Directory for the Ministry and Life of Permanent Deacons (Directorium pro ministerio et vita diaconorum permanentum)*, 28.
2. Ibid.
3. Ibid.

The Biblical Readings for Each Sacrament

Each sacrament includes suggested Old Testament readings, Responsorial Psalms, passages from the New Testament epistles, and appropriate selections from the Gospels, all chosen to highlight different aspects of the sacrament being celebrated. For example, one of the Old Testament options for the Sacrament of Penance and Reconciliation is 2 Samuel 12:1–9, 13. In this passage the prophet Nathan confronts David concerning his affair with Bathsheba and arranging the death of Uriah her husband. David acknowledges his sinful actions, and Nathan replies that God has forgiven his sin. This Old Testament account prefigures several important aspects of the Sacrament of Penance: grave sin, contrition, and the announcement of forgiveness by God's representative.

Catechism of the Catholic Church

A third source for exploring the Old Testament roots of each sacrament is the *Catechism of the Catholic Church*. The Old Testament reveals many facets of sickness and healing, for "the man of the Old Testament lives his sickness in the presence of God" (CCC, 1502). The summary in the *Catechism* suggests five different aspects of the Sacrament that are expressed by the man of the Old Testament. First, he "laments his illness" and "implores healing" from God (CCC, 1502), as we hear in Psalm 38: "Foul and festering are my sores because of my folly. . . . My loins burn with fever; there is no wholesomeness in my flesh. . . . LORD, it is for you that I wait; O Lord, my God, you respond. . . . I am very near to falling; my wounds are with me always. . . . Come quickly to help me, my Lord and my salvation!" (Ps 38:6, 8, 16, 23). It is to the Lord that he recounts his suffering and from the Lord begs healing and salvation.

Lamentation, prayer and response are present in the illness of King Hezekiah as described in Isaiah 38. "In those days, when Hezekiah was mortally ill, the prophet Isaiah, son of Amoz, came and said to him: 'Thus says the LORD: Put your house in order, for you are about to die; you shall not recover.' Hezekiah turned his face to the wall and prayed to the LORD: 'Ah, LORD, remember how faithfully and wholeheartedly I conducted myself in your presence, doing what was good in your sight'" (Isaiah 38:1–3). After Hezekiah had heard Isaiah's prophecy, St. Cyril of Jerusalem asks, "What expectation was left? What hope of recovery was there?" He continues, "But Hezekiah remembered what was written—'In the hour that you turn and lament, you will be saved.' He turned his face to the wall, and from his bed of pain his mind soared up to heaven (for no wall is so thick as to stifle fervent prayer). He said, 'Lord, remember me.' . . . He whom the prophet's sentence had forbidden to hope was granted further years of life, the sun turning back its course as a witness."[4]

A second aspect of the man of the Old Testament living his sickness before God is that illness can become a way to conversion. Concerning King Hezekiah St. Cyril of Jerusalem writes, "Do you want to know the power of repentance? Do you want to understand this strong weapon of salvation and the might of confession? . . . The same king's repentance won the repeal the sentence God had passed on him."[5] Furthermore, "God's forgiveness initiates healing" (CCC, 1502), as we see in Psalm 107: "Some fell sick from their wicked ways, afflicted because of their sins. They loathed all manner of food; they were at the gates of death. In their distress they cried to the LORD, who saved them in their peril, sent forth his word to heal them, and snatched them from the grave" (Ps 107:17–20). Sin can lead to sickness, repentance to forgiveness and healing.

A third aspect is the relationship between illness and sin. "It is the experience of Israel that illness is mysteriously linked to sin and evil, and that faithfulness to God according to his law restores life" (CCC, 1502).[6] The first trial that Israel encountered during its wilderness wanderings was the spring of bitter water at Marah (Ex 15:22ff.). Moses besought the Lord, who instructed him to throw into the water a piece of wood, and "the water became fresh" (Ex 15:25). The narrator tells us that here God "put them to the test. He said: 'If you listen closely to the voice of the LORD, your God, and do what is right in his eyes: if you heed his commandments and keep his statutes, I will not afflict you with any of the diseases with which I afflicted the Egyptians; for I, the LORD, am your

4. Steven A. McKinion, ed., *Isaiah 1–39*, vol. OT 10 of *Ancient Christian Commentary on Scripture* (Downers Grove, IL: InterVarsity Press, 2004), 262.

5. Ibid., 261.

6. We should note however, that the Church does not teach that all sickness is a result of sin, as St. John Paul II has noted: "*it is not true that all suffering is a consequence of a fault and has the nature of punishment*" (SD, 11, italics original). When Jesus and his disciples pass a man born blind, his disciples ask him who sinned, the man or his parents, "that he was born blind?" Jesus replied that the man's blindness was not the result of sin, "but that the works of God might be made manifest in him" (Jn 9:2–3).

healer'" (Ex 15:26). This first trial is a deliberate allusion to the first Egyptian plague, the blood waters. The lesson is clear: "If Israel opens its heart, then its fate will be different from the Egyptians' for it will experience Yahweh as healer (v. 26) rather than sender of plagues."[7]

Fourth, the man of the Old Testament also understood that suffering can also have a redemptive meaning for the sins of others. This is clearly expressed in Isaiah 53: "My servant, the just one, shall justify the many, their iniquity he shall bear" (Is 53:11). We will discuss this passage in detail later in this chapter. Finally, a time will come when God "will pardon every offense and heal every illness" (CCC, 1502). In a future Jerusalem, Isaiah prophesies that "No one who dwells there will say, 'I am sick'; the people who live there will be forgiven their guilt" (Is 33:24). Commenting on this prophecy of salvation, Clement of Alexandria writes, "This is the greatest and noblest of all God's acts: saving humanity. But those who labor under some sickness are dissatisfied if the physician prescribes no remedy to restore their health. How, then, can we withhold our sincerest gratitude from the divine Educator when he corrects the acts of disobedience that sweep us on to ruin and uproots the desires that drag us into sin, refusing to be silent and connive at them, and even offers counsels on the right way to live? Certainly we owe him the deepest gratitude."[8]

The Old Testament illuminates some of the fundamental aspects of sickness and anticipates the definitive healing of body and soul—salvation—that Christ will accomplish through the Paschal Mystery.

Mystagogical Catechesis: Meaning of the Signs

An effective mystagogical catechesis *explains the meaning of the different signs contained in the rites*. The liturgical signs are essential because they are "bearers of the saving and sanctifying action of Christ" (CCC, 1189). Furthermore, we need to understand these signs because only when we understand them are we able to pass from the signs to the mystery they contain. The sacraments differ in their complexity and in the number and variety of the signs and symbols. The Mass, for example, employs

7. Raymond E. Brown, SS, Joseph A. Fitzmyer, SJ, and Roland E. Murphy, OCARM, *New Jerome Biblical Commentary* (Upper Saddle River, NJ: Prentice Hall, 1990), 50.

8. McKinion, *Isaiah 1–39*, 234.

a greater number of liturgical signs than the Sacrament of Penance and Reconciliation. In addition, while many signs are common to many if not all of the sacraments (see again chapter 2), each sacrament has some elements that are unique to that sacrament.

To illustrate this, let's look at three sacramental signs that comprise the Ordination of a Priest: vesting with stole and chasuble, anointing with sacred chrism, and the presentation of the paten and chalice. These three elements follow the imposition of hands and the Prayer of Consecration, the essential elements that *make* the sacrament, and so they are called "explanatory rites" since they *explain* the meaning of the sacrament just received. We'll begin with the vesting with stole and chasuble.

Immediately after the Prayer of Consecration, the newly ordained priest is vested with stole and chasuble, assisted by some of the priests present. The stole was originally a sort of protective towel or scarf that became a symbol of priestly authority, worn around the neck and falling in vertical strips in front. Current liturgical law stipulates that the stole be worn underneath the chasuble. The chasuble began as the outdoor cloak worn by citizens of the Greco-Roman world until the fifth century. It was originally a large square or circular garment with a hole cut in the middle for the wearer's head, hence the name chasuble, from the Latin word *casula*, meaning "little house." St. Isidore of Seville in the seventh century described it as "a garment furnished with a hood, which is a diminutive of *casa*, a cottage, as, like a small cottage or hut, it covers the entire person."[9] By the tenth century the chasuble was seen as a symbol of charity, as St. Ivo of Chartres (d. 1115) explained: "Over all the vestments is superimposed the chasuble . . . which, because it is the common vestment, signifies charity, which is superimposed over all the virtues [see Col 3:12–14], for the other virtues produce nothing profitable without it."[10] The chasuble is worn over the stole because "in the context of celebrating the Eucharistic Sacrifice, this symbol of charity should surely take precedence over the symbol of

9. Herbert Thurston, "Chasuble," in *The Catholic Encyclopedia* (New York: Robert Appleton, 1908), 639.

10. Monti, *A Sense of the Sacred*, 169.

authority."[11] Together, the stole and chasuble outwardly manifest "the ministry they will henceforth fulfill in the Liturgy" (RO, 113).

The newly ordained priests are anointed while kneeling before the consecrating bishop. Kneeling as a liturgical sign has many meanings. In Old Testament thought, the knees were a symbol of strength: "to bend the knee is, therefore, to bend our strength before the living God, an acknowledgement of the fact that all that we are we receive from him."[12] In several Old Testament passages—2 Chr 6:13; Ezr 9:5; Ps 22:29—it is also an expression of worship. In the Middle Ages it was also a sign of homage.[13] "One kneels as a human gesture of submission. In Christian tradition, kneeling is an acknowledgment of one's creatureliness before God. It can signify penitence for sin, humility, reverence, and adoration" (IOM, 31). In the ordination rite, it signifies the obedience of priests to the bishop. Newly ordained priests are anointed on the palms their hands. While performing the anointing, the bishop says the following words: "The Lord Jesus Christ, whom the Father anointed with the Holy Spirit and power, guard and preserve you that you may sanctify the Christian people and offer sacrifice to God" (RO, 133). This anointing "symbolizes the Priests' distinctive participation in Christ's Priesthood" (RO, 113).

Following the anointing, the bishop presents to the new priests a paten holding the bread and a chalice containing wine mixed with water for the celebration of the Mass. As the bishop hands them to the newly ordained, he says, "Receive the oblation of the holy people, to be offered to God. Understand what you do, imitate what you celebrate, and conform your life to the mystery of the Lord's Cross" (RO, 163). The priest will spend the rest of his earthly life fulfilling this command —understanding the profound spiritual reality of the Holy Sacrifice of the Mass, imitating Christ's gift of himself made present at every Mass, and conforming his life ever more completely to Christ's Paschal Mystery. This rite signifies priests' "duty of presiding at the celebration of the Eucharist and of following Christ crucified" (RO, 113).

---

11. Peter J. Elliott, *Ceremonies of the Modern Roman Rite: The Eucharist and the Liturgy of the Hours,* rev. ed. (San Francisco: Ignatius, 1995), 46.

12. Ratzinger, *Spirit,* 191.

13. United States Conference of Catholic Bishops, *Praying with Body, Mind, and Voice* (Washington, DC: United States Conference of Catholic Bishops, 2010).

These three sacramental signs—vesting with stole and chasuble, anointing with chrism while kneeling, and the presentation of the paten and chalice—signify essential aspects of the priesthood, authority exercised in charity, participation in the one priesthood of Christ, and the celebration of the Eucharist.

Significance of the Rites for Christian Life

The third aspect of effective mystagogical catechesis brings "out the *significance of the rites for the Christian life* in all its dimensions—work and responsibility, thoughts and emotions, activity and repose. Part of the mystagogical process is to demonstrate how the mysteries celebrated in the rite are linked to the missionary responsibility of the faithful. The mature fruit of mystagogy is an awareness that one's life is being progressively transformed by the holy mysteries being celebrated" (SacCar, 64). The sacraments both invite and enable us to conform our lives to the image of Christ.

Sacramental Grace

The sacraments have the power to transform our lives because they communicate God's grace to us. The *Catechism* defines grace as "the *free and undeserved help* that God gives us to respond to his call to become children of God, adoptive sons, partakers of the divine nature and of eternal life" (CCC, 1996). It is "a *participation in the life of God*" that "introduces us into the intimacy of Trinitarian life" (CCC, 1997). Grace is "the gift of the Spirit who justifies and sanctifies us," but it also includes gifts that are proper to each of the sacraments, which is our concern here (CCC, 2003). The gifts or graces that are specific to each sacrament are signified by the corresponding sacramental signs, because each liturgical sign "points to what it specifically signifies."[14] For example, the Eucharistic bread and wine are signs of the Body and Blood of Christ. Furthermore, "the sacraments are given to us humans for the 'different situations of our life,' and consequently they must contain different effects of grace."[15] Put another way, "the grace imparted by

---

14. Johann Auer, *A General Doctrine of the Sacraments and the Mystery of The Eucharist* (Washington, DC: The Catholic University of America Press, 1995), 49.

15. Ibid., 49.

the sacraments renders God's love, presence and power available in the present moment, in a way that is specific to each sacrament."[16] Reconciliation, for example, effects "a new today in Christ after we fall."[17] Through the gifts specific to each sacrament, "the Spirit heals and transforms those who receive him by conforming them to the Son of God" (CCC, 1129). God bestows on us the love and power to deepen our participation in the life of the Trinity.

However, it is also true that the sacraments are not equally fruitful in everyone who receives them. While everyone at Mass may receive the Body and Blood of Christ, the fruitfulness of this sacramental communion will vary. This is because "the fruits of the sacraments also depend on the disposition of the one who receives them" (CCC, 1128). The most obvious example is when someone receives a sacrament in a state of mortal sin, but other dispositions such as indifference or a lack of faith can affect the fruitfulness of sacramental grace. This was true during Jesus' earthly ministry. When he went to Nazareth, his hometown, the people "took offense at him. . . . And he did not work many mighty deeds there because of their lack of faith" (Mt 13:57–58). On the other hand, Jesus praised the Canaanite woman who asked him to heal her daughter: "'O woman, great is your faith! Let it be done for you as you wish.' And her daughter was healed from that hour" (Mt 15:28). There is an intimate and reciprocal relationship between the sacraments and faith: "They not only presuppose faith, but by words and objects they also nourish, strengthen, and express it. That is why they are called 'sacraments *of faith*'" (CCC, 1123). Through the sacraments God imparts his help and life to us, but we must prepare ourselves to receive them with faith and humility.

Transformation of Life

As an example of the transforming power of the sacraments, let us look at the marital bond of the Sacrament of Matrimony. God himself establishes the marital bond "in such a way that a marriage concluded and consummated between baptized persons can never be dissolved" (CCC, 1640). This bond, which results from the free human act of the spouses, is a reality and cannot be revoked. It gives rise to the marital covenant

16. Haffner, *The Sacramental Mystery*, 21.

17. Ibid., 22.

that is "guaranteed by God's fidelity" (CCC, 1640). Rooted in the covenantal love of God, it is perpetual and exclusive. This means that the marital bond is not some sacred "thing"; rather, it brings the spouses into a new and perpetual relationship with the Blessed Trinity, which springs from Christ's covenant with his Bride, the Church.

St. Paul explains the relationship between the married couple on the one hand, and Christ and the Church on the other, in his Letter to the Ephesians. After exhorting husbands to love their wives as Christ loved the Church (Eph 5:25–30), he writes, "For this reason a man shall leave his father and his mother and be joined to his wife, and the two shall become one flesh. This is a great mystery, but I speak in reference to Christ and the church" (Eph 5:31–32). It is of great significance that in this explanation, the mystery of Christ and the Church precedes the mystery of Christian marriage. "What the sacrament adds is . . . the love of Christ and his Church in which the husband and wife will share. The mystery comes first; it both reveals the divine meaning of the union of the spouses and makes that meaning a reality in them."[18] What takes place through the sacrament is a mysterious identity between sacramental sign and spiritual reality: "In a sacramental marriage there is a personal covenant uniting bridegroom and bride, but 'bridegroom and bride' here refer inseparably to Christ and the Church and to this man and this woman."[19]

This new, covenantal relationship with the Blessed Trinity is effected by the Holy Spirit, bestowed through the Nuptial Blessing. "The covenant . . . is the Holy Spirit himself. He is the source of the unity of this undivided love; he is its divine bond, which human sin cannot break."[20] This work of the Holy Spirit is vividly expressed in the Nuptial Blessing. The epiclesis asks the Lord to send down upon the couple "the grace of the Holy Spirit and pour your love into their hearts, that they may remain faithful in the Marriage covenant" (RM, For the Celebration of Marriage, A). Another form implores God to "Graciously stretch out your right hand over these your servants (N. and N.), we pray, and pour into their hearts the power of the Holy Spirit" (RM, For the Celebration of Marriage, B). The third form asks, "May the power

18. Jean Corbon, *The Wellspring of Worship*, trans. Matthew J. O'Connell, 2nd ed. (San Francisco: Ignatius, 2005), 173.

19. Ibid.

20. Ibid.

of your Holy Spirit set their hearts aflame from on high" (RM, For the Celebration of Marriage, C). In the Sacrament of Marriage, as in every liturgical celebration, "the Holy Spirit is sent in order to bring us into communion with Christ and so to form his Body. The Holy Spirit is like the sap of the Father's vine which bears fruit on its branches" (CCC, 1108). This new relationship with the Blessed Trinity, guaranteed by God's own fidelity, endures for the whole of married life.

Participation

In its *Constitution on the Sacred Liturgy*, the Second Vatican Council put special emphasis on "full, conscious, and active participation in liturgical celebrations" by all the faithful (SC, 14). "In the reform and promotion of the liturgy, this full and active participation by all the people is *the aim to be considered before all else*" (SC, 14, italics added). The Council's vision of participation has two dimensions, interior and exterior. Interior participation requires "a good understanding of the rites and prayers" so all present are "conscious of what they are doing, with devotion and full involvement" (SC, 48). Exterior participation means participating "by means of acclamations, responses, psalmody, antiphons, and songs, as well as by actions, gestures, and bearing. And at the proper times all should observe a reverent silence" (SC, 30). It also means that those who have a role to perform, whether minister or layperson, "should do all of, but only, those parts" proper to their office (SC, 28). The Church urges this full, conscious, and active participation because "it is the primary and indispensable source from which the faithful are to derive the true Christian spirit" (SC, 14).

Conclusion

The method of mystagogical catechesis proposed by Pope Benedict XVI and illustrated in this chapter can facilitate the kind of interior and exterior participation envisioned by the Church. Looking at the Old Testament roots of a sacrament reveals the unity of God's revelation in word and deed, a revelation that finds its fulfillment in Christ. Understanding the meaning of the liturgical signs, which carry within them the saving power of Christ's Paschal Mystery, enables us to pass from the signs to the mysteries they contain and to encounter Christ, who is the meaning of all of the signs. This in turn opens us up to the transforming power of each sacrament so that we may know the love of Christ which surpasses knowledge and adore the one who "is able to accomplish far more than all we ask or imagine" (Eph 3:20).

PART II

The Sacrament of Baptism

"From the time of the apostles, becoming a Christian has been accomplished by a journey and initiation in several stages" (CCC, 1229). This sacramental journey, which "can be covered rapidly or slowly" (CCC, 1229), begins with Baptism, continues with Confirmation, and reaches its fulfillment in the Eucharist. "In the sacraments of Christian initiation we are freed from the power of darkness and joined to Christ's death, burial, and resurrection. We receive the Spirit of filial adoption and are part of the entire people of God in the celebration of the memorial of the Lord's death and resurrection" (GICI, 1). In this section, chapters 4–6, we will look closely at the Sacrament of Baptism, which "is the basis of the whole Christian life, the gateway to life in the Spirit . . . and the door which gives access to the other sacraments" (CCC, 1213).

In chapter 4 we will begin with an overview of the Sacrament of Baptism. We will then look in detail at its Old Testament roots, focusing on passages mentioned in the baptismal liturgy and interpreted by the Church Fathers as prefiguring Baptism. We will begin with the account of creation in Genesis 1, in which the spirit or breath of the Lord hovered over the waters and brought forth life. We will next consider the flood, through which God brought an end to sin and rebellion and the beginning of righteousness in the person of righteous Noah. Then we will study Israel's miraculous crossing of the Red Sea, through which the Israelites were freed from slavery in Egypt and their oppressors were destroyed. We will also examine the Moses' song of victory. The last event we will consider is Israel's crossing the Jordan to enter the Promised Land and to receive the promises of new covenant. Each of these events provides insight into the meaning and power of the Sacrament of Baptism.

In Chapter 5 we will look at the liturgical signs which comprise the celebration of the Baptism of Children, which is divided into five sections. The participants and the sign of the cross are the central signs of the Reception of the Child. This is followed by the Liturgy of the Word, whose signs include scripture readings, a homily, a litany, the prayer of exorcism, and anointing with the oil of catechumens. This leads into the Celebration of the Sacrament: the blessing of the baptismal water, followed by the renunciation of sin and profession of faith, and the threefold immersion or pouring of water and the essential words. This is followed by the Explanatory Rites, liturgical signs that indicate the different effects of the sacrament, including anointing with Chrism, clothing with a white garment, the lighted candle, and the Ephphetha rite (Prayer over the Ears and Mouth). The Sacrament of Baptism concludes with the Lord's Prayer, a blessing, and dismissal. The variety and richness of the sacramental signs convey the profound transformative power of Baptism.

We will conclude our study of Baptism by looking in chapter 6 at the transforming power of this sacrament. As "the door to life and to the kingdom of God" (RBC, 3), the effects of Baptism are manifold and dynamic. The principal effects of Baptism are the forgiveness of sin and a new birth as an adopted child of God. Union with Christ also means union with his Body, the Church, which is the third effect of Baptism. Furthermore, all who are united to Christ are united in a certain way to each other, so that Baptism is the sacramental basis for our communion with all Christians. Finally, Baptism confers an indelible seal or character that configures us to Christ. This journey will continue with "the outpouring of the Holy Spirit" (CCC, 1229) at Confirmation, which we will study in chapters 7–9, and the journey culminates in "admission to Eucharistic communion" (CCC, 1229), the subject of chapters 10–12.

Chapter 4

Baptism: Overview and Old Testament Roots

During the time of Elisha the prophet, Naaman was the army commander of the king of Aram, a man "highly esteemed and respected by his master, for through him the LORD had brought victory to Aram. But valiant as he was, the man was a leper" (2 Kgs 5:1). Providentially, his wife had a servant girl from Israel, an Aramean, who knew about Elisha. She tells Naaman's wife that Elisha can cure her husband's leprosy. With the king's permission, Naaman goes to meet Elisha, who tells him to wash seven times in the Jordan, "and your flesh will heal, and you will be clean" (2 Kgs 5:10). However, Elisha's prescribed cure angers Naaman, and he leaves, followed by his servants, who urge him to do as Elisha has commanded. He reluctantly agrees, and "his flesh became again like the flesh of a little child, and he was clean" (1 Kgs 5:14).

The Church Fathers saw in the miraculous healing of Naaman a prefiguring of the Sacrament of Baptism. St. Irenaeus noted several ways that this miracle was a type of Baptism: "It was not for nothing that Naaman of old, when suffering from leprosy, was purified upon his being baptized, but [it served] as an indication to us. For as we are lepers in sin, we are made clean, by means of the sacred water and the invocation of the Lord, from our old transgressions; being spiritually regenerated as new-born babes."[1] Naaman's leprosy was a visible sign of sin, his washing in the Jordan a sign of Baptism, and the restoration of his flesh to that of a child's a sign of spiritual rebirth.

St. Gregory of Nyssa noted the significance of Naaman washing in the Jordan: "Elisha, when Naaman the Syrian, who was diseased with leprosy, had come to him as a suppliant, cleanses the sick man by washing him in Jordan, clearly indicating what should come, both by the use of water generally, and by the dipping in the river in particular. For the Jordan alone of rivers, receiving in itself the first-fruits of

1. Irenaeus, "Fragments from the Lost Writings of Irenaeus," New Advent, accessed August 12, 2015, http://www.newadvent.org/fathers/0134.htm.

sanctification and benediction, conveyed in its channel to the whole world, as it were from some fount in the type afforded by itself, the grace of Baptism. These then are indications in deed and act of regeneration by Baptism."[2] Although Naaman had first objected to the Jordan—"Are not the rivers of Damascus, the Abana and the Pharpar, better than all the waters of Israel? Could I not wash in them and be cleansed?" (2 Kgs 5:11)—after he was cleansed, "he understood that it is not of the waters but of grace that a man is cleansed."[3] Read in the light of Christ, the cleansing of Naaman prefigures both the signs and the effects of the Sacrament of Baptism.

Baptism in the New Testament

Baptism is woven throughout Jesus' public ministry, beginning with John the Baptist, who preached a baptism of repentance to prepare the way for the Messiah (Mk 1:2–4, quoting Mal 3:1 and Is 40:3). So powerful was his ministry that "all were asking in their hearts whether John might be the Messiah" (Lk 3:15). John replied by predicting the coming of one "mightier than I" (Lk 3:16). This one, however, would not baptize with water but "with the holy Spirit and fire" (Lk 3:16). In Old Testament thought, fire, "a purifying element more refined and efficacious than water, was already a symbol of God's supreme intervention in history and of his Spirit, which comes to purify hearts (see Sir 2:5; Is 1:25; Zec 13:9; Mal 3:2–3)."[4] St. Cyril of Alexandria said that John the Baptist combined fire and Spirit "to indicate through the designation *fire* that the life-giving energy of the Spirit is given."[5]

Jesus then comes to be baptized by John, blending "into the gray mass of sinners waiting on the banks of the Jordan."[6] John objects, knowing that his baptism is intended for sinners, but Jesus replies that "it is fitting for us to fulfill all righteousness" (Mt 3:15). In the Jordan at

---

2. Gregory of Nyssa, "On the Baptism of Christ," New Advent, accessed July 4, 2015, http://www.newadvent.org/fathers/2910.htm.

3. Ambrose, "On the Mysteries," New Advent, http://www.newadvent.org/fathers/3405.htm.

4. NJB, 1613, n. 3i.

5. Manlio Simonetti, ed., *Matthew 1–13*, vol. NT 1a of *Ancient Christian Commentary on Scripture* (Downers Grove, IL: InterVarsity Press, 2001), 47.

6. Benedict XVI, *Jesus of Nazareth: From the Baptism in the Jordan to the Transfiguration* (New York: Doubleday, 2007), 16.

the hands of the John of the Baptist Jesus "goes down in the role of one whose suffering-with-others is transforming suffering that turns the underworld around, knocking down and flinging open the gates of the abyss. . . . Looked at from this angle, the sacrament of Baptism appears as the gift of participation in Jesus' world-transforming struggle in the conversion of life that took place in his descent and ascent."[7] In this event there is also a reference to Jesus inaugurating a new creation. "The Spirit who had hovered over the waters of the first creation descended then on the Christ as a prelude of the new creation, and the Father revealed Jesus as his 'beloved Son'" (CCC, 1224).

Jesus alludes to Baptism in his discussion with Nicodemus, recorded in John 3. Confused by Jesus' reference to being "born from above" (3:3), Nicodemus asks if he means a second physical birth. Jesus replies, "No one can enter the kingdom of God without being born of water and Spirit" (3:5). Commenting on this verse, St. Basil the Great explained that rebirth is an appropriate—and striking—image for Baptism, for "in making a change in lives it seems necessary for death to come as mediator between the two, ending all that goes before and beginning all that comes after."[8]

Jesus also referred to his own Death as a "baptism" (CCC, 1225). When two of his disciples, James and John, ask for seats of honor when Jesus reigns in glory, he answers with a question: "Can you drink the cup that I drink or be baptized with the baptism with which I am baptized?" (Mk 10:38). Later, as he is journeying to Jerusalem and his passion, he tells his disciples, "There is a baptism with which I must be baptized, and how great is my anguish until it is accomplished" (Lk 12:50). According to St. John Chrysostom Jesus called his Death a baptism "because by it he cleansed the world."[9] The power of the sacrament comes from the Paschal Mystery. "See where you are baptized," wrote St. Ambrose, "see where Baptism comes from, if not from the cross of Christ, from his death. There is the whole mystery: he died for you. In him you are redeemed, in him you are saved" (quoted in CCC, 1225).

---

7. Ibid., 20.

8. Joel C. Elowsky, ed., *John 1–10*, vol. NT 4a of *Ancient Christian Commentary on Scripture* (Downers Grove, IL: InterVarsity Press, 2007), 143.

9. Thomas C. Oden and Christopher A. Hall, eds., *Mark*, vol. NT 2 of *Ancient Christian Commentary on Scripture* (Downers Grove, IL: InterVarsity Press, 1998), 143.

Finally, before his Ascension Jesus commanded the eleven Apostles, "Go, therefore, and make disciples of all nations, baptizing them in the name of the Father, and of the Son, and of the holy Spirit" (Mt 28:19). Tertullian explained the importance of this charge to the apostles: "For the law of baptizing has been imposed and the formula prescribed: 'Go,' he says, 'teach the nations, baptizing them into the name of the Father and of the Son and of the Holy Spirit.'"[10] He then connects this to Jesus' words to Nicodemus: "The comparison with this law of that definition, 'Unless one has been reborn of water and Spirit, he shall not enter into the kingdom of the heavens' [Jn 3:5], has tied faith to the necessity of baptism."[11]

The Apostles' obedience to this command is described throughout the Acts of the Apostles. On the day of Pentecost Peter explains to the crowd the gift of the Spirit (Acts 2:14–36). At the conclusion of his sermon, the people "were cut to the heart" and asked him and the other apostles, "What are we to do, my brothers?" (Acts 2:37). Peter tells them, "Repent and be baptized, every one of you, in the name of Jesus Christ for the forgiveness of your sins; and you will receive the gift of the holy Spirit. . . . Those who accepted his message were baptized, and about three thousand persons were added that day" (2:39, 41). The Apostle Philip baptized many men and women in the city of Samaria (Acts 8:12). Peter baptized Cornelius, the first Gentile convert, as well as his relatives and close friends (Acts 10:48). Paul baptized the first European Christians, Lydia and her household, in the Greek city of Philippi (Acts 16:15). The Church has never ceased, from the day of Pentecost, to celebrate and administer holy Baptism (CCC, 1226).

Names of the Sacrament

The names for this sacrament reveal the different effects of its celebration. The most common name, *Baptism*, comes from the Greek word *baptizein*, which means to "plunge" or "immerse" (CCC, 1214). The catechumen is plunged or immersed in the water symbolizing his participation in Christ's Death, "from which he rises up by resurrection with him, as 'a new creature'" (CCC, 1214). The Letter to Titus refers to Baptism as "*the washing of regeneration and renewal by the Holy Spirit*"

10. Elowsky, *John 1–10*, 112.
11. Ibid.

(Ti 3:5), because "it signifies and actually brings about the birth of water and the Spirit without which no one 'can enter the kingdom of God'[Jn 3:5]" (CCC, 1215). It is also called *enlightenment* because the baptized person receives Christ who is "the true light that enlightens every man" (Jn 1:9) and so is "enlightened" (Heb 10:32) and becomes a "son of light" (1 Thes 5:5) and even "light" himself (Eph 5:8) (CCC, 1216). St. John Chrysostom explained additional names for "this mystic cleansing. . . . It is called a burial. *For you were buried,* says St. Paul, *with Him by means of baptism into death.* It is called a circumcision. *In Him, too, you have been circumcised with a circumcision not wrought by hand but through putting off the body of the sinful flesh.* It is called a cross. *For our old self has been crucified with Him, in order that the old body of sin may be destroyed.*"[12]

St. Gregory of Nazianzus explained these and other names—gift, grace, anointing, clothing, seal—concisely and elegantly:

> Baptism is God's most beautiful and magnificent gift. . . . We call it gift, grace, anointing, enlightenment, garment of immortality, bath of rebirth, seal, and most precious gift. It is called *gift* because it is conferred on those who bring nothing of their own; *grace* since it is given even to the guilty; *Baptism* because sin is buried in the water; *anointing* for it is priestly and royal as are those who are anointed; *enlightenment* because it radiates light; *clothing* since it veils our shame; *bath* because it washes; and *seal* as it is our guard and the sign of God's Lordship. (CCC, 1216)

In this brief description St. Gregory includes important elements of the rite such as washing, anointing and clothing, important effects such as enlightenment and sealing, and the generosity of God—gift and grace.

The Minister and the Recipient

"The ordinary ministers of baptism are bishops, priests, and deacons" (GICI, 11). However, because God wants all to be saved (1 Tm 2:4) and because Baptism is necessary for salvation (CCC, 1256), when the danger of death is imminent or at the moment of death, if no priest or deacon is available, "any member of the faithful, indeed anyone with the right intention, may and sometimes must administer baptism" (CIGI, 16). The "right intention" is the intention to do what the Church does when

12. Anthony M. Coniaris, ed., *Daily Readings from the Writings of St. John Chrysostom* (Minneapolis: Light and Life Publishing, 1988), 13.

she baptizes. Furthermore, the Church requires that "pastors of souls, especially the pastor of a parish, are to be concerned that the Christian faithful are taught the correct way to baptize" (CIC, c. 861 §2). On this point the Rite of Baptism of Children specifically mentions parents, catechists, midwives, family or social workers, nurses, physicians, and surgeons (CIGI, 17). These, and all lay persons, should be taught the proper method of baptizing in an emergency "since they belong to the priestly people" (CIGI, 17).

The proper recipient of Baptism is anyone not yet baptized. Unbaptized adults, known as catechumens, undergo a period of formation "by successive sacred rites" (CCC, 1248) known as the catechumenate and contained in the *Rite of Christian Initiation of Adults* (RCIA), in preparation for Baptism, Confirmation, and the Eucharist. Parents are urged to have infants baptized "in the first few weeks" (CIC, c. 867 §1), for they are born with a fallen human nature that is tainted by Original Sin (CCC, 1250). Infant Baptism has been practiced by the Church since the second century, and the Baptism of entire households recorded in the Acts of the Apostles (Acts 16:15; 16:33; 18:8) may have included infants (CCC, 1252). It is the desire of the Church that at least one parent consent to the Baptism, and "there must be a founded hope that the infant will be brought up in the Catholic religion" (CIC, c. 868 §1, 2°). However, in danger of death it is permitted to baptize an infant "even against the will of the parents" (CIC, c. 868 §2) if it can be done "in a way that avoids scandal or hatred of the faith," for example, when the parents are not present.[13] "Insofar as possible," the one being baptized should have a sponsor (a man, woman, or one of each), sometimes referred to as a godparent, who "helps the baptized person to lead a Christian life in keeping with baptism and to fulfill faithfully the obligations inherent in it" (CIC, c. 872). The sponsor must be a Catholic at least sixteen years old who has received the Sacraments of Confirmation and Eucharist, but not the parents, and is "able and ready to help the newly baptized—child or adult—on the road of Christian life" (CCC, 1255).

Baptism as the sacrament of faith requires the community of believers, for each Christian can believe "only within the faith of the Church" (CCC, 1253). For the baptized, whether adult or infant,

13. John M. Huels, *The Pastoral Companion: A Canon Law Handbook for Catholic Ministry*, 4th updated ed. (Montreal: Wilson & Lafleur, 2009), 63.

the necessary faith is only "a beginning that is called to develop" (CCC, 1253). This is why when "the catechumen or the godparent is asked: 'What do you ask of God's Church? The response is: 'Faith!'" (CCC, 1253). This faith is modeled and nourished in the family, supported by the sponsor(s), and "lived within the community of the Church, part of a common 'We'" (LF, 43). "The whole ecclesial community bears some responsibility for the development and safeguarding of the grace given at Baptism" (CCC, 1255).

Celebrating the Sacrament of Baptism

In the sacrament of Baptism the believer enters into communion with the Death, burial, and Resurrection of Christ. St. Paul explained this participation in the Paschal Mystery of Christ in his Letter to the Romans: "Or are you unaware that we who were baptized into Christ Jesus were baptized into his death? We were indeed buried with him through baptism into death, so that, just as Christ was raised from the dead by the glory of the Father, we too might live in newness of life" (Rom 6:3–4). Citing this passage and Ephesians 2:5–6 the Church teaches us that "baptism recalls and makes present the paschal mystery itself, because in baptism we pass from the death of sin into life" (CIGI, 6). "In baptism, the pledges of our covenant with God are fulfilled: burial and death, resurrection and life. And these all take place at once," explained St. John Chrysostom, "For by the immersion of our heads in the water, the old person disappears and is buried as it were in a tomb below and wholly sunk forever. Then as we raise them again, the new person rises in his place. As easy as it is for us to dip and to lift our heads again, that is how easy it is for God to bury the old person and to show forth the new. And this is done three times so that you may learn that the power of the Father, the Son and the Holy Spirit fulfills all this."[14]

In Baptism we are "consecrated to the Trinity and enter into communion with the Father, the Son, and the Holy Spirit" (CIGI, 5). The rite prepares us "for this high dignity" and leads us to it "by the scriptural readings, the prayers of the community," and our profession of faith in the Trinity. The essential elements of baptism are the triple immersion or pouring of water accompanied by the words, "I baptize you in the name of the Father, and of the Son, and of the Holy Spirit"

14. Elowsky, *John 1–10*, 113.

(CCC, 1240). This is followed by several explanatory rites, such as anointing with chrism and the presentation of a lighted candle, which clearly manifest the important aspects of this sacrament.

The sacrament is found in two ritual books, *The Rite of Baptism for Children* (RBC) and *The Rite of Christian Initiation of Adults* (RCIA). In this book we will follow the *Rite of Baptism for Children,* citing texts for the RCIA that shed additional light on specific aspects of Baptism. The RBC contains several baptismal rites, beginning with the rite for baptizing several children, followed by the rite for baptizing one child, the rite for baptizing a large number of children, the rite for baptism by a catechist, the rite for baptizing children in danger of death in the absence of a priest or deacon, and the rite for bringing a baptized child to the church. The RBC also has texts for use in Baptism, including biblical texts, different options for intercessions, and options for other elements of the baptismal rite. The RBC concludes with the text of the Litany of the Saints. Adults normally receive the sacraments of initiation "during the Vigil of the Holy Night of Easter" (RM, 207) but *The Roman Missal* also contains the Ritual Mass for the Conferral of Baptism outside of the Easter Vigil.

The Necessity of Baptism

In his discussion with Nicodemus (see above), "the Lord himself affirms that Baptism is necessary for salvation" (CCC, 1257). "The Church does not know of any means other than Baptism that assures entry into eternal beatitude; this is why she takes care not to neglect the mission she has received from the Lord to see that all who can be baptized are 'reborn of water and the Spirit'" (CCC, 1257). Although "God has bound salvation to the sacrament of Baptism . . . he himself is not bound by his sacraments" (CCC, 1257). In the case of Baptism, this divine "freedom" is understood especially in situations where those desiring and/or preparing for Baptism are prevented from receiving the sacrament. The Church has always believed in the Baptism of blood: "those who suffer death for the sake of the faith without having received Baptism are baptized by their death for and with Christ" (CCC, 1258). Although they have not received the sacrament, they receive its fruits. Similarly, if catechumens (those preparing for Baptism) die before receiving the sacrament, "their explicit desire to receive it, together with repentance for their sins, and charity, assures them the salvation that they were not able to receive through the sacrament" (CCC, 1259). Analogously, because Christ died for all and all are called to eternal life, "we must hold that the Holy Spirit offers to all the possibility of being made partakers, in a way known to God, of the Paschal mystery. Every man who is ignorant of the Gospel of Christ and of his Church, but seeks the truth and does the will of God in accordance with his understanding of it, can be saved" (CCC, 1260). Since all have been created for eternal communion with the Trinity, the Church confidently supposes "that such persons would have desired Baptism explicitly if they had known its necessity" (CCC, 1260). Finally, concerning children who die without Baptism, the knowledge that God is "rich in mercy" (Eph 2:4) and that Jesus showed great care and affection for children (cf. Mk 10:14) "allow us to hope that there is a way of salvation for children who have died without Baptism" and to stress the importance of bringing infants and children to Jesus for Baptism (CCC, 1261).

Old Testament Roots

The rite itself, in the blessing of the baptismal water during the liturgy of the Easter Vigil, identifies the Old Testament events "that already prefigured the mystery of Baptism" (CCC, 1217). The opening stanza introduces the sacramental principle: "O God, who by invisible power accomplish a wondrous effect through sacramental signs" (RM, Easter Vigil, Blessing of Baptismal Water, 46). God communicates the power and fruits of the Paschal Mystery to us through sacramental signs to "accomplish a wondrous effect." This stanza further explains that God has used water "in many ways" to express the grace of Baptism: "and who in many ways have prepared water, your creation, to show forth the grace of Baptism" (RM, Easter Vigil, Blessing of Baptismal Water, 46). The succeeding stanzas will give three different Old Testament examples—creation, the Flood, and the crossing of the Red Sea—of how God prepared water "to show forth the grace of Baptism." Each stanza cites one Old Testament example and explains how it reveals a specific aspect of Baptism.

Creation

The first Old Testament event cited in this prayer is the account of creation in Genesis 1.

> O God, whose Spirit
> in the first moments of the world's creation
> hovered over the waters,
> so that the very substance of water
> would even then take to itself the power to sanctify.
> (RM, Easter Vigil, 46)

At the beginning of the creation account—"in the first moments of the world's creation"—the world "was without form or shape" (Gn 1:2). To be formless or shapeless means "to be uninhabitable by humans—metaphorically, groundless or unreal."[15] Furthermore, there was "darkness over the abyss" (Gn 1:2), introducing "two chaotic elements [that] obstruct the emergence of the peopled cosmos—the deep and primordial night."[16] However, there is more than formlessness, darkness, and abyss, there is also "a mighty wind sweeping over the waters" (Gn 1:2). The word "wind" is a translation of the Hebrew word *rûah* that means "air in motion" and so can in different contexts can be translated as "mighty wind," "breath," or "spirit," so this passage can also be translated "the Spirit of God was moving over the face of the waters" (RSVCE translation). The point is clear: "The wind of God sweeping over the waters shows that chaos was never beyond God's control."[17] The creation of light on the first day vanquishes the night, and the abyss is overcome by the separation of the waters on the second day and the creation of the sea on the third day.[18]

Tertullian, in his interpretation of this passage from Genesis, specifically emphasized the power of water to sanctify: "The Holy One was carried over that which was holy, or, rather, over that which could receive holiness from Him Who was carried. It is thus that the nature of water, sanctified by the Spirit, received the capability of itself becoming sanctifying. This is why all waters, by reason of their ancient original prerogative, may obtain the sacrament of sanctification [Baptism] by

---

15. NJBC, 10.
16. Ibid.
17. Ibid.
18. Ibid.

the invocation of God."[19] St. Jerome emphasized the necessity of both water and the Spirit: "In the beginning of Genesis, it is written: 'And the Spirit was stirring above the waters' . . . Now for its mystical meaning—'The Spirit was stirring above the waters'—already at that time baptism was being foreshadowed. It could not be true baptism, to be sure, without the Spirit."[20] The Spirit moving over the waters is seen as a sort of primordial epiclesis (see ch. 1, p. 18), as St. Ambrose explained: "You have seen water. But all water does not heal, if the Spirit has not descended and consecrated that water."[21] St. Ephrem the Syrian emphasized the power of water to bring forth new life: "Here then, the Holy Spirit foreshadows the sacrament of holy baptism, prefiguring its arrival, so that the waters made fertile by the hovering of that same divine Spirit might give birth to the children of God."[22] As the Church Fathers saw, God chose "so humble and wonderful a creature" as water to be "the source of life and fruitfulness" (CCC, 1218).

The Flood

The blessing of the baptismal water next invokes the Flood.

> O God, who by the outpouring of the flood
> foreshadowed regeneration,
> so that from the mystery of one and the same element of water
> would come an end to vice and a beginning of virtue . . .
> (RM, Easter Vigil, 46)

The story of the Flood is recounted in Genesis 6–8 and is most likely based on "the memory of one or more disastrous floods in the valley of the Euphrates and Tigris which tradition had enlarged to the dimensions of a worldwide catastrophe."[23] The Lord, grieved at "how great the wickedness of human beings was on earth" and their continual evil desires, "regretted making human beings on the earth" (Gn 6:5–6), and determines to wipe out all living creatures except for Noah (Gn 6:9).

19. Jean Daniélou, SJ, *The Bible and the Liturgy* (Notre Dame: University of Notre Dame Press, 1956), 72–73.

20. Andrew Louth, ed., *Genesis 1–11*, vol. OT 1 of *Ancient Christian Commentary on Scripture* (Downers Grove, IL: InterVarsity Press, 2001), 6.

21. Daniélou, *The Bible and the Liturgy*, 73.

22. Ibid.

23. NJB, 25, n. 6c.

However, God's punishment is not arbitrary; rather, he "simply brings to its completion the corruption initiated by human beings."[24]

What follows is well-known. God instructs Noah to build an ark through which Noah's family and pairs of all living creatures are to be saved and promises to establish a covenant with Noah (Gn 6:18). Heavy rains flood the earth, destroying all life outside the ark. Only then does God send a wind and eventually the waters subside. God blesses Noah and his sons and commands them to be fruitful, multiply, and fill the earth. This story expresses "the tension between divine mercy and justice . . . destruction will not be the last word."[25] The memory of disastrous floods becomes for the inspired authors "a vehicle for teaching eternal truths—that God is just and merciful, that human beings are perverse, that God saves his faithful ones,"[26] truths that find their definitive expression in the Sacrament of Baptism.

"The Church," says the *Catechism*, "has seen in Noah's ark a prefiguring of salvation by Baptism, for by it 'a few, that is, eight persons, were saved through water' [1 Pt 3:20]" (CCC, 1219). Let's listen to a few of the Church Fathers. St. John of Damascus prefaces his interpretation of the Flood by noting the power of water to sanctify: "over and again Scripture testifies to the fact that water is purifying. It was with water that God washed away the sin of the world in the time of Noah."[27] St. Augustine offers a more expanded interpretation: "Who does not know, indeed, that in other times the earth was purified from its stains by the Flood. And that the mystery of holy Baptism, by which all the sins of man were cleansed by the water, was preached already beforehand?"[28] The Fathers, like the diligent scribe in the Gospels, bring forth from the Church's Scriptures treasures both old and new. We will give St. Maximus of Turin the last word: "For the very same thing is at issue with regard to Noah and in our own day: baptism is a flood to the sinner and a consecration to the faithful; by the Lord's washing, righteousness is preserved and unrighteousness is destroyed."[29] Water, then,

---

24. NABRE, 13, n. 6:11.
25. NJBC, 16.
26. NJB, 25, n. 6c.
27. Louth, *Genesis 1–11*, 132.
28. Daniélou, *The Bible and the Liturgy*, 279.
29. Louth, *Genesis 1–11*, 140.

is the perfect sacramental sign of "an end to vice and a beginning of virtue" (RM, Easter Vigil, Blessing of Baptismal Water, 46).

Crossing the Red Sea

The next Old Testament event cited in the Blessing of Baptismal Water is Israel's exodus from Egypt.

> O God, who caused the children of Abraham
> to pass dry-shod through the Red Sea,
> so that the chosen people,
> set free from slavery to Pharaoh,
> would prefigure the people of the baptized . . .
> (RM, Easter Vigil, 46)

Israel's liberation from Egyptian servitude, the liturgy teaches us, prefigures the spiritual freedom granted the sinner through Baptism.

Israel's exodus from Egypt is described in Exodus 14. Following the tenth plague, the death of every firstborn Egyptian (Ex 12:29), Pharaoh orders the Israelites to leave Egypt (Ex 12: 31). Soon after their departure, however, Pharaoh and his leaders have "a change of heart. . . . 'What in the word have we done!' they said" (Ex 14:5), and the Egyptian army sets out in pursuit of Moses and the Israelites, who God has "rerouted . . . toward the Red Sea by the way of the wilderness road" (Ex 13:18). At the sight of Pharaoh and his army, the Israelites cry out in terror to Moses. God commands Moses: "lift up your staff and stretch out your hand toward the sea, and slit it in two that the Israelites may pass through the sea on dry land. But I will harden the hearts of the Egyptians so that they will go in after them, and I will receive glory through Pharaoh and all his army" (Ex 14:16–17). And so it happened. The Israelites "walked on dry land through the midst of the sea" (Ex 14:29) while "of all Pharaoh's army which had followed the Israelites into the sea, not even one escaped" (Ex 14:28).

St. Basil the Great explains how this event prefigured Baptism: "The sea is the figure of Baptism, since it delivered the people from Pharaoh, as Baptism from the tyranny of the devil. The sea killed the enemy; so in Baptism, our enmity to God is destroyed. The people came out of the sea whole and safe; we also come out of the water as living men from among the dead."[30] St. Gregory of Nyssa imagines the

30. Ibid., 90.

catechumens coming to the baptismal found just as the Israelites approached the Red Sea pursued by the Egyptians: "when the people approach the water of rebirth as they flee from Egypt, which is sin, they themselves are freed and saved, but the devil and his aids, the spirits of wickedness, are destroyed.[31]" "Above all," teaches the *Catechism*, "the crossing of the Red Sea, literally the liberation of Israel from the slavery of Egypt, announces the liberation wrought by Baptism" (CCC, 1219).

Song of Victory: The Bath of Holy Grace

Following the destruction of the Egyptian army, Moses and the Israelites praise God for their deliverance in what is probably one of the oldest compositions in the Old Testament, the Song of the Sea, Exodus 15:1–18. "In the Bible one renders thanks by reciting publicly what God has done; the public report of the rescue makes known on earth the glory God has in heaven (cf. Ps 18, 30, 118, 138)."[32] This song is part of the official prayer of the Church, the *Liturgy of the Hours*, as part of Morning Prayer on Saturday of Week 1. The Church Fathers interpreted a number of passages from this song as prefiguring different aspects of Baptism.

The song begins with praise of the Lord who "is glorious triumphant; horse and chariot he has cast into the sea" (Ex 15:1). This, according to Augustine, anticipates the forgiveness of our sins through Baptism. "All our past sins, you see, which have been pressing on us, as it were, from behind, he has drowned and obliterated in baptism. These dark things of ours were being ridden by unclean spirits as their mounts, and like horsemen they were riding them wherever they liked. . . . We have been rid of all this through baptism, as through the Red Sea, so called because sanctified by the blood of the crucified Lord. Let us not turn back to Egypt in our hearts, but with him as our protector and guide let us wend our way through the other trials and temptations of the desert toward the kingdom."[33] The horses and chariots of Pharaoh are a type of our sins that are forgiven in Baptism through the power of Christ's Paschal Mystery.

31. Ibid.
32. NJBC, 50.
33. Ibid.

The song continues, praising God as strength, refuge, and warrior (Ex 15:2–3) and returning to the destruction of "Pharaoh's chariots and army . . . the elite of his officers" (Ex 15:4). The chariots and army, says St. Augustine, are figures of our sin and the enemy's attacks. "And the worldly pride and arrogance and the troops of innumerable sins which were fighting for the devil in us, he obliterated in baptism."[34] The Greek version of the Old Testament, the *Septuagint*, refers to "teams of three" in each chariot. These "teams of three," says St. Augustine, refer to a trio of sins with which the Devil terrorizes us "by haunting us with the fear of pain, the fear of humiliation, the fear of death. All these things were sunk in the Red Sea, because 'together with him,' together with the One who for our sakes was scourged, dishonored and slain, 'we were buried through baptism into death' [Rom 6:4]. Thus he overwhelmed all our enemies in the Red Sea, having consecrated the waters of baptism with the blood death which was utterly to consume our sins."[35] Baptism frees us from our sins and the torment of our enemy through the saving Passion of Christ.

The song recalls the enemy's boast of victory, "I will pursue and overtake them" (Ex 15:9). Just as Pharaoh was ignorant of Yahweh's power to deliver Israel, neither does our enemy comprehend God's power working through the sacrament. "The enemy does not understand the power of the Lord's sacrament, which is available in saving baptism for those who believe and hope in him. He still thinks that sins can prevail even over the baptized, because they are being tempted by the frailty of the flesh. He doesn't know where and when and how the complete renewal of the whole person is to be perfected, which is begun and prefigured in baptism and is already grasped by the most assured hope."[36]

The song next praises God who summoned the sea with his breath so that the Egyptian army sank "like lead . . . in the mighty waters" (Ex 15:10). The breath of God, says St. Ambrose, is his Spirit. "Moses himself says in his song, 'You sent your Spirit, and the sea covered them.' You observe that even then holy baptism was prefigured in

34. Joseph T. Lienhard, SJ, in collaboration with Ronnie J. Rombs, *Exodus, Leviticus, Numbers, Deuteronomy*, vol. OT 3 of *Ancient Christian Commentary on Scripture* (Downers Grove, IL: InterVarsity Press, 2001), 80.

35. Ibid., 80–81.

36. Ibid., 81.

that passage of the Hebrews, wherein the Egyptian perished, the Hebrew escaped. For what else are we daily taught in this sacrament but that guilt is swallowed up and error done away, but that virtue and innocence remain unharmed?"[37]

This song of the victorious and liberated Israelites is also our song, says St. Augustine: "This is what Moses sang and the sons of Israel with him, what Miriam the prophetess sang and the daughters of Israel with her. It is what we too now should sing, whether it means men and women or means our spirit and our flesh."[38] In a sense, the Blessing of the Baptismal Waters at the Easter Vigil is our "Song of the Sea." It is the public recitation of what God has done definitively in Christ, the proclamation of our rescue that "makes known on earth the glory God has in heaven."[39] Just as God delivered the Israelites from Egypt through the waters of the Red Sea, so "we were set free by the bath of holy grace."[40]

Crossing the Jordan

Israel's crossing the Jordan River is the fourth Old Testament event that prefigures Baptism, although it is not cited in the Blessing of Baptismal Water that we have been analyzing. This event is recounted in chapters 3 and 4 of Joshua. Assured by his spies that "the LORD has given all this land into our power" (Jos 2:24), Joshua leads Israel to the edge of Jordan. There he instructs the people to sanctify themselves for the crossing, "for tomorrow the LORD will perform wonders among you" (3:5).

The following day, priests carrying the ark of the covenant, "the visible sign of Yahweh's presence,"[41] lead Israel across the Jordan. The people are instructed to follow the ark at a distance of 2,000 cubits, approximately 3,000 feet—"do not come nearer to it" (3:4), "a scruple inspired by Yahweh's awesome presence resting on the ark."[42] The details of this crossing parallel those of crossing the Red Sea.[43] When the priests carrying the ark step into the Jordan River, "the waters flowing from upstream halted, standing up in a single heap" (3:16), enabling

37. Ibid., 81.
38. Ibid., 82.
39. NJBC, 50.
40. Lienhard, *Exodus*, 80.
41. NJBC, 114.
42. NJB, 287, note b.
43. See other parallels in NJB, 287, note 3a.

Israel once again to cross "on dry ground, until the whole nation had completed the crossing of the Jordan" (3:17). The Lord instructs Israel to commemorate the crossing with twelve stones which "are to be a sign among you . . . a perpetual memorial to the Israelites" (4:6–7).[44] In Israel's inspired reflection, "the exodus from Egypt came to be thought of in the light of the entry into Canaan, and both ideas are intertwined in [Ex] ch. 14."[45]

Drawing on this Old Testament event, St. Gregory of Nyssa exhorted those about to be baptized: "Imitate Jesus, the son of Nave [Joshua]. Carry the Gospel as he carried the Ark. Leave the desert, that is to say, sin. Cross the Jordan. Hasten toward Life according to Christ, toward the earth which bears the fruits of joy, where run, according to the promise, streams of milk and honey. Overthrow Jericho, the old dwelling-lace, do not leave it fortified. All these things are a figure (typos) of ourselves. All are prefigurations of realities which now are made manifest."[46] When Israel crossed the Jordan River "the People of God received the gift of the land promised to Abraham's descendants, an image of eternal life. The promise of this blessed inheritance is fulfilled in the New Covenant" (CCC, 1222).

Conclusion

These Old Testament passages reveal important aspects of the Sacrament of Baptism. From creation we learn that the baptismal waters receive from the Spirit the power to sanctify believers. Like the Flood, Baptism brings an end to the reign of sin and the beginning of holiness. Like the Exodus, Baptism frees us from slavery to sin and brings us into "the glorious freedom children of God" (Rom 8:21). In the assembly and in our spirits we praise God for the marvelous victory he has won for us. Finally, like the crossing of the Jordan River, Baptism introduces believers into the promises and riches of the New Covenant sealed by the blood of Christ.

44. The details of the twelve stones appear to reflect two separate traditions interwoven in the final narrative. One tradition places the stones on the west bank of the Jordan (Jos 4:20), while a separate tradition has the stones placed in the bed of the Jordan (Jos 4:9) (cf. NJBC, 114).

45. NJB, 99, n. 14.

46. Daniélou, *The Bible and the Liturgy*,103.

Chapter 5

Baptism: Signs and Symbols

Baptism is "the gateway to the sacraments" (CIC, c. 849), uniting the recipient to Christ and his Church. "In the rite of this initiation we have a more elaborate ceremony, both as better befitting the uniqueness of the occasion, which occurs but once in a lifetime for each member of Christ, and as better impressing upon us the importance of the occasion."[1] The rite consists of five parts. It begins with the Reception of the Child/Children, whose signs include the participants, the sign of the cross, and liturgical vestments. This is followed by the Liturgy of the Word, composed of readings from Scripture, a homily, general intercessions, a litany, a prayer of exorcism, and anointing with the oil of catechumens. This brings us to the high point of the rite, the Celebration of the Sacrament. This begins with the blessing of the baptismal water, followed by the renunciation of sin and profession of faith, culminating in the celebration of Baptism. The Explanatory Rites come next: anointing with chrism, clothing with a white garment, the lighted candle, and the Ephphetha rite. The Sacrament of Baptism concludes with the Lord's Prayer, a blessing, and the dismissal.

As we noted above, every sacramental celebration is "a meeting of God's children" with the Holy Trinity "that takes the form of a dialogue, through actions and words" (CCC, 1153). In the Sacrament of Baptism, dialogues are part of the Reception of the Child, the Liturgy of the Word, and the Celebration of the Sacrament. This dialogical element "is a striking illustration for us of the mind of the Church in regard to active participation by the faithful in her liturgy."[2] Dialogues help those present to "take part fully aware of what they are doing, actively engaged in the rite, and enriched by its effects" (SC, 11). "By following the gestures and words of this celebration with attentive participation,

1. Dom Virgil Michel, OSB, *The Liturgy of the Church According to the Roman Rite* (New York: MacMillan, 1937), 217.

2. Ibid., 219.

the faithful are initiated into the riches this sacrament signifies and actually brings about in each newly baptized person" (CCC, 1234).

The Reception of the Children

Liturgical celebrations, including the Sacrament of Baptism, "are not private functions, but celebrations belonging to the Church," and so they "involve the whole Body of the Church" (SC, 26). The parents, assisted by the godparents, "present the child to the Church for baptism" (RBC, 33). This, as Pope Francis has noted, is a fundamental responsibility of Christian parents: "Parents are called, as Saint Augustine once said, not only to bring children into the world but also to bring them to God, so that through baptism they can be reborn as children of God and receive the gift of faith" (LF, 43). The godparents are signs of "both the expanded spiritual family of the one to be baptized and the role of the Church as mother" (GICI, 8). "The people of God, that is, the Church, made present by the local community" (RBC, 4), includes not only the parents, godparents, and relatives, but also friends, neighbors, and members of the parish, all of whom "should take an active part" (GICI, 7). The assembly also signifies the child's right "to the love and help of the community," both before and after his or her reception of the sacrament.

The celebrant—a bishop, priest, or deacon—acts "in the name of Christ and by the power of the Holy Spirit" (GICI, 11). Since Baptism "recalls and makes present the paschal mystery itself" by which "we pass from the death of sin into life," its celebration "should therefore reflect the joy of the resurrection" (GICI, 6). To signify this joy, the celebrant should be vested "with a stole of festive color" (RBC, 35).

The celebrant begins by greeting those present, reminding all of the joy with which the children were welcomed "as gifts from God, the source of life, who now wishes to bestow his own life on these little ones" (RBC, 36). He then addresses the parents, asking them what name they are giving or have given their children, and what they are asking of God's Church for their children, to which the parents reply, "Baptism" (RBC, 37). He continues by speaking to them about the responsibility that Baptism imposes on them and their duty to raise their children to keep Christ's command to love God and neighbor. He concludes with a third question: "Do you clearly understand what you are undertaking?" to which they reply, "We do" (RBC, 39). He then asks the godparents if they are ready assist the parents in this endeavor, and they reply, "We are" (RBC, 40). These dialogues "indicate the desire of the parents and godparents, as well as the intention of the Church, concerning the celebration of the sacrament of baptism" (RBC, 15).

The dialogue with the parents and godparents is followed by signing each child on the forehead with the sign of the cross. The celebrant, in the name of the Church, addresses the child in these words: "N., the Christian community welcomes you with great joy. In its name I claim you for Christ our Savior by the sign of his cross. I now trace the cross on your forehead, and invite your parents (and godparents) to do the same" (RBC, 41). The sign of the cross "marks with the imprint of Christ the one who is going to belong to him and signifies the grace of the redemption Christ won for us by his cross" (CCC, 1235). At the same time, it expresses the desire of the parents and godparents and the intention of the Church in the sacramental celebration to follow (RBC, 16).

Baptismal Priesthood

In *The Spirit of the Liturgy*, Cardinal Ratzinger (Pope Emeritus Benedict XVI) describes how his parents would make the sign of the cross on the forehead, mouth, and chest of their children whenever they left home. It was, he writes, "like an escort that we knew would guide us on our way. It made visible the prayer of our parents, which went with us, and it gave us the assurance that this prayer was supported by the blessing of the Savior. The blessing was also a challenge to us not to go outside the sphere of this blessing. Blessing is a priestly gesture, and so in this sign of the Cross we felt the priesthood of parents, its special dignity and power."[3] He urges a return to the giving of this blessing in our daily life in order to "permeate it with the power of the love that comes from the Lord," for it is "a perfect expression of the common priesthood of the baptized."[4] What are ways that you can practice this expression of your baptismal priesthood?

3. Ratzinger, *Spirit,* 184.
4. Ibid.

The Liturgy of the Word

The celebration continues with the Liturgy of the Word: one or more readings from Sacred Scripture, a brief homily, general intercessions, a litany, the prayer of exorcism, and anointing with the oil of catechumens. It "is directed toward stirring up the faith of the parents, godparents, and congregation and toward praying in common for the fruits of baptism before the sacrament itself" (RBC, 17). The recommended readings are taken from the Gospels: John 3:1–6; Matthew 28:18–20; Mark 1:9–11; or Mark 10:13–16. However, other options from the Old and New Testaments are given in chapter 7 of the RBC. The purpose of the homily that follows is to lead all "to a deeper understanding of the mystery of baptism and to encourage parents and godparents to a ready acceptance of the responsibilities which arise from the sacrament" (RBC, 45). The general intercessions follow, with petitions for those to be baptized, their parents and godparents, and a renewal of the grace of the Baptism of all those present (RBC, 47).

The intercessions continue with an invocation of the saints known as the Litany of the Saints. A litany is a form of prayer consisting of a series of petitions, said or sung, with a fixed response, such as "Lord, have mercy" or "pray for us." It is divided into two parts: a series of petitions addressed directly to God, and the invocation of a series of saints. The origins of this prayer are obscure, although there are examples from Jewish and pagan sources. The litany was used in the early Church before the dismissal of the catechumens (those preparing for Baptism), who did not participate in the prayers of the faithful. There is evidence that this litanic prayer form was used in Rome before 225. Litanies are part of the Sacraments of Baptism, Holy Orders, and the Anointing of the Sick, the Dedication of a Church and an Altar, and the celebration of the sacraments of initiation at the Easter Vigil. They are also part of private devotions, such as the Litany of the Sacred Heart and the Litany of Loreto.

The Litany of Supplication is an example of the union of the earthly Church with the heavenly Church that occurs in every liturgical celebration. The liturgy, as we noted in chapter 2, is unceasingly celebrated in heaven by Christ, our high priest, "with the holy Mother of God, the apostles, all the saints, and the multitude of those who have already entered the kingdom" (CCC, 1187). When we celebrate the liturgy, we are "entering into the liturgy of the heavens that has always been taking place. Earthly liturgy is liturgy because and only because it joins what is already in process, the greater reality."[5] We seek the intercession of the saints because they are present at our liturgical celebrations, and their intercession is efficacious.

The litany in the RBC is brief, invoking the Blessed Virgin Mary, Saint John the Baptist, Saint Joseph, and Saints Peter and Paul.[6] However, other saints can be added, "especially the patrons of the children to be baptized, and of the church or locality" (RBC, 48). It concludes with a summary invocation of "all holy men and women" (RBC, 48).

The general intercessions conclude with a prayer "drawn up in the style of an exorcism" (RBC, 17), "since Baptism signifies liberation from sin and from its instigator the devil" (CCC, 1237). The prayer of exorcism is an example of a *sacramental.* Sacramentals are sacred signs instituted by the Church "which bear a resemblance to the sacraments" (CCC, 1667). The effects which they signify "are obtained through the intercession of the Church" (CCC, 1667). They differ from sacraments in three important ways.

1. The seven sacraments have been instituted by Christ, while sacramentals are instituted by the Church.
2. The sacraments are effective whenever they are celebrated using the rite approved by the Church by the proper minister who, in doing so, intends what the Church intends.[7] Sacramentals are effective through the prayer of the Church.
3. Sacraments confer grace whenever they are celebrated "in accordance with the intention of the Church" (CCC, 1128), while sacramentals "prepare us to receive grace and dispose us to cooperate with it" (CCC, 1670) and "sanctify different circumstances of life" (CCC, 1677).

---

5. Joseph Ratzinger, *A New Song to the Lord: Faith in Christ and Liturgy Today*, trans. Martha M. Matesich (New York: Crossroad, 1996), 166.

6. For an example of a more elaborated litany, see the Litany in *The Roman Missal* as part of the Easter Vigil (RM, Easter Vigil, 43).

7. "This is the meaning of the Church's affirmation that the sacraments act *ex opere operato* (literally: 'by the very fact of the action's being performed'), i.e., by virtue of the saving work of Christ, accomplished once for all. . . . From the moment that a sacrament is celebrated in accordance with the intention of the Church, the power of Christ and his Spirit acts in and through it, independently of the personal holiness of the minister" (CCC, 1128).

Sacramentals usually include a prayer and a sign such as the sign of the cross or the sprinkling of holy water. Examples of sacramentals include blessings of persons, places, meals, and things, as well as exorcisms.

The Church distinguishes two kinds of exorcisms, simple or minor exorcisms, and solemn or major exorcisms. The exorcisms found in the RBC and RCIA are examples of simple or minor exorcisms. "Minor exorcisms are prayers used to break the influence of evil and sin in a person's life, whether as a catechumen preparing for Baptism or as one of the baptized faithful striving to overcome the influence of evil and sin in his or her life."[8] The proper minister of a minor exorcism is "the designated authorized minister of the sacrament," which in the case of Baptism means a bishop, priest, or deacon, or in the RCIA, a priest, deacon, or "qualified catechist appointed by the bishop for this ministry" (RCIA, 91). In addition to effecting a true liberation from evil and its author, the exorcism emphasizes "the real nature of Christian life, the struggle between flesh and spirit, the importance of self-denial for reaching the blessedness of God's kingdom, and the unending need for God's help" (RCIA, 90).

The RBC offers two prayers of exorcism. Both begin by recalling Christ's victory over sin and Satan: "Almighty and ever-living God, you sent your only Son into the world to cast out the power of Satan, spirit of evil, and to rescue man from the kingdom of darkness, and bring him into the splendor of your kingdom of light [Col 1:13–14]" (RBC, 49A). The Christian battle that the children will face is frankly acknowledged: "We now pray for these children who will have to face the world with its temptations, and fight the devil in all his cunning" (RBC, 49B). The prayers conclude with several petitions: "cleanse these children from the stain of original sin" (RBC, 49B); "make them temples of your glory" (RBC, 49A); "strengthen them with the grace of Christ" (RBC, 49B); "send your Holy Spirit to dwell within them" (RBC, 49A); "and watch over them at every step in life's journey" (RBC, 49B).

This leads directly into the anointing with the oil of catechumens. In the early Church those preparing for Baptism were anointed over their entire body—"from the hair of your head to your toes," in the

8. "29 Questions on Exorcism and Its Use in the Church, Part One," *Newsletter*, Committee on Divine Worship, vol. 50 (November 2014): 44.

words of St. Cyril of Jerusalem.[9] St. Cyril refers to it as "exorcised oil . . . the token which drives away every trace of the enemy's power."[10] This oil, he explains, "through invocation of God and through prayer, is invested with such power as not merely to cleanse all traces of sin with its fire, but also to pursue all the invisible powers of the wicked one out of our persons."[11]

It still retains this exorcistic function today. The introduction to the blessing of this oil in the *Roman Pontifical* says that "The Oil of Catechumens extends the effects of the baptismal exorcisms: it strengthens the candidates with the power to renounce the devil and sin before they go to the font of life for rebirth."[12] The RCIA expresses a similar thought, explaining that this anointing with the Oil of Catechumens "symbolizes their need for God's help and strength so that, undeterred by the bonds of the past and overcoming the opposition of the devil, they will forthrightly take the step of professing their faith and will hold fast to it unfalteringly throughout their lives" (RCIA, 99).

In addition to combatting the devil, the oil also communicates more broadly God's strength and wisdom. The prayer of blessing of the Oil of Catechumens asks God to bless the oil and so "give wisdom and strength to all who are anointed with it in preparation for their Baptism."[13] The words that accompany the anointing express the same thought: "We anoint you with the oil of salvation in the name of Christ our Savior; may he strengthen you with his power, who lives and reigns for ever and ever" (RBC, 50). The prayer of blessing, said by the bishop, explains a final dimension to this anointing. The prayer asks God to "Bring them to a deeper understanding of the Gospel, help them to accept the challenge of Christian living, and lead them to the joy of new birth in the family of your Church."[14]

9. Edward Yarnold, SJ, *The Awe-Inspiring Rites of Initiation: The Origins of the RCIA*, 2nd ed. (Collegeville, MN: The Liturgical Press, 1994), 77.

10. Ibid.

11. Ibid.

12. RPont, *The Rite for the Blessing of Oils and the Consecration of Chrism*, 2.

13. Ibid.

14. Ibid.

The Celebration of the Sacrament

The celebration now moves to the baptismal font (see chapter 2 on movement).[15] It begins with the epiclesis to consecrate the baptismal water (CCC, 1238).[16] St. Ambrose has left us a description of this epicletic prayer from the fourth century, emphasizing the presence and action of the Trinity: "The priest comes, he says a prayer at the font, he invokes the name of the Father, the presence of the Son and the Holy Spirit; he uses heavenly words. They are heavenly words, because they are the words of Christ which say that we must baptize in the name of the Father and of the Son and of the Holy Spirit."[17] St. Ambrose then compares it to an event in the Old Testament, Elijah's encounter with the prophets of Baal in which at his prayer God sends down fire to consume the sacrifice he has prepared (see 1 Kgs 18:20): "If at a word of men, at the invocation by one of the saints [Elijah's prayer], the Trinity was present, how much more efficacious this presence is where the eternal word is working."[18] In another passage St. Ambrose describes the Spirit's consecration of the baptismal water: "You have seen the water, but all water does not heal; that water heals which has the grace of Christ. The water is the instrument, but it is the Holy Spirit Who acts. The water does not heal, if the Spirit does not descend to consecrate it."[19] St. Ambrose's older contemporary, St. Cyril of Jerusalem, describes the transformation of the water by the Trinity: "Ordinary water, by the invocation of the Holy Spirit, of the Son and of the Father, acquires a sanctifying power."[20] The Church Fathers remind us of the activity of the three Persons of the Trinity in the Sacrament of Baptism.

The RBC offers three options for the epiclesis: an extended blessing of the water (RBC, 54A) that is also found in *The Roman Missal* for the liturgy of the Easter Vigil (RM, Easter Vigil, 44) and the RCIA (RCIA, 311), and two shorter options in the form of litanies with responses for the congregation—"Blessed be God" in response to praise for God's saving works (RBC, 54B and C), and "Hear us, Lord" in

15. If the assembly is large for the baptistery, the baptism can be celebrated at another place within the church (RBC, 52).

16. See the section entitled "Epiclesis" in chapter 1, page 18.

17. Yarnold, *The Awe-Inspiring Rites*, 1115.

18. Yarnold, *The Awe-Inspiring Rites*, 1115.

19. Daniélou, *The Bible and the Liturgy*, 42.

20. Ibid.

response to petitions for the Lord's blessing of the water (RBC, 54B). Here we will look at the first option, the extended blessing found in *The Roman Missal*. The opening stanzas of this prayer recall several Old Testament events that illustrate how God "prepared water, your creation, to show forth the grace of Baptism" (RM, Easter Vigil, 44). These events, discussed in the previous chapter, include creation, illustrating that water could "take to itself the power to sanctify" (RM, Easter Vigil, 44); the flood, showing how water can bring "an end to vice and a beginning of virtue" (RM, Easter Vigil, 44); and the crossing of the Red Sea, foreshadowing how baptism frees the people of God from sin.

Here we will look more carefully at the section of the prayer invoking the Holy Spirit, a moment whose importance can go unnoticed, for "the faithful, and perhaps even celebrants, are too often unconscious of the consecration of the baptismal water."[21] After recounting Jesus' baptism, suffering, Death, and Resurrection—the Paschal Mystery—and commission to the eleven to teach and baptize all nations (cf. Mt 28:16–20), the prayer asks God to send the Holy Spirit upon the water.

> look now, we pray, upon the face of your Church
> and graciously unseal for her the fountain of Baptism.
> May this water receive by the Holy Spirit
> the grace of your Only Begotten Son,
> so that human nature, created in your image
> and washed clean through the Sacrament of Baptism
> from all the squalor of the life of old,
> may be found worthy to rise to the life of newborn children
> through water and the Holy Spirit.
> [At this point the paschal candle may be lowered into the water once or three times]
> May the power of the Holy Spirit,
> O Lord, we pray,
> come down through your Son
> into the fullness of this font [holding the candle in the water]
> so that all who have been buried with Christ by Baptism into death
> may rise again to life with him."
> (RM, Easter Vigil, 46)

This part of the prayer, the epiclesis proper, explains and brings about the Spirit's power to act through the water to effect the saving

21. Corbon, *The Wellspring of Worship*, 164.

work of Baptism, cleansing from sin, restoring the radiance of God's image in the recipient, and making him or her a sharer in the death and resurrection of Christ. "When catechumens are immersed in the waters of baptism . . . they are really 'baptized' because they participate in what the epiclesis has made real beforehand . . . the epiclesis that makes baptism possible has consisted in the coming of the Holy Spirit into the water in which the catechumens are to be baptized."[22]

The prayer also helps us understand that this is not just an individual event, but an ecclesial action, an action of the Church, Christ's body, "the fullness of the one who fills all things in every way" (Eph 1:23). "Every epiclesis is a sacramental Pentecost, but here the Spirit really descends, enters into the water, and transforms it into a 'divine milieu'. This new reality is the maternal womb of the Church, in which a man who is born of flesh and blood and human desire will be immersed in order that it may be born of the Spirit and the Bride. The virginal fruitfulness of the Church is the masterpiece of the Spirit. This is how the sons of God are born (Jn 1:13)."[23] This is a wondrous work of the Trinity, the Father sending forth his Spirit to make fruitful the Body of his Son, the Church.

The Blessing of the Water is followed by the Renunciation of Sin. The celebrant addresses the parents and godparents, exhorting them to have "constant care" that "the divine life" God is giving the children may be "kept safe from the poison of sin, to grow always stronger in their hearts" (RBC, 56). He then invites them to reject sin, for which there are two options, both in the form of a dialogue of three questions and answers ("I do"). The first option asks them to reject Satan, all his works, and all his empty promises (RBC, 57A), while the second form asks them if they first "reject sin, so as to live in the freedom of God's children", then reject "the glamor of evil, and refuse to be mastered by sin," and finally, "reject Satan, father of sin and prince of darkness" (RBC, 57B).

The question-and-answer form of renunciation is ancient. St. Ambrose describes a dialogue that is almost identical to that found in the current rite. "When the question was put to you, Do you renounce the devil and his works? What was your reply? I do renounce

22. Ibid.

23. Ibid.

them. And: Do you renounce the world and its pleasures? What was your reply? I do renounce them. Keep what you said in mind. The terms of the guarantee you gave must never fade from your memory."[24] The early Church Fathers emphasized the importance of this renunciation. St. Cyril of Jerusalem urged his newly baptized, "Now realize this: all that you say, especially at that most awesome moment, is written in God's books. So when you are found contravening your promise, you will be judged a transgressor."[25] St. John Chrysostom spoke in similarly strong language: "There is great power in these few words. For the angels who are present and the invisible powers rejoice at your conversion and, receiving the words from your lips, carry them to the common master of all things, where they are inscribed in the books of heaven."[26]

The renunciation of Satan leads directly into the profession of faith, for which it is an essential preparation: "Thus prepared, he [the catechumen] is able to confess the faith of the Church, to which he will be 'entrusted' by Baptism" (CCC, 1237, italics original). This too takes the form of a dialogue, using the Apostles' Creed, and concludes with an expression of assent by the assembly and the celebrant. In so doing, "the community exercises its duty. . . . In this way it is clear that the faith in which the children are baptized is not the private possession of the individual family, but the common treasure of the whole Church of Christ" (RBC, 4). Children, however, cannot accept "the faith by a free act, nor are they yet able to profess that faith on their own; therefore the faith is professed by their parents and godparents in their name" (LF, 43). This solemn moment is recalled and celebrated each year as part of the Easter Vigil, in which the baptismal liturgy concludes with the assembly renewing its baptismal promises. Why? "For all the baptized, children or adults, faith must grow after Baptism. For this reason the Church celebrates each year at the Easter Vigil the renewal of baptismal promises" (CCC, 1254).

We come now to the essential rite, the triple infusion with water accompanied by the prescribed Trinitarian formula. Baptism must be conferred by either a triple immersion or triple pouring of water. Both

24. Yarnold, *The Awe-Inspiring Rites* 102. St. Ambrose's reference to a "guarantee" may be an allusion to the Profession of Faith.

25. Ibid., 72.

26. Ibid., 159.

the matter—water—and the manner in which it is administered, especially immersion, are powerful sacramental signs.

Baptism must be conferred using "true water" (CIC, c. 849) which, "both for the sake of authentic sacramental symbolism and for hygenic reasons, should be pure and clean" (RBC, 18). St. Thomas Aquinas described the different characteristics of water that make it the appropriate sacramental sign of baptism. Water, he wrote, "symbolizes regeneration into spiritual life, just as it is a principle of generation in the natural life of men, animals and plants. By reason of its moistness, it symbolizes cleansing, because of its freshness it symbolizes the cooling of the passions of sin, by reason of its transparency it allows the light to pass, symbolizing the illumination of the faith. . . . Since water is so common and abundant, it is opportune that it is the matter of this necessary sacrament for salvation (Aquinas, ST, III, 66, 3)."[27] The ability to give life as well as moistness, freshness, and transparency are natural qualities of water that point to deeper spiritual realities.

St. Ambrose offers a somewhat more playful explanation of the fittingness of water for Baptism. Addressing the newly baptized, he asks, "But what conclusions do you draw from the fact that it is in water that you are immersed? Are you a little lost here? Does some doubt creep in?"[28] He begins his answer by summarizing how, in the account of creation in Genesis 1, water brought forth living things, an event with a deeper spiritual meaning: "but this gift was kept for you: that the waters should regenerate you into grace, even as those other waters generated life."[29] He then continues with a surprising exhortation: "Imitate the fish. . . . On the sea the tempest rages, violent winds blow; but the fish swims on. . . . In the same way, this world is the sea for you. It has various currents, huge waves, fierce storms. You too must be a fish, so that the waves of this world do not drown you."[30] The sanctifying and strengthening waters of Baptism prepare us to swim safely through the sea of this world.

Baptism is administered by either a threefold immersion or pouring over the head of blessed water accompanied by the essential words: "N., I baptize you in the name of the Father" (immerse or pour water),

27. Haffner, *The Sacramental Mystery*, 38.

28. Yarnold, *The Awe-Inspiring Rites*, 120.

29. Ibid., 121.

30. Ibid.

"and of the Son" (immerse or pour water), "and of the Holy Spirit" (immerse or pour water).

Although pouring is permitted, immersion is "the original and full sign" of Baptism and so "is more suitable as a symbol of participation in the death and resurrection of Christ" (RBC, 22). Baptism by immersion "efficaciously signifies the descent into the tomb by the Christian who dies to sin with Christ in order to live a new life" (CCC, 628). This is based on Romans 6:4: "We were indeed buried with him through baptism into death, so that, just as Christ was raised from the dead by the glory of the Father, we too might live in newness of life." For this reason St. Gregory of Nazianzus urged his catechumens, "Let us be buried with Christ by Baptism to rise with him; let us go down with him to be raised with him; and let us rise with him to be glorified with him" (CCC, 537).

St. Hilary of Poitiers explained how this is truly an efficacious sacramental sign, a sign that accomplishes what it signifies: "Everything that happened to Christ lets us know that, after the bath of water, the Holy Spirit swoops down upon us from high heaven and that, adopted by the Father's voice, we become sons of God" (CCC, 537). St. Cyril of Jerusalem summarizes this sacramental reality in two striking images, tomb and mother: "In one and the same action you died and were born; the water of salvation became both tomb and mother for you. . . . [Y]our begetting was simultaneous with your death."[31]

The triple immersion or pouring of blessed water accompanied by the words, "N., I baptize you in the name of the Father, and of the Son, and of the Holy Spirit," constitutes the essential rite of Baptism. This rite "signifies and actually brings about [efficaciously signifies] death to sin and entry into the life of the Most Holy Trinity through configuration to the Paschal mystery of Christ" (CCC, 1239).

The Explanatory Rites

The celebration of the sacrament is followed by four explanatory rites, entitled Anointing after Baptism, Clothing with White Garment, Lighted Candle, and Ephphetha or Prayer over Ears and Mouth. We will consider each in turn.

31. Ibid., 8.

The first explanatory rite is the Anointing after Baptism, in which the newly baptized is anointed with sacred chrism. Chrism is plant oil scented with an aromatic substance such as balsam or perfume and consecrated by the bishop that signifies the Holy Spirit. In addition to the Sacraments of Baptism and Confirmation, it is also used in the Sacrament of Holy Orders to anoint the hands of priests and the heads of bishops, and "in the rites of anointing pertaining to the dedication of churches and altars" (CB, 274).[32]

In the Sacrament of Baptism, chrism has two principal meanings. First, "the anointing of the baptized person with chrism in the presence of God's people" is a sign of the "unchangeable effect" of Baptism (RBC, 4). Second, it "signifies the royal priesthood of the baptized and enrollment into the company of the people of God" (RBC, 18.3). This is clearly expressed by the words which introduce the anointing: "God the Father of our Lord Jesus Christ has freed you from sin, given you a new birth by water and the Holy Spirit, and welcomed you into his holy people. He now anoints you with the chrism of salvation. As Christ was anointed Priest, Prophet, and King, so may you live always as members of his body, sharing everlasting life" (RBC, 62). The child is the anointed on the crown of the head with Chrism in silence (RBC, 62).[33]

The reference to the threefold office of Christ—Priest, Prophet, and King—is taken from "the Old Testament usage of anointing kings, priests, and prophets with consecratory oil because they prefigured Christ, whose name means 'the anointed by the Lord.'"[34] As examples of the anointing of kings the *Catechism* cites Saul (1 Sm 10:1), David (1 Sm 16:13), and Solomon, (1 Kgs 1:39); an example of the anointing of priests is Aaron and his sons, (Ex 29:7); and an example of the anointing

32. "It is on account of this chrism that the houses of prayer help us to pray. They become for us what they are called by being anointed with chrism. . . . As for the altars, they imitate the Saviour's hand. From the anointed table we receive the bread as from the undefiled hand, receiving the Body fo Christ and drinking His Blood like those whom the Master first made partakers of the sacred table as He pledged them with that awesome cup of friendship" (Nicholas Cabasilas, *The Life in Christ* [Crestwood, NY: St. Vladimir's Seminary Press, 1998], 111).

33. This anointing is omitted for adult catechumens since they are anointed with Chrism in the sacrament of Confirmation, which they receive immediately after Baptism. The RCIA omits this reference except when Confirmation is deferred, an omission that Yarnold laments: "it is a pity that all reference to the Christian's union with Christ the Priest, Prophet and King is lost" (Yarnold, *The Awe-Inspiring Rites*, 30).

34. RPont, *Rite for the Blessing of Oils*, 2.

of prophets is Elisha (1 Kgs 19:19). In the new covenant, "the Chrism is a sign that Christians, incorporated by Baptism into the Paschal Mystery of Christ, dying, buried, and rising with him [SC, 6], are sharers in his kingly and prophetic Priesthood and that by Confirmation they receive the spiritual anointing of the Spirit who is given to them."[35] The Church provides a choice of two prayers for the consecration of chrism, and both include a reference to this threefold ministry of Christ: "Through this sign of Chrism grant them royal, priestly, and prophetic honor, and clothe them with incorruption"; "Through that anointing you transform them into the likeness of Christ your Son and give them a share in his royal, priestly, and prophetic work."[36] The baptismal anointing with chrism anticipates the Sacrament of Confirmation and helps us understand the integral relationship between these two sacraments as distinct but complementary impartations of the Holy Spirit. "[T]he post-baptismal anointing announces a second anointing with sacred chrism to be conferred later by the bishop at Confirmation, which will as it were 'confirm' and complete the baptismal anointing" (CCC, 1242).

Pope St. Leo the Great described the faithful's participation in the kingly and priestly offices of Christ this way: "What, indeed, is as royal for a soul as to govern the body in obedience to God? And what is as priestly as to dedicate a pure conscience to the Lord and to offer the spotless offerings of devotion on the altar of the heart" (CCC, 786). The faithful participate in the prophetic office of Christ when they "cooperate with the bishops and priests in the exercise of the ministry of the word" by word and example.[37] Evangelization is a participation in the prophetic ministry of Christ, efforts directed toward the "sanctification of men" a priestly participation, and efforts "to have the Gospel spirit permeate and improve the temporal order" a kingly participation.[38] The liturgy expresses this threefold participation in Preface I of the Sundays in Ordinary Time, which praises God for "summoning us to the glory of being now called a chosen race, a royal priesthood, a holy nation, a people for your own possession, to proclaim everywhere your mighty

35. Ibid.

36. Ibid., 25.

37. Haffner, *The Sacramental Mystery*, 47.

38. *Apostolicam Actuositatem (The Decree on the Apostolate of the Laity)*, Second Vatican Council, November 18, 1965.

works, for you have called us out of darkness into your own wonderful light" (RM, 52). This passage is based on 1 Peter 2:9: "But you are 'a chosen race, a royal priesthood, a holy nation, a people of his own, so that you may announce the praises of him who called you out of darkness into his wonderful light." These different titles "underline its [the Church] relationship with God and its responsibility in the world."[39]

The next explanatory rite is the clothing of the newly baptized in a white garment, a symbol that he or she has "put on Christ" (CCC, 1243), which is a reference to Galatians 3:27: "For as many of you as were baptized into Christ have put on Christ" (RSVCE rev.) St. John Chrysostom calls this verse "awe-inspiring. For if Christ is the Son of God and you put him on, having the Son inside yourself and being made like him, you have been made one in kind and form."[40]

In the early Church the neophytes were baptized naked and then clothed in a white garment. St. Cyril of Jerusalem explained the meaning of this garment: "Once you have stripped off the old garments and put on those which are spiritually white, you must be clad in white always. I am not of course saying that you must always wear white clothing on your body, but that your spiritual dress must be truly white and shining, so that you may say, in the words of the blessed Isaiah: 'Let my soul rejoice in the Lord: he has clothed me with the garment of salvation, and with the robe of gladness he has covered me' [61:10]."[41] St. John Chrysostom sees it as a uniform and compares it to the uniform worn by those who work in the world. They wear on their clothes, he says, "an imperial badge as a sign to the public of their trustworthiness. They would not permit themselves to do anything unworthy of their uniform; and even if they attempted it, there are many people to stop them. . . . Now the neophytes carry Christ himself, not on their clothes, but dwelling in their souls with his Father, and the Holy Spirit has descended on them there. They are even more obliged, then, to prove themselves reliable, and show everyone by their scrupulous conduct and careful lives that they wear the imperial badge."[42] The

39. NJB, 2003, n. 2d.

40. Mark J. Edwards, ed., *Galatians, Ephesians, Philippians*, vol. NT 8 of *Ancient Christian Commentary on Scripture Ancient Christian Commentary on Scripture* (Downers Grove, IL: InterVarsity Press, 1999), 51.

41. Yarnold, *The Awe-Inspiring Rites*, 89.

42. Ibid., 32.

white garment invited other interpretations. St. Ambrose said it was a reminder of Christ's radiant white garments at the Transfiguration, John the Deacon saw it as a sort of wedding-garment, and for Zeno it was a reminder of the fleece of Christ the Lamb.[43]

In the current rite, the newly baptized is addressed in these words: "you have become a new creation, and have clothed yourselves in Christ. See in this white garment the outward sign of your Christian dignity. With your family and friends to help you by word and example, bring that dignity unstained into the everlasting life of heaven" (RBC, 63). A white garment, preferably provided by the family, is then put on the child (RBC, 63, rubric).

This is followed by the third explanatory rite, the lighted candle, lit from the Easter candle, also known as the Paschal Candle, which "is the symbol of the light of Christ, rising in glory, scattering the darkness of our hearts and minds."[44] Taking the Paschal Candle, the celebrant says, "Receive the light of Christ." A family member lights the child's candle from the Easter candle, and the celebrant then addresses them in these words: "Parents and godparents, this light is entrusted to you to be kept burning brightly. These children of yours have been enlightened by Christ. They are to walk always as children of the light. May they keep the flame of faith alive in their hearts. When the Lord comes, may they go out to meet him with all the saints in the heavenly kingdom" (RBC, 64). This final admonition—to go out to meet the Lord—is "also apparently an allusion to the lamps of the bridesmaids of the parable [Mt 25]."[45] This rite is a sign that the newly baptized have been enlightened by Christ and in him they "are 'the light of the world'" (CCC, 1243).

This rite signifies in a simple yet profound way the communal nature of the faith. Faith, wrote Pope Francis, "is a reality lived within the community of the Church, part of a common 'We'" (LF, 43). For this reason, children need the support of their parents, godparents and the local community, and are "welcomed into their faith, which is the faith of the Church; this is symbolized by the candle which the child's father lights from the paschal candle" (LF, 43). Pope Francis explains how

43. Ibid.

44. Committee on Divine Worship, USCCB, *Ten Years of the Newsletter:* 2001–2010 (Washington, DC, 2011), 226.

45. Yarnold, *The Awe-Inspiring Rites*, 33.

baptism expresses the integral relationship between the Church and the family, the domestic church: "The structure of baptism, then, demonstrates the critical importance of cooperation between Church and family in passing on the faith. Parents are called, as Saint Augustine once said, not only to bring children into the world but also to bring them to God, so that through baptism they can be reborn as children of God and receive the gift of faith" (LF, 43).

The final explanatory rite is the Ephphetha Rite, the prayer over the ears and mouth. This rite is taken from one of the healing miracles recorded in the Gospel of Mark. People brought a deaf man with a speech impediment to Jesus. Jesus took the man apart from the crowd, put his finger into the man's ear, and touched his tongue with some of his spittle. Jesus then "looked up to heaven and groaned, and said to him, 'Ephphatha!' (that is, 'Be opened!'). And [immediately] the man's ears were opened, his speech impediment was removed, and he spoke plainly" (Mk 7:35). One of the Church Fathers, Prudentius, praised this and other miracles in a hymn:

> Deafened ears, of sound unconscious,
> every passage blocked and closed,
> At the word of Christ responding,
> all the portals open wide,
> Hear with joy friendly voices and
> the softly whispered speech
> Every sickness now surrenders,
> every listlessness departs,
> Tongues long bound by chains of silence
> are unloosed and speak aright,
> While the joyful paralytic
> bears his pallet through the streets.[46]

In the current rite the celebrant touches the ears and mouth of the child with his thumb and says, "The Lord Jesus made the deaf hear and the dumb speak. May he soon touch your ears to receive his word, and your mouth to proclaim his faith, to the praise and glory of God the Father" (RBC, 65). As the words indicate, in the Baptism of infants this rite looks ahead to when the child will be able to hear and understand God's word and to proclaim it by word and deed. For newly baptized adults, the rite expresses the truth that it is by God's grace that

46. Oden and Hall, *Mark*, 99.

believers are able to hear and profess the word of God: "By the power of its symbolism the ephphetha rite, or rite of opening the ears and mouth, impresses on the elect their need of grace in order that they may hear the word of God and profess it for their salvation" (RCIA, 197). Whether celebrated with children or adults, this rite affirms our fundamental vocation to hear and proclaim the Gospel.

The Conclusion of the Rite

The Rite of Baptism concludes with the Lord's Prayer, a Blessing, and the Dismissal. It begins with a procession from the baptismal font to the altar, with a parent or godparent carrying the lighted candle. As we explained in chapter 2, processions are important liturgical signs. Just as the anointing with chrism looks ahead to Confirmation, so the procession to the altar looks ahead to the Eucharist. The Church "expresses the orientation of Baptism to the Eucharist by having the newly baptized child brought to the altar for the praying of the Our Father" (CCC, 1244). The invitation to the assembly explains the unity of the sacraments of initiation:

> Dearly beloved, these children have been reborn in baptism. They are now called children of God, for so indeed they are. In confirmation they will receive the fullness of God's Spirit. In holy communion they will share the banquet of Christ's sacrifice, calling God their Father in the midst of the Church. In their name, in the Spirit of our common sonship, let us pray together in the words our Lord has given us. (RBC, 68)

Through this prayer the newly baptized—now or when they are old enough—will "learn to share in Christ's spiritual experience and to see all things through his eyes" (LF, 46).

The celebration concludes with a three-part solemn blessing: first, over the mother holding the child, then over the father, and finally over the assembly (RBC, 70). The tripartite structure of the solemn blessing is modeled on the threefold blessing God instructed Aaron to give the Israelites:

> The LORD bless you and keep you!
> The LORD let his face shine upon you, and be gracious to you!
> The LORD look upon you kindly and give you peace!"
> (Nm 6:26)

The Roman Missal contains a large number of solemn blessings for other occasions. There are twenty different solemn blessings For Celebrations in the Different Liturgical Times, such as Advent, The Beginning of the Year, Easter Time, The Holy Spirit, and six options for Ordinary Time. There are four solemn blessings For Celebrations of the Saints, one for the Dedication of a Church, and one for Celebrations for the Dead. Several Ritual Masses also include optional solemn blessings: Confirmation, Anointing of the Sick, Holy Orders, the Blessing of an Abbot or Abbess, the Consecration of Virgins, and Religious Profession. Appropriate solemn blessings can be used not only at the end of Mass, but also to conclude liturgies of the word and the *Liturgy of the Hours*.[47] The solemn blessings are "undoubtedly a great acquisition, because they add appropriate aspects to the general formula of blessing and interpret them as well."[48]

The three-part blessing begins with a blessing of the mother, a blessing which "occupies a special place" (CCC, 1245). The blessing begins by invoking God the Father, his Son, and the Virgin Mary, for through them joy has come "to all Christian mothers . . . as they see the hope of eternal life shine on their children" (RBC, 105A). God the Father is then asked to bless the mother who "now thanks God for the gift of her child" and to grant that she may "be one with him/her in thanking him for ever in heaven, in Christ Jesus our Lord" (RBC, 105A). The father is then blessed by invoking "God . . . the giver of all life, human and divine" (RBC, 105). The prayer acknowledges the parents' responsibility in communicating the faith to the child: "He and his wife will be the first teachers of their child in the ways of faith. May they be also the best of teachers, bearing witness to the faith by what they say and do, in Christ Jesus our Lord" (RBC, 105). Finally, those present are blessed with a prayer that begins by recalling their Baptism: "By God's gift, through water and the Holy Spirit, we are reborn to everlasting life" (RBC, 105). The Lord is then petitioned to "make them always, wherever they may be, faithful members of his holy people. May he send his peace upon all who are gathered here" (RBC, 105).

---

47. Johannes H. Emminghaus, *The Eucharist: Essence, Form, Celebration*, trans. Linda M. Maloney, revised and edited by Theodor Mass-Ewerd (Collegeville, MN: The Liturgical Press, 1997), 213.

48. Ibid., 214.

This three-part blessing reveals important aspects of the Sacrament of Baptism. The blessings for the mother and father emphasize the importance of the family as the domestic church, for it is within the family "that parents are 'by word and example . . . the first heralds of the faith with regard to their children'" (CCC, 1656). It is also within the family that the members "exercise *the priesthood of the baptized* in a privileged way 'by the reception of the sacraments, prayer and thanksgiving, the witness of a holy life, and self-denial and active charity'" (CCC, 1657, italics original). The blessing of the assembly highlights the community of faith to which the child belongs and the fact that liturgical celebrations, regardless of the number of those present, are always celebrations of the Church (SC, 26). This tripartite blessing brings the celebration of the Sacrament of Baptism to a solemn and beautiful conclusion.

Conclusion

The Sacrament of Baptism unfolds through the rich and dynamic sacramental signs of the celebration. The water reveals how a simple element of the natural world can become the vehicle for God's transforming power and invested with layers of meaning. The signs which comprise the sacrament engage the whole person—hearing the word of God, the light of fire, the scent of the perfumed chrism, the touch of water and oil, the sight of the white garment. Gestures such as the sign of the cross and touching the water during the prayer of blessing convey the power of God. The various dialogues between minister, parents, and the assembly make present in this place and time the eternal dialogue between God and his children. Signs such as chrism and the Our Father prayed before the altar point to the fulfillment of Baptism in the Sacraments of Confirmation and the Eucharist. Taken together the signs make present the mystery of God's power in our lives through the Paschal Mystery of Christ, and we can make our own the words of St. John Chrysostom when he said, "I was right, then—was I not?—to speak of the need we have of the eyes of faith if we are to believe in what is unseen instead of despising what our sense perceives."[49]

49. Yarnold, *The Awe-Inspiring Rites*, 155.

Chapter 6

Baptism: Living the Sacrament

Baptism, is "the door to life and to the kingdom of God . . . the first sacrament of the New Law" (RBC, 3). These words indicate the profound importance of Baptism and its transforming effects on the believer, effects which we will consider in this chapter. According to the *Catechism of the Catholic Church*, the first principal effect is "purification from sins," the forgiveness of original and personal sin (CCC, 1262). Baptism's second principal effect is "new birth in the Holy Spirit" (CCC, 1262), a new birth that brings us into intimate communion with the Most Holy Trinity. Union with the Blessed Trinity is also union with the Body of Christ, the Church, and also communion with all other members of his Body, the third and fourth effects of Baptism. Finally, Baptism imprints an indelible seal or character that configures us to Christ.

Forgiveness of Sin

The first principal effect of Baptism is "purification from sins" (CCC, 1262). "Baptism, the cleansing with water by the power of the living word [cf. Eph 5:25]," says the RBC, "washes away every stain of sin, original and personal" (5). In addition to forgiveness of original and personal sin, Baptism also forgives "all punishment for sin. In those who have been reborn nothing remains that would impede their entry into the Kingdom of God, neither Adam's sin, nor personal sin, nor the consequences of sin, the gravest of which is separation from God" (CCC, 1263).

Original Sin is the sin in which Adam, "tempted by the devil, let his trust in his Creator die in his heart and, abusing his freedom, disobeyed God's command. This is what man's first sin consisted of" (CCC, 397). In his Letter to the Romans, St. Paul teaches that all are affected by Adam's sin: "through one person sin entered the world, and through sin, death, and thus death came to all, inasmuch as all sinned . . . through the disobedience of one person the many were made sinners" (Rom 5:12, 19). Although the Church acknowledges that "the transmission of original sin is a mystery that we cannot fully understand" (CCC, 404), she "has always taught that the overwhelming misery which oppresses men and their inclination toward evil and death cannot be understood apart from their connection with Adam's sin and the fact that he has transmitted to us a sin with which we are all born afflicted, a sin which is the 'death of the soul'" (CCC, 403). The personal sin of Adam and Eve "affected the human nature that they would then transmit *in a fallen state*" (CCC, 404). The *Catechism* further explains that Original Sin "is a sin 'contracted' and not 'committed'—a state and not an act" (CCC, 404). Original Sin "does not have the character of a personal fault" (CCC, 405); rather, human nature is deprived "of original holiness and justice . . . it is wounded in the natural powers proper to it; subject to ignorance, suffering, and the dominion of death" (CCC, 405). Baptism erases Original Sin and "turns man back toward God" (CCC, 405).

Although Baptism forgives Original Sin, it does not eradicate some of the "temporal consequences of sin . . . such as suffering, illness, death, and such frailties inherent in life as weakness of character" (CCC, 1264). Because of these remaining temporal consequences, our desires and appetites are still disordered and incline us to sin, as St. Augustine explains: "Whatever our sin was previously, it was wiped out in baptism. But because all our iniquity has been blotted out, does that mean there is no weakness left? If there were no weakness left, then that would mean that we should be living here without sin. Yet who would venture to say such a thing except someone who is proud but also unworthy of the Deliverer's mercy."[1] This weakness that remains, the "inclination to sin," is called concupiscence, "or metaphorically, 'the tinder of sin'" (CCC, 1264). Concupiscence is not *in and of itself* sinful, but rather is an inclination to sin which we must resist, for "it cannot harm those who do not consent but manfully resist it by the grace of Jesus Christ.' Indeed, 'an athlete is not crowned unless he competes according to the rules'" (CCC, 1264).

Finally, Baptism also forgives all personal sin, sin which we commit and for which we are responsible once we have reached the age of

1. Elowsky, *John 1–10*, 298.

discretion, which the Church has established as the age of seven (CIC, c. 97 §2).Tradition has recognized a basic distinction regarding the seriousness of personal sin, a distinction based on 1 John 5:16–17: "If anyone sees his brother sinning, if the sin is not deadly, he should pray to God and he will give him life. This is only for those whose sin is not deadly. There is such a thing as deadly sin, about which I do not say that you should pray. All wrongdoing is sin, but there is sin that is not deadly." In this passage, John distinguishes between sins that are "deadly" and sins that are "not deadly." The Tradition of the Church calls deadly sin mortal or grave sin, and sin that is not deadly venial sin. Mortal sin is "a grave infraction of the law of God that destroys the divine life in the soul of the sinner (sanctifying grace), constituting a turn away from God" (CCC, glossary). For a sin to be mortal or grave, three conditions must be present: it must be grave or serious matter, the sinner must know that it is grave matter, and he or she must freely choose to commit the sin. Only when these three conditions are present can one be *held responsible* for committing a grave sin.

In assessing this responsibility for grave sin, Pope Francis reminds us of the Church's teaching that one's *responsibility* for a sinful action, which *in and of itself* is grave, is affected by other factors: "pastors and the lay faithful who accompany their brothers and sisters in faith or on a journey of openness to God must always remember what the *Catechism of the Catholic Church* teaches quite clearly: 'Imputability and responsibility for an action can be diminished or even nullified by ignorance, inadvertence, duress, fear, habit, inordinate attachments, and other psychological or social factors' [CCC, 1735]" (EG, 44). A clear understanding of sin helps us enter into the love of the Trinity and live in the joy and freedom God wants for all of his children—sin is a rejection of God's desire to bring us into a communion of love and freedom.

The significance of forgiveness is not always fully appreciated in our day. In 1946, Pope Pius XII stated that "the sin of the century is the loss of the sense of sin,"[2] an observation echoed by his successors. Pope Blessed Paul VI observed in 1972, "Ours is an age that desperately needs to recover a clear, well-founded moral consciousness and that yearns for liberation from the force that most interiorly and oppressively holds

---

2. Pope Pius XII, Radio Message to the U.S. National Catechetical Congress in Boston (October 26, 1946): *Discorsi e Radiomessaggi VIII* (1946), 288.

people prisoner."[3] St. John Paul in *Reconciliation and Penance* quoted this assertion by Pope Pius XII: "words that have almost become proverbial" (RaP, 18) and stated in the strongest terms: "The sacrament of penance is in crisis" (RaP, 28). At the close of the Great Jubilee Year of 2000, seventeen years later, he again acknowledged "the crisis of 'the sense of sin' in today's culture" and proposed to the universal Church as a pastoral priority encouraging "persuasively and effectively" the Sacrament of Reconciliation.[4]

St. John Paul II has not only noted the crisis of the sense of sin and its effect on the sacrament of penance but has discussed at length various factors that have contributed to this crisis (RaP, 18). He begins by looking at four social-cultural factors that contribute to this loss of the sense of sin. First, he notes the influence of a secularism that emphasizes production, consumerism, and pleasure seeking and reduces sin to anything that offends man. Teachings that place the blame for sin upon society or the influences of environment and historical conditioning and declare the individual free of all responsibility are a second factor. Added to this is a denial that certain actions or attitudes are always wrong and sinful—everything is relative, there are no absolutes. Finally, he noted a false identification of sin with "a morbid feeling of guilt or with the mere transgression of legal norms and precepts"—breaking the rules rather than hurting a relationship rooted in love.

In addition to these factors, St. John Paul II also acknowledges certain trends in the thought and life the Church that "inevitably favor the decline of the sense of sin" (RaP, 18). In some cases, he observes, a tendency to see sin everywhere has been replaced by a failure to recognize it anywhere. Also, an exaggerated emphasis on the fear of eternal punishment has given way "to preaching a love of God that excludes any punishment deserved by sin" (RaP, 18). Finally, some have passed "from severity in trying to correct erroneous consciences . . . to a kind of respect for conscience which excludes the duty of telling the truth" (RaP, 18).

A third set of factors noted by the saint concerns sacramental practice. Sin has both an individual and a communal dimension—it

3. Paul VI, Address to a General Audience, on the sacrament of reconciliation, 19 July 1972, note 8 (1972), 305–307, in *Documents on the Liturgy 1963–1979: Conciliar, Papal, and Curial Texts* (Collegeville, MN: The Liturgical Press, 1982), n. 363, 953.

4.. John Paul II, *Novo Millennio Ineunte* (Boston: Pauline Books and Media, 2001), n. 37.

wounds our relationship with God, and it hurts our relationship with others and the Church. Today, notes the saint, there is "the tendency to obscure the ecclesial significance of sin and of conversion and to reduce them to merely personal matters; or vice versa, the tendency to nullify the personal value of good and evil and to consider only their community dimension" (RaP, 18). Finally, he notes "the danger, never totally eliminated, of routine ritualism that deprives the sacrament of its full significance and formative effectiveness" (RaP, 18). What is needed, he says, is "a rediscovery of Christ as . . . the one in whom God shows us his compassionate heart and reconciles us fully with himself. It is this face of Christ that must be rediscovered through the Sacrament of Penance."[5]

Each believer first experiences the compassion of Christ and reconciliation with the Trinity in the forgiveness of his/her sins granted in Baptism. The wonder and amazement of forgiveness is proclaimed in the Eucharistic Prayer, the Church's great prayer of praise, thanksgiving, sacrifice, offering, and intercession directed to the Father through Christ in the Holy Spirit. In the Ritual Mass for the Conferral of Baptism, the Church provides special inserts for the Eucharistic Prayer, and one of the themes is forgiveness. In Eucharistic Prayer I, the Roman Canon, God is petitioned to accept the Eucharistic Sacrifice in a particular way for the newly baptized, "granting them forgiveness of all their sins so as to find them in Christ Jesus our Lord" (RM, Ritual Masses I, 3A, Eucharistic Prayer [EP] I, proper *Hanc igitur*). The insert for Eucharistic Prayer III brings before God "your servants who by the cleansing waters of rebirth . . . have today been joined to your people" (RM, Ritual Masses I, 3A, EP III). Baptism is for us the occasion of the same joy experienced by the Israelites when they were miraculously "set free from slavery to Pharoah," for they "prefigure the people of the baptized" (RM, Easter Vigil, Blessing of the Water, 46).

An Adopted Child of God

The second principal effect of Baptism is "regeneration and renewal . . . new birth in the Holy Spirit" (CCC, 1262). Baptism makes one "'a new creature,' an adopted son of God" (CCC, 1265). This new birth by Baptism is reflected in the prayers of the Eucharistic Liturgy for

5. Ibid.

Baptism, where special mention is made of the newly baptized. The opening prayer (Collect) prays specifically for those "strengthened by the spirit of adoption as your children" (RM, Ritual Masses I, 3A, Collect). The special inserts for the Eucharistic Prayer also mention the grace of new birth. In addition to the petitions for the pope, bishop and others, God is asked to "be mindful of . . . especially the newly baptized, whom today you have brought to new birth by water and the Holy Spirit" (RM, EP IV), or in the words of the insert for Eucharistic Prayer I, "those to whom you have been pleased to give the new birth of water and the Holy Spirit" (RM, Ritual Masses I, 3A, proper *Hanc igitur*).

The Apostle Paul described the radical nature of this new birth in his second letter to the Church at Corinth: "So whoever is in Christ is a new creation: the old things have passed away; behold, new things have come" (2 Cor 5:17). In his commentary on this verse, St. Basil the Great spoke of three creations, the first "from nonexistence into existence," and the third, "the resurrection from the dead." [6] The middle or second creation is "the change from worse to better," a change brought about by Baptism: "Now, humanity is created a second time through baptism, 'for if any man is in Christ, he is a new creature.'"[7] In his commentary on this same passage, St. John Chrysostom described the newly baptized as "citizens of a new world": "Let us forget the whole past and, like citizens in a new world, let us reform our lives, and let us consider in our every word and deed the dignity of him who dwells within us."[8] St. John Chrysostom's exhortation to preserve diligently our citizenship "in a new world" is reflected in the Eucharistic Liturgy for Baptism. Here too we pray that "we may always walk in newness of life" (RM, Ritual Masses I, 3A, Collect). This is also the petition for the newly baptized in the insert for Eucharistic Prayer III: "grant that they may always walk in newness of life" (RM, Ritual Masses I, 3A, EP III).

In formal theological language this new birth and creation is called "sanctifying grace, the grace of justification," and is the work of the Most Holy Trinity (CCC, 1266; italics original). This grace grants the newly baptized the theological virtues of faith, hope, and charity, which enable them "to believe in God, to hope in him, and to love him"

6. Gerald L. Bray, ed., *1–2 Corinthians*, vol. NT 7 of *Ancient Christian Commentary on Scripture* (Downers Grove, IL: InterVarsity Press, 1999), 247.

7. Ibid.

8. Ibid.

(CCC, 1266). It also makes them docile to the Holy Spirit, able to live and act at his prompting "through the gifts of the Holy Spirit" (CCC, 1266). Grace is associated in a particular way with the Holy Spirit, for according to the *Catechism*, "Grace is first and foremost the gift of the Spirit" (CCC, 2003). But the *gift* of the Spirit "also includes the *gifts* that the Spirit grants us to associate us with his work, to enable us to collaborate in the salvation of others and in the growth of the Body of Christ, the Church" (CCC, 2003; italics added). Finally, this grace allows the recipients "to grow in goodness through the moral virtues" (CCC, 1266).

The sanctifying and justifying grace of Baptism is the work of the Most Holy Trinity, and the ultimate goal of this Trinitarian work is Trinitarian communion. "The blessed Trinity is invoked over those who are to be baptized, so that all who are signed in this name are consecrated to the Trinity and enter into communion with the Father, the Son, and the Holy Spirit" (RBC, 5). One of the Greek Fathers, St. Gregory of Nazianzus, has left us a glimpse of the heights of this Trinitarian communion into which Baptism introduces us: "my eyes have been blinded by the light of the Trinity, whose brightness surpasses all that the mind can conceive; for from a throne high exalted the Trinity pours forth upon all, the ineffable radiance common to the Three. This is the source of all that is here below, separated by time from the things on high."[9]

Adoption, new birth, a new creation—in these powerful and resonant images we see the fulfillment of the Genesis Flood, that "from the mystery of one and the same element of water would come an end to vice and a beginning of virtue" (RM, Easter Vigil, 46). The entire dynamic "of the Christian's supernatural life has its roots in Baptism" (CCC, 1266).

One of the Church Fathers, Ambrosiaster, explained the interrelationship between the two principal effects of Baptism—forgiveness and adoption—and the perseverance they entail. Commenting on St. Paul's First Letter to the Corinthians (6:9–11), he wrote, "In baptism the believer is washed clean from all sins and is made righteous in the name of the Lord, and through the Spirit of God he is adopted as God's child. . . . But afterward, by thinking which is contrary to this

9. Vladimir Lossky, *The Mystical Theology of the Eastern Church* (Crestwood, NY: St. Vladimir's Seminary Press, 2002), 44.

baptismal rule of faith, they had stripped themselves of these benefits. For this reason, he is trying to bring them back to their original way of thinking, so that they can recover what they had once received."[10]

Digging into the Catechism

As we discussed in chapter 4, grace is "a participation in the life of God" (CCC, 1997). It is "favor, the free and undeserved help that God gives us to respond to his call to become children of God" (CCC, 1996). To learn more about how God helps us and deepens our participation in his divine life, look up the following terms in the *Catechism*.

Habitual grace (CCC, 2000)

Actual graces (CCC, 2000)

Sacramental graces (CCC, 2003)

Special graces/charisms (CCC, 2003)

Graces of state (CCC, 2004)

Incorporated into the Church

Baptism initiates us into communion with the Most Holy Trinity and gives us the gift of the Spirit. A further effect, one that in a sense follows from these, is incorporation into the Church, the Body of Christ (Eph 1:22–23; CCC, 795) and Temple of the Holy Spirit (1 Cor 6:19; CCC, 797). "From the baptismal fonts is born the one People of God of the New Covenant, which transcends all the natural or human limits of nations, cultures, races, and sexes: 'For by one Spirit we were all baptized into one body' [1 Cor 12:13]" (CCC, 1267). In Baptism we "are incorporated into the Church and are built up together in the Spirit into a house where God lives [cf. Eph 2:22], into a holy nation and a royal priesthood [cf. 1 Pt 2:9; also Preface]" (GICI, 4). In the words of the liturgy, "the newly baptized . . . have today been joined to your family" (RM, Ritual Masses I, 3A, EP II), they "have today been joined to your people" (RM, Ritual Masses I, 3A, EP III).

10. Bray, *1–2 Corinthians*, 53.

As members of Christ's Church, the newly baptized have both responsibilities and rights. The responsibilities and duties of the newly baptized stem from the communal and hierarchical nature of the Church. "From now on, he is called to be subject to others, to serve them in the communion of the Church, and to 'obey and submit' to the Church's leaders, holding them in respect and affection" (CCC, 1269). As members of the Church, the new baptized also share in the Church's mission. "'Reborn as sons of God, [the baptized] must profess before men the faith they have received from God through the Church' and participate in the apostolic and missionary activity of the People of God" (CCC, 1270). But Baptism also confers rights that equip the newly baptized to carry out their responsibilities. The newly baptized have the right "to receive the sacraments, to be nourished with the Word of God and to be sustained by the other spiritual helps of the Church" (CCC, 1269).

Baptism incorporates us into "a royal priesthood" (GICI, 4), recalling the baptized's participation in the priestly, prophetic, and kingly offices of Christ. Following Baptism, infants and children are anointed on the crown of their head with chrism as the celebrant says: "As Christ was anointed Priest, Prophet, and King, so may you live always as members of his body, sharing everlasting life" (RBC, 62). The *Catechism* explicitly connects this participation in Christ's priestly, prophetic and kingly offices to our incorporation into the Church. The newly baptized have become "'living stones' to be 'built into a spiritual house, to be a holy priesthood. By Baptism they share in the priesthood of Christ, in his prophetic and royal mission'" (CCC, 1268). Here we will develop our discussion—begun in the previous chapter—of the participation of the baptized in Christ's priestly, prophetic, and kingly offices.

At the heart of the faithful's participation in Christ's priestly and sanctifying office is the offering of sacrifice, understood in the most comprehensive way and oriented to the Holy Sacrifice of the Mass. "For all their works, prayers, and apostolic undertakings, family and married life, daily work, relaxation of mind and body, if they are accomplished in the Spirit—indeed even the hardships of life if patiently born—all these become spiritual sacrifices acceptable to God through Jesus Christ. In the celebration of the Eucharist these may most fittingly be offered to the Father along with the body of the Lord" (CCC, 901). Parents participate in the office of sanctifying by living their married life "in the Christian spirit" and providing for "the Christian education of their children" (CCC, 902). The faithful participate in the priestly office of Christ when they serve as liturgical ministers in the Eucharistic liturgy (CCC, 903). "And so, worshipping everywhere by their holy actions, the laity consecrate the world itself to God, everywhere offering worship by the holiness of their lives" (CCC, 901).

The laity also contribute to the building up of the Church by participating in Christ's prophetic office. "By virtue of their prophetic mission, lay people 'are called . . . to be witnesses to Christ in all circumstances and at the very heart of the community of mankind'" (CCC, 942). St. Thomas Aquinas reminds us that proclaiming the Gospel is not just the job of priests and religious: "To teach in order to lead others to faith is the task of every preacher and of each believer" (CCC, 904). All Christians are to proclaim Christ both by word and example. The evangelization by the lay faithful has "a specific property and peculiar efficacy because it is accomplished in the ordinary circumstances of the world" (CCC, 905). The laity also exercise their prophetic office when they serve in catechetical formation.

Finally, the faithful also build up the Church when they participate in Christ's kingly office through his "gift of royal freedom" (CCC, 908). The newly baptized must start by rightly ordering his or her own life, as St. Ambrose taught in the fourth century. "That man is rightly called a king who makes his own body an obedient subject and, by governing himself with suitable rigor, refuses to let his passions breed rebellion in his soul, for he exercises a kind of royal power over himself. And because he knows how to rule his own person as king, so too does he sit as its judge. He will not let himself be imprisoned by sin, or thrown headlong into wickedness" (CCC, 908). Through the practice of self-denial and a holy way of life, the newly baptized "have the power to uproot the rule of sin within themselves and in the world" (CCC, 943). The faithful are called to work for the transformation of the sinful and broken institutions and circumstances of the world and thereby "impregnate culture and human works with a moral value" (CCC, 909). Their participation in Christ's kingly office also includes participation in the life of the Church, diocese, and parish through "particular councils, diocesan synods, pastoral councils; the exercise of the pastoral care of a parish, collaboration in finance committees, and participation in ecclesiastical tribunals" (CCC, 911). Possessing rights and duties both as members of human society and as members of Christ's Church, the faithful must always strive to harmoniously unite these two spheres, "remembering that in every temporal affair they are to be guided by a Christian conscience, since no human activity, even of the temporal order, can be withdrawn from God's dominion" (CCC, 912). In these ways the baptized, incorporated into the Church and anointed as sharers in Christ's priestly, prophetic, and kingly offices, contribute to the growth and sanctification of the Church and the world.

The Sacramental Basis for Communion with All Christians

As we have seen, Baptism brings us into communion with the Blessed Trinity and unites us to the Church, which is the Body of Christ and the Temple of the Holy Spirit. This is true for every validly baptized person, every person who is baptized with water in the name of the Father, and of the Son, and of the Holy Spirit, with the intention of doing what the Church does, what she accomplishes through Baptism. For this reason, "Baptism is a sacramental bond of unity linking all who have been signed by it" (RBC, 4) and "the foundation of communion among all Christians, including those who are not yet in full communion with the Catholic Church. . . . They therefore have a right to be called Christians, and with good reason are accepted as brothers by the children of the Catholic Church" (CCC, 1271).

This, however, also indicates the dynamic nature of Baptism, which "is only a beginning, a point of departure" (UR, 22). Introduced into communion with the Trinity and the life of grace and united to Christ's Church, the newly baptized "is thus ordained toward a complete profession of faith, a complete incorporation into the system of salvation such as Christ himself willed it to be, and finally, toward a complete integration into eucharistic communion" (UR, 22). Thus, this sacramental bond of unity with all the baptized compels us to work for the unity for which Christ himself prayed, died, rose and ascended to the Father. On the night of his betrayal, Christ prayed not only for his apostles, "but also for those who will believe in me through their word, so that they may all be one, as you, Father, are in me and I in you, that they also may be in us" (Jn 17:20–21). "But we must realize," acknowledges the *Catechism*, "'that this holy objective—the reconciliation of all Christians in the unity of the one and only Church of Christ—transcends human powers and gifts'" (CCC, 822). Baptism unites us to God, to whom we proclaim, "you never cease to gather a people to yourself" (RM, EP III, 108), and to whom we pray, "gather to yourself all your children scattered throughout the world" (RM, EP III, 113). The desire to restore the unity of all Christians "is a gift of Christ and a call of the Holy Spirit" (CCC, 820).

> **Digging into the Catechism**
>
> What, according to CCC, 821, are the seven requirements for us to respond to the gift and call for the unity of all Christians?

The Sacramental Character

Baptism, Confirmation, and Holy Orders, are the three sacraments that confer not only grace but also "a sacramental character or 'seal'" (CCC, 1121). This character or seal makes the Christian a sharer in Christ's priesthood and a member of his Church. It is an indelible configuration both to Christ and his Church (CCC, 1121). This seal "remains forever in the Christian as a positive disposition for grace, a promise and guarantee of divine protection, and as a vocation to divine worship and to the service of the Church" (CCC, 1121). Note in particular the three effects of this sacramental character: first, it gives the believer "a positive disposition for grace," the right disposition "to share in the divine life" (2 Pt 1:4) and to receive God's gifts; second, it is God's "promise and guarantee of divine protection," God's commitment to us; and third, it equips us for our vocation—our calling—"to divine worship and to the service of the Church" (CCC, 1121). The biblical concept of "the seal is a symbol close to that of anointing," and in all three sacraments "this seal indicates the indelible effect of the anointing with the Holy Spirit" (CCC, 698).

We can think of this sacramental character or seal as "a sign, sculptured by God within the person configuring them to Christ."[11] The Sacraments of Baptism, Confirmation, and Holy Orders each

11. Haffner, *The Sacramental Mystery*, 23–24.

impart a distinctive sacramental character. "The baptized person is consecrated and united with Christ as a confessor of the faith, the confirmed person is set apart as a defender of the faith, and the ordained man is denoted as a servant of Christ (in the diaconal order) or as a mediator of Christ (in the presbyteral and episcopal orders) within the Church."[12] We will consider the meaning of the seal in the Sacrament of Confirmation in chapter 9; here we will look specifically at the meaning of the seal in the Sacrament of Baptism.

The New Testament teaches us that God set his seal on Christ, his anointed one (Jn 6:27), and he seals us in him (2 Cor 1:22; Eph 1:13; 4:30). The citations in 2 Corinthians and Ephesians are all references to Baptism. In a passage that is explicitly Trinitarian, St. Paul reminded the Corinthian Church that "the one who gives us security with you in Christ and who anointed us is God; he has also put his seal upon us and given the Spirit in our hearts as a first installment" (2 Cor 1:21–22). Commenting on this passage, St. Ambrose writes, "Because you have been baptized in the name of the Trinity, in all that we have done the mystery of the Trinity has been preserved. Everywhere the Father, the Son and the Holy Spirit, one operation, one sanctification. . . . How? God, who anointed you, and the Lord sealed you and placed the Holy Spirit in your heart. Therefore, you have received the Holy Spirit in your heart." [13] According to Severian of Gabala, this seal indicates our belonging to Christ: "Shepherds brand their sheep so as to distinguish the ones which belong to them from others. This is what Christ has done to us."[14] Concerning St. Paul's reference to the seal as a "first installment," St. Augustine wrote this: "Let the faith and hope and charity, which are diffused through the hearts of the faithful by the Holy Spirit, be your consolation. We receive a little of it in this life as a pledge to make us learn how to long for its fullness. You must not think of yourself as left alone, since in the interior life you have Christ, present in your heart by faith."[15]

The seal is also mentioned twice in the Letter to the Ephesians. St. Paul reminds the Ephesians that in Christ they heard the Gospel, they believed in him, and they 'were sealed with the promised holy

12. Haffner, *The Sacramental Mystery*, 23–24.

13. Bray, *1–2 Corinthians*, 200.

14. Ibid.

15. Ibid., 201.

Spirit, which is the first installment of our inheritance toward redemption as God's possession, to the praise of his glory" (Eph 1:13–14). "By this seal," said St. John Chrysostom, "God shows great forethought for humanity. He not only sets apart a people and gives them an inheritance but secures it as well. It is just as if someone might stamp his heirs plainly in advance; so God set us apart to believe and sealed us for an inheritance of future glory."[16]

In Ephesians 4, in the midst of exhortations to unity and godly conduct, there is another reference to the seal: "And do not grieve the holy Spirit of God, with which you were sealed for the day of redemption" (Eph 4:30). St. Jerome, in his commentary on this passage, touches on the notion of belonging, restoration, and the promise of future glory: "That we have been 'sealed' with the Holy Spirit means that both our spirit and our soul are impressed with God's own seal, signifying that we belong to him. By this we receive in ourselves that image and likeness in which we were created at the outset. . . . You are sealed so that you may be preserved to the end. You may show that seal on the day of redemption, pure and unblemished and not damaged in any part. You are thereby ready to be counted with those who are redeemed."[17]

Our present understanding of the seal incorporates the insights of the Church Fathers. The seal marks us as Christ's sheep: "Baptism seals the Christian with an indelible spiritual mark (character) of his belonging to Christ. No sin can erase this mark" (CCC, 1272). It is the pledge of future glory. "The faithful Christian who has 'kept the seal' until the end, remaining faithful to the demands of his Baptism, will be able to depart this life 'marked with the sign of faith' [RM, EP I, 97] with his baptismal faith, in expectation of the blessed vision of God—the consummation of faith—and in the hope of resurrection" (CCC, 1274).

The sacramental character imprinted by Baptism is also oriented to the Eucharist, the culmination of Christian initiation. "Incorporated in the Church by Baptism, the faithful are appointed by their baptismal character to Christian religious worship" (LG, 11). The sacramental seal makes possible full and active participation in the liturgy as well as the abundant and overflowing fruitfulness of Eucharistic Communion for the whole of life: "The baptismal seal enables and commits Christians

16. Edwards, *Galatians*, 118.

17. Ibid., 179.

to serve God by a vital participation in the holy liturgy of the Church and to exercise their baptismal priesthood by the witness of holy lives and practical charity" (CCC, 1273). The sacramental character received at Baptism is a dynamic force that impels us to full sacramental communion and a life radiant with the presence and power of Christ through the Holy Spirit to the glory of God the Father.

This dynamic power of the sacramental character is based on Jesus' encounter with the Samaritan woman at the well in John 4. Jesus' physical thirst—he begins by asking her for a drink of water—leads to the recognition of a deeper spiritual thirst and the offer of a water that eternally quenches: "whoever drinks the water I shall give will never thirst; the water I shall give will become in him a spring of water welling up to eternal life" (Jn 4:13–14). This spring of water welling up to eternal life becomes an image of the sacramental character imprinted in Baptism. The character or seal is like "a fountain which is inserted at baptism, while the life of grace is the water that flows from that fountain."[18]

Conclusion

Baptism is "the door to life and to the kingdom of God" (GICI, 3). We pass through this door and enter the kingdom by the forgiveness of our sins and a new birth as God's adopted children, new creations. At the same time we are incorporated into the Church, enter into communion with all the baptized, and are imprinted with an indelible character that marks us as Christ's own. But any summary of the effects of Baptism fails to do justice to the spiritual reality, which one might say is explosive in its power and radicalness. Listen to just a few of St. Paul's descriptions of this kingdom, a kingdom that "is not a matter of talk but of power" (1 Cor 4:20), a kingdom in which "everything belongs to you . . . the world or life or death, or the present or the future: all belong to you, and you to Christ, and Christ to God" (1 Cor 3:21–22). In this kingdom we, the baptized, will know "what is the surpassing greatness of his power for us who believe" (Eph 1:19) and will know "him who is able to accomplish far more than all we ask or imagine, by the power at work with us" (Eph 3:20).

---

18. Haffner, *The Sacramental Mystery*, 46.

One spiritual writer uses the images of seed and fire to convey the explosive power of Baptism. In Baptism "we have already received the fullness of Christ in principle. It is like a seed which will soon demand the whole life of the believer in order later to let all its hidden power unfold. It is like a fire which is only a spark at first and then quietly begins to smolder and finally, especially through testings and affliction, breaks out in flames for good and consumes everything it touches. It is a fire like the Holy Spirit himself, who ignites in us the fire of his love and consumes everything which cannot be made into building material for his love. It is a fire which makes us malleable and enables us to become one with that God of whom Scripture says that he is a consuming fire."[19]

19. André Louf, *Mercy in Weakness: Meditations on the Word*, trans. John Vriend (Kalamazoo, MI: Cisterican Publications, 1998), 23–24.

PART III

The Sacrament of Confirmation

Confirmation, Pope Francis reminds us, is not our work but God's, "who cares for our lives in such a manner as to mold us in the image of his Son, to make us capable of loving like him."[1] In the Sacrament of Confirmation God imparts to us his Holy Spirit, "whose action pervades the whole person and his entire life" through the Spirit's seven gifts—Wisdom, Understanding, Counsel, Fortitude, Knowledge, Piety, and Fear of the Lord.[2] Through the action of the Spirit, "Christ makes himself present in us and takes shape in our lives; through us, it will be—Christ himself—who prays, forgives, gives hope and consolation, serves the brethren, draws close to the needy and to the least, creates community and sows peace."[3] In this section, we will examine in detail the Sacrament of Confirmation to understand better and to participate more fully in the sacrament which produces these wondrous effects.

We will begin our study in chapter 7 with an overview of the Sacrament of Confirmation. We will then look in detail at the five Old Testament passages that are options for the first reading for the celebration of the sacrament. All of these passages are taken from the prophets and announce a future outpouring of God's Spirit. The first passage we will look at is Isaiah 11:1–4ab, in which the prophet announces the gifts of the Holy Spirit. This passage is the source for the prayer for the seven gifts of the Holy Spirit. The next passage is Isaiah 42:1–3, known as the first Servant Song because it describes a future servant of the Lord who will

1. Francis, General Audience, January 29, 2014, http://m.vatican.va/content/francescomobile/en/audiences/2014/documents/papa-francesco_20140129_udienza-generale.html.

2. Ibid.

3. Ibid.

come in peace and gentleness. The third passage is Isaiah 61:1–3abcd, 6ab, 8c–9 and describes the servant who will be anointed with the Spirit to proclaim the mercy of the Lord to the brokenhearted and the captives. We next listen to the words of the prophet Ezekiel, who in 36:24–28 looks ahead to the gift of a new spirit and a new heart for the people of God. We will conclude with Joel 2:23a, 26, 3:1–3a in which the prophet predicts an outpouring of the Spirit on all regardless of age or social status, a prophecy cited by the Apostle Peter on the day of Pentecost. In distinct yet complementary ways, these Old Testament prophecies prefigure the power and effects of the Sacrament of Confirmation.

In chapter 8 we will walk through the celebration of the Sacrament of Confirmation and explore the meaning of its liturgical signs. The participants, the bishop, parents, and sponsor, signify different dimensions of the sacrament, as does its celebration within the Mass. The words of the rite are another important sign, including the essential words, the Renewal of Baptismal Promises, the Sign of Peace, and the Lord's Prayer. We will also examine in depth the meaning of the sacred chrism with which the bishop anoints the candidates. And we will also look at the different gestures of the rite, such as the imposition of hands both "over" and "on" the candidates, as well as the sign of the cross. Throughout this chapter we will also highlight the connection between the sacramental signs of Baptism and Confirmation in order to enable the readers to understand readily the sacramental signs of Confirmation as well as its relationship to the Sacrament of Baptism.

Finally, in chapter 9 we will look at the transforming power of the Sacrament of Confirmation. We will begin by looking at Confirmation as a personal Pentecost that strengthens baptismal grace (CCC, 1302). We will then consider the specific ways in which it builds upon the grace of Baptism. Like Baptism, Confirmation imparts an indelible character. It also deepens our configuration to Christ, our identity as sons and daughters of God. It also strengthens our baptismal bond with Christ's Body, the Church, and further equips us to bear witness to the Gospel, a duty first received at Baptism. Finally, Confirmation imparts the seven gifts of the Holy Spirit, whose dwelling place we became at Baptism. A deeper understanding of the Old Testament roots of Confirmation, the meaning of its liturgical signs, and its power to transform our lives will enrich our participation in the sacramental celebration and deepen our ability to live out the sacrament in every aspect of our life.

A Note on the "Restored Order" of the Sacraments of Initiation

In this book we are presenting the sacraments of initiation in their traditional order: Baptism, Confirmation, and the Eucharist.[4] This is the ancient order of initiation. "The rites which theologians have identified as constitutive of baptism, confirmation, and the Eucharist, formed one single celebration in ancient times."[5] This is still true for the Christian initiation of adults in both the Latin and Eastern Churches, which is conferred in "a single celebration of the three sacraments of initiation: Baptism, Confirmation, and the Eucharist" (CCC, 1233). It is also the sequence for infants in the Eastern rites: "In the Eastern rites the Christian initiation of infants also begins with Baptism followed immediately by Confirmation and the Eucharist" (CCC, 1233).

However, in the Roman Rite, Confirmation came to be separated from Baptism (CCC, 1233). In the early fourth century Emperor Constantine ended the persecution of Christianity and in 380 Emperor Theodosius made it the state religion, events that contributed to the dramatic growth of the Church. While the Church reserved "the completion of Baptism [Confirmation] to the bishop" (CCC, 1290), several factors made it increasingly difficult for the bishop to celebrate Confirmation at the time of Baptism, as the *Catechism* explains: "the multiplication of infant baptisms all through the year, the increase of rural parishes, and the growth of dioceses often prevented the bishop from being present at all baptismal celebrations" (CCC, 1290). The development of the sacraments of initiation during the following centuries is complex and beyond the scope of this book. However, by the thirteenth century the initiation for children comprised "three distinct and separate sacramental rites—baptism, confirmation and Eucharist."[6] Also by the thirteenth century, the

4. Confirmation did not exist as a separate sacrament during the first four centuries of the Church. Rather, what we have is an initiatory rite that included various combinations of the following elements: water baptism, a prebaptismal anointing, a postbaptismal anointing, a consignation, and the imposition of hands, all under the governance of the bishop.

5. Marcel Metzger, *History of the Liturgy: The Major Stages*, trans. Madeleine Beaumont (Collegeville, MN: The Liturgical Press, 1997), 98.

6. Liam G. Walsh, OP, *The Sacraments of Initiation: A Theology of Life, Word, and Rite,* 2nd ed. (Chicago: Hillenbrand Books, 2011), 153.

order in which Confirmation and Eucharist were conferred varied.[7] Nevertheless, the conferral of the Eucharist prior to Confirmation was not fixed until the early twentieth century (1910) by Pope Pius X: "it was only after the introduction by Pope Pius X of first communion for children once they had reached the use of reason that it became standard practice for children to be admitted to the Eucharist before they were confirmed."[8]

To recap, we know that in the early Church the sacraments of initiation were conferred in a single continuous rite. Then, due to a number of different factors, Confirmation came to be conferred separately from Baptism, and in some cases Confirmation was conferred after the Eucharist, altering the original order. In 1910 St. Pius X lowered the age of first communion so that it was received before Confirmation. As a result, the traditional order of the sacraments of initiation—Baptism, Confirmation, Eucharist—became *for children* Baptism, Eucharist, Confirmation, thus disrupting the sacramental reality that "the holy Eucharist completes Christian initiation" (CCC, 1322). Unfortunately, the conferral of the Eucharist before Confirmation can create the impression that it is Confirmation, *not the Eucharist*, which completes Christian initiation.

This placement of Confirmation after First Communion led Pope Benedict XVI to address the order of the sacraments of initiation. Contrasting on the one hand "the practice of the West regarding the initiation of adults [Baptism-Confirmation-Eucharist], and, on the other hand, the procedure adopted for children [Baptism-Eucharist-Confirmation]," he stated that "attention needs to be paid to the order of the sacraments of initiation" (SacCar, 18). Furthermore, because these differences "are not properly of the dogmatic order, but are pastoral in character" (SacCar, 18), they are open to reflection and revision. The pope affirmed the need for such consideration: "Concretely, it needs to be seen which practice better enables the faithful to put the sacrament of the Eucharist at the center, as the goal of the whole process of initiation" (SacCar, 18).

This is the context and the impetus for a return to the "restored order" of the sacraments of initiation *for children*, which means conferring the Sacrament of Confirmation *before* First Communion, not after. The reasons are compelling. A return to the original "restored" order of the sacraments

7. Ibid.

8. Ibid.

of initiation actuates the integral relationship that exists among the sacraments of initiation, confers the grace of Confirmation to children before the challenges of adolescence, and restores the intrinsic relationship of Baptism and Confirmation to the Eucharist. "It must never be forgotten," writes Pope Benedict XVI, "that our reception of Baptism and Confirmation is ordered to the Eucharist" (SacCar, 17).

A number of dioceses in the United States have restored the ancient order of the sacraments of initiation, celebrating Confirmation before First Communion. The change presents challenges. A transition must be formulated to move the celebration of Confirmation from middle school or high school to second or third grade, a process that can take three to five years. It may also require a revised approach to youth ministry, which currently devotes considerable time and energy to sacramental preparation. A few dioceses in the United States instituted the restored order, only to encounter pastoral problems and decide to return to the celebration of Confirmation in middle school or high school.

Yet it is also true that the current order of Baptism–Eucharist–Confirmation poses problems. Pope Francis has acknowledged that Confirmation is often an exit sacrament: "The sacrament of Confirmation— what is this sacrament called? Confirmation? No. Its name has changed: the 'Sacrament of Farewell.' They do this and then they leave the Church. Is this true or not?"[9] It is significant that the traditional order of the sacraments of initiation is the order in which they are presented in the *Catechism of the Catholic Church* and the *Code of Canon Law*, as well as the *Rite of Christian Initiation of Adults*, which we noted above. "We need to ask ourselves," wrote Pope Benedict XVI, "whether in our Christian communities the close link between Baptism, Confirmation and Eucharist is sufficiently recognized" (SacCar, 17). It is hoped that this book will contribute to the discussion concerning the proper order of the sacraments of initiation and help "the faithful to put the sacrament of the Eucharist at the center, as the goal of the whole process of initiation" (SacCar, 18).

---

9. Francis, address to the young people of Cagliari, September 22, 2013, http://archden.org/saints/in-depth-examination-of-the-restored-order/restored-priorities-initiation-not-graduation/.

Chapter 7

Confirmation: Overview and Old Testament Roots

In the Old Testament, the prophets announced that the Messiah would be anointed with the Spirit of the Lord for his saving mission (CCC, 1256). "The spirit of the Lord GOD is upon me," wrote Isaiah, "because the LORD has anointed me; He has sent me to bring good news to the afflicted, to bind up the brokenhearted, to proclaim liberty to the captives, release to the prisoners" (Is 61:1). This anointing of the Spirit, however, would not be given exclusively to the Messiah, but "was to be communicated to the *whole messianic people*" (CCC, 1287; italics original). During Israel's exile in Babylon, the Lord promised through Isaiah, "I will pour out water upon the thirsty ground, streams upon the dry land; I will pour out my spirit upon your offspring, my blessing upon your descendants. . . . One shall say, 'I am the LORD's,' another shall be named Jacob, and this shall write on his hand, "The LORD's,' and receive the name Israel" (44:3, 5). This gift of the spirit would enable Israel to extend "new life through her offspring" and transform her land "into a new paradise."[1]

This promise of the gift of the Spirit to the messianic people was fulfilled in Jesus' gift of the Spirit (Jn 15:26), poured out upon the nascent Church at Pentecost (Acts 2). However, the Pentecost event continues sacramentally in Confirmation, for "the effect of the sacrament of Confirmation is the full outpouring of the Holy Spirit as once granted to the apostles on the day of Pentecost" (CCC, 1302). Strengthened by the Holy Spirit through the Sacrament of Confirmation, God's people in union with Christ proclaim good news to the afflicted, comfort and heal the broken hearted, and announce freedom to captives and prisoners.

1. NJBC, 336.

INSTITUTED BY CHRIST

In his Apostolic Constitution on the Sacrament of Confirmation, *Sharing in the Divine Nature* (*Divinae Consortium Naturae*, henceforth DCN), Bl. Paul VI explained Jesus' institution of the Sacrament of Confirmation, beginning with his baptism. When Jesus was baptized in the Jordan by John the Baptist, the Spirit descended on him "like a dove" and remained on him (Mk 1:10; Jn 1:32). At this moment Isaiah's prophecy (Isaiah 61, quoted above) that the Messiah would be anointed with the Spirit, was fulfilled. Jesus himself confirmed this fulfillment in the synagogue after reading Isaiah's prophecy—"Today this scripture passage is fulfilled in your hearing" (Lk 4:21).

Jesus taught his disciples about the gift and work of the Holy Spirit during his earthly ministry. He assured them that the Spirit would help them when they were persecuted: "For the holy Spirit will teach you at that moment what you should say" (Lk 12:12). On the night he was betrayed he told the apostles that he would send the Spirit of truth (Jn 15:26), who would be with them forever (Jn 14:16) and "help them to be his witnesses (cf. Jn 15:26)" (DCN). Following his resurrection, Jesus told the apostles, "You will receive power when the Holy Spirit comes upon you; and you will be my witnesses" (Acts 1:8; cf. Lk 24:49; DCN).

On Pentecost, "the Holy Spirit did indeed descend in a marvelous way on the Apostles as they were gathered together with Mary the Mother of Jesus and the group of disciples" (DCN). Under the Spirit's inspiration they began to proclaim in the different languages of those present "the mighty acts of God" (Acts 2:11). Peter, quoting Joel 3:1–5 and Isaiah 2:2, and 44:3, "regarded the Spirit . . . as the gift of the Messianic age" (DCN). Those who believed that day were baptized and received the "the gift of the Holy Spirit" (Acts 2:38; DCN). "From that time on the Apostles, in fulfillment of Christ's will, imparted to the newly baptized, by the laying on of hands, the gift of the Spirit that completes the grace of Baptism" (DCN). This practice is further attested in the Letter to the Hebrews, which says that "the basic teaching of Christ" includes "instruction about baptism and laying on of hands" (Heb 6:12). "This laying on of hands is rightly recognized by Catholic tradition as the beginning of the Sacrament of Confirmation, which in a certain way perpetuates the grace of Pentecost in the Church" (DCN).

Names of the Sacrament

The Eastern Churches refer to this sacrament as Chrismation because recipients are anointed with perfumed oil, known as chrism or *myron*, blessed by the bishop. In the West it is called Confirmation, which "suggests both the ratification of Baptism, thus completing Christian initiation, and the strengthening of baptismal grace—both fruits of the Holy Spirit" (CCC, 1289).[2] This ratification or "confirming" of Baptism is expressed in the liturgy for Confirmation:

> Remember also, Lord,
> your servants reborn in Baptism
> whom you have been pleased to confirm
> by bestowing the Holy Spirit,
> and in your mercy, keep safe in them your grace.
> (Proper EP III, Ritual Mass 4, For the Conferral of Confirmation).

Confirmation is also called "perfecting," for "the original meaning of the term 'confirmation' seems to have been 'completion'; the gift of the Holy Spirit at confirmation completed or sealed the effect of baptism."[3] Confirmation as a perfecting of Baptism is also alluded to in the Confirmation liturgy, which asks that the Holy Spirit "may make of us a perfect temple of his glory" (RM, Ritual Masses I, 4A, Collect) and that the recipients may be "conformed more perfectly to your Son" (RM, Ritual Masses I, 4A, Prayer over the Offerings).

These three names—Chrismation, Confirmation and Perfecting—reveal distinctive aspects of the celebration and effects of this sacrament while also highlighting its integral relationship to the Sacrament of Baptism.[4]

---

2. The reference here to Confirmation "completing Christian initiation" means "that the reception of the sacrament of Confirmation is necessary for the completion of baptismal grace" (CCC, 1285); but "The holy Eucharist completes Christian initiation" (CCC, 1322).

3. Yarnold, *The Awe-Inspiring Rites*, 36.

4. As we noted in chapter 5, the anointing with chrism after the Baptism of children anticipates the Sacrament of Confirmation.

The Minister and the Recipient of the Sacrament

The bishop is the ordinary minister of the Sacrament of Confirmation. Priests, however, may confirm in three specific situations. First, a priest possesses the faculty to confirm if he "holds rank equivalent in law to a diocesan bishop," such as a territorial abbot, apostolic administrator, or diocesan administrator (OC, 7a). Second, with a mandate from the bishop, a priest who baptizes an adult or receives a person already baptized "into the full communion of the Catholic Church" has the faculty to also confirm him or her (OC, 7b). Finally, any priest can confirm "those who are in danger of death" (OC, 7c), for "the Church desires that none of her children, even the youngest, should depart this world without having been perfected by the Holy Spirit with the gift of Christ's fullness" (CCC, 1314).

The recipient of the Sacrament of Confirmation must be baptized. In addition, those who possess the use of reason "must be in a state of grace, be properly instructed, and be capable of renewing the baptismal promises" (OC, 12). However, those "who lack the use of reason should be confirmed at the age that other children are confirmed. The use of reason is not a requirement for confirmation."[5] In "the event of danger of death or serious problems of another kind," children should receive the sacrament, "even before the use of reason, so that they are not left without the benefits of this Sacrament" (OC, 11). St. Thomas Aquinas reminds us of the sometimes astonishing spiritual maturity present in children: "Age of body does not determine age of soul. Even in childhood man can attain spiritual maturity: as the book of Wisdom says: 'For old age is not honored for length of time, or measured by number of years' [Wis 4:8]. Many children, through the strength of the Holy Spirit they have received, have bravely fought for Christ even to the shedding of their blood" (CCC, 1308).

The OC also stipulates that, "as a rule," those being confirmed should be supported by a sponsor who "will bring them to receive the Sacrament, will present them to the minister of Confirmation for the sacred anointing, and afterwards will help them to fulfill their baptismal promises faithfully in accordance with the Holy Spirit whom they have received" (OC, 5). Sponsors should be "spiritually fit to take on

---

5. Huels, *The Pastoral Companion*, 72.

this responsibility" and possess specific qualities: the maturity to fulfill the role of sponsor; be a fully-initiated member of the Catholic Church; and "not be impeded by law" from fulfilling this role (OC, 5). Parents cannot serve as sponsors for their children.

Celebrating the Sacrament

The Sacrament of Confirmation is normally conferred within Mass. Following the Gospel, the candidates are presented to the bishop. They may be "called by name and individually approach the sanctuary," or, if children, come forward with "one of their sponsors or parents and stand before the celebrant" (OC, 21). If there is a large number to be confirmed, "they are assigned to a suitable place before the Bishop" instead of being called individually (OC, 21). This is followed by the homily and the renewal of baptismal promises. Next the bishop and concelebrating priests lay hands over those to be confirmed, after which the bishop says the prayer for the seven gifts of the Holy Spirit. The OC carefully notes, however, that while this imposition of hands "does not pertain to the validity of the Sacrament, [it] should still be considered to be of great importance with regard to the integrity of the rite and a fuller understanding of the Sacrament" (OC, 9).

Then follow the essential elements of the sacrament. Each candidate may go to the bishop or the bishop may go to each candidate. "The sponsor who presents the person to be confirmed places his (her) right hand on his (her) shoulder and says the name of the one to be confirmed to the Bishop; or the one to be confirmed alone says his (her) name" (OC, 26). The essential elements of the Sacrament of Confirmation are anointing the forehead with chrism "done by the laying on of the hand" (OC, 9),[6] accompanied by the words, "Be sealed with the Gift of the Holy Spirit." Through these words and actions the recipient receives "the indelible character, the seal of the Lord" (OC, 9; we will look at the seal as a sign in chapter 8 and explore the meaning and effect of this character or seal in chapter 9). The rite concludes with the exchange of peace between the bishop and each of the newly confirmed.

---

6. Regarding the imposition of hands, "it is sufficient for the minister to apply the chrism with his thumb, and that he need not impose his hand at the same time on the candidate's head" (Haffner, *The Sacramental Mystery*, 79).

The Mass then continues with the Universal Prayer. The Creed is omitted, replaced by the Renewal of Baptismal Promises. Some of the newly confirmed may participate by joining "those who bring forward the offerings" (OC, 31b). There are special, or proper, inserts for Eucharistic Prayers I, II, and III (OC, 58). Mass concludes with either a special blessing or Prayer over the People (OC, 33).

The official ritual book, *The Order of Confirmation*, includes an introduction and five chapters. Chapter 1 is "The Order for the Conferral of Confirmation within Mass" and chapter 2, "The Order for the Conferral of Confirmation without Mass." Chapter 3, consisting of only two paragraphs, summarizes the conferral of the sacrament when celebrated by an extraordinary minister—in other words, a priest in one of the three situations described above. Chapter 4 is the rite for a person in danger of death, and chapter 5 contains "Texts to Be Used in the Conferral of Confirmation." Finally, the OC permits the celebrant to adapt the Rite of Confirmation by introducing, "in individual cases and with due consideration for the capacity of those to be confirmed . . . some explanations into the rite" as well as making "appropriate accommodations in the existing texts, for example, by expressing these in a kind of dialogue, especially with children" (OC, 18).

Old Testament Roots of the Sacrament

The OC offers a number of Old Testament readings for the Conferral of Confirmation. The OC stresses the importance of the Liturgy of the Word as an integral part of the celebration of the sacrament, urging that "great emphasis . . . be placed" on its celebration: "For it is from the hearing of the word of God that the many-sided work of the Holy Spirit flows out upon the Church and upon each one of the baptized and confirmed and that the Lord's will is made known in the life of Christians" (OC, 13). The OC gives five options for the first (Old Testament) reading, all prophetic texts that announce a future outpouring of God's Spirit: Isaiah 11:1–4ab; Isaiah 42:1–3; Isaiah 61:1–3abcd, 6ab, 8c–9; Ezekiel 36:24–28; and Joel 2:23a, 26—3:3a. We will look at each of these passages, which prefigure important but different aspects of the Sacrament of Confirmation.

The New Davidic King: "The Spirit of the Lord Shall Rest upon Him"

The first text, Isaiah 11:1–4a, is a passage that "seems to come from late in Isaiah's career."[7] It prophesies the coming of a new, ideal king from the line of David: "a shoot shall sprout from the stump of Jesse [David's father], and from his roots a bud shall blossom" (11:1). The imagery of new growth from a "stump" and "roots" presents a sharp contrast between past rulers and the king to come, an indictment of "the bankruptcy of the monarchy as embodied by the historical kings, along with the need for a new beginning, to spring from the very origin from which David and his dynasty arose."[8]

This ideal king will be empowered by the Lord, for "the spirit of the LORD shall rest upon him" (11:2). The Lord's spirit "was a divine force given to individuals to enable them to fulfill missions otherwise beyond them, as in the case of Moses (Nm 11:17), the judges (Jgs 3:10; 6:34; 11:29), prophets (Mi 3:8), David (1 Sm 16:13), and others; this king would represent a return to the charismatic tradition so long an ideal in Israel."[9] The prophet then enumerates the gifts to be given to the king: "a spirit of wisdom and of understanding, a spirit of counsel and of strength, a spirit of knowledge and of fear of the LORD, and his delight shall be the fear of the LORD" (11:2–3). Readers will likely recognize in this list of gifts the source of the gifts of the Spirit, but also note six gifts, not seven, since "fear of the Lord" is listed twice. However, the Greek version of the Old Testament, the Septuagint, and the Latin Vulgate translate the first occurrence of "fear of the Lord" as "piety," resulting in the traditional seven gifts. This passage is the source for the prayer in the OC said by the bishop over those being confirmed. We will look at the prayer in chapter 8 and in more detail at the individual gifts in chapter 9.

These gifts "reflect Isaiah's experience with Ahaz and Hezekiah, especially in that wisdom, understanding, and counsel would make the king independent of foolish advisers (see 5:21; 9:5; 29:14)."[10] Strength is

---

7. NJBC, 237. Isaiah's ministry spanned the years 742 BC to approximately 701 BC (NJBC, 229).

8. NABRE, 876, n. 11:1.

9. NJBC, 237.

10. Ibid., 237–238.

given to make "good counsel effective,"[11] and fear of the Lord is a favored quality in wisdom literature. "Fear of the LORD," says the writer of Proverbs, "is the beginning of knowledge" (Prv 1:7), understood not as an emotion but as a disposition of "reverential awe and respect toward God combined with obedience to God's will."[12] This bud that will blossom from seemingly dead roots will be endowed with "the outstanding virtues of his great ancestors: the wisdom and insight of Solomon, the heroism and prudence of David, the knowledge and fear of God characteristic of patriarch and prophet, of Moses, Jacob and Abraham."[13] Empowered by these divine virtues, the king will not judge by appearance nor render decisions based on hearsay (11:3). Rather, "he shall judge the poor with justice, and decide fairly for the land's afflicted" (11:4).

This ideal king who combines the qualities of Abraham, Jacob, Moses, David, and Solomon is Jesus, anointed with the Spirit at his baptism and sharing the fullness of the Spirit with his disciples through the Sacrament of Confirmation.

"Here Is My Servant upon Whom I Have Put My Spirit"

The Song of the Servant, Isaiah 42:1–3, is another Old Testament option for the Sacrament of Confirmation. It comes from the section of Isaiah known as Second Isaiah, chapters 40–55. While chapters 1–39 of Isaiah call Israel to repentance and warn of judgment, chapters 40–55 address a very different situation. Known as the Book of Comfort from the opening words of Isaiah 40:1—"Comfort, give comfort to my people, says your God"—Second Isaiah is addressing a defeated nation taken into exile in Babylon. The author is speaking to "a people discouraged, dazed, and destitute, severely tempted to apostasy. The people in exile must be consoled, not punished; their faith must be sustained, not further tried."[14] The Four Songs of the Servant of YHWH (42:1–7; 49:1–7; 50:4–9; 52:13—53:12) are the jewels of Second Isaiah, poems that "depict a perfect servant of Yahweh—re-gatherer of his people and light

11. Ibid., 238.
12. NABRE, 728, note 1:7.
13. NJB, 1207, note d.
14. NJBC, 330.

of nations—one who preaches the true faith, who expiates the people's sins by his own death and is glorified by God."[15] Let us now look at the First Song.

This passage begins with God's introduction of his servant, addressed possibly "to the heavenly court (cf. 40:1–2)"[16]: "Here is my servant whom I uphold, my chosen one with whom I am pleased" (42:1). This servant "is a 'chosen one' like Moses (Ps 106:23), David (Ps 89:4), and all Israel (1 Chr 16:13; Is 41:8); as servant, he fulfills the role of Davidic king (2 Sm 2:18) and messianic king (Ez 34:23–24)."[17] He is anointed by Yahweh for his mission: "Upon him I have put my spirit" (42:1). This promise of the spirit, "important for any extraordinary redemptive work, was promised the messianic king (Is 11:1; *see above*) and will later be given to the entire messianic community (Jl 3; *see below*)."[18] Furthermore, the scope of his redemptive mission is universal, for "he shall bring forth justice to the nations" (42:1). The Hebrew word for *justice* connotes "a legal decision ratifying and executing the divine will."[19] With a few exceptions, it was a power "reserved to kings, priests, and local magistrates."[20] In addition, the servant also "imparts teaching (tôrâ), a task never done by kings but only by prophets (Is 8:16; Zec 7:12) and priests (Jer 2:8; Ez 7:26)."[21]

The Lord also speaks of the gentleness of his chosen servant. "He will not cry out, nor shout, nor make his voice heard in the street" (42:2); rather, he will accomplish his mission quietly. "'To cry out' normally indicates a person in special need, so that the servant stands quiet and strong."[22] Two images convey the sensitive manner of the servant: "A bruised reed he will not break, and a dimly burning wick he will not quench" (42:3). His care for the bruised reed and the dimly burning wick reveals "a gentle respect for others, even a detection of strength in

15. Ibid., 1169.
16. Ibid.
17. Ibid.
18. Ibid.
19. Ibid.
20. Ibid., 334.
21. Ibid.
22. Ibid., 334–335.

their weakness."[23] The passage concludes by restating the servant's mission to "faithfully bring forth justice" (42:3).

The First Servant Song has been called the "Confirmation of the peaceful servant,"[24] for "the servant is presented as a prophet, the object of a mission and a divine destiny, v. 6, cf. v. 4; Jeremiah 1:5, quickened by the Spirit, Isaiah 42:1, to teach the entire world, vv. 1 and 3, discreetly and firmly, vv. 2–4, in spite of opposition."[25] However, if we may be permitted to transpose it into a "sacramental key," we can see how it also anticipates the Sacrament of Confirmation. Here, too, the Lord "confirms" in his servants the relationship and mission begun at Baptism with an anointing of the Spirit so that they may stand "quiet and strong" and proclaim the Gospel to the world with "a gentle respect for others."

"The Lord Has Anointed Me"

Our next passage also comes from Isaiah, but from a section known as Third Isaiah, chapters 56–66. Second Isaiah, the setting for the previous passage, addressed a nation defeated and in exile and emphasized comfort and consolation. Third Isaiah addresses a nation that has returned to its homeland and rebuilt the Temple. There is now a "new emphasis on Temple, worship, Sabbath, fasting, and law [that] reflects a different spirituality."[26] Words of comfort are now mixed with condemnation for falling into sin and idolatry. These chapters "reflect the tensions between the *vision* of a renewed Israel and the plain, hard *reality* which the exiles found on their return."[27]

The passage chosen for Confirmation, Isaiah 61, has several points of similarity with the Servant Song in Isaiah 42: both are soliloquys spoken by the servant, both speak of an anointing by the spirit, and both proclaim a "mission of mercy."[28] In this passage the prophet announces that the spirit of the Lord is upon him, and in a messianic ("messiah" means "the anointed one") reference proclaims that the Lord

---

23. Ibid.

24. Ibid., 334.

25. NJB, 1253, note a.

26. NJBC, 346.

27. Lawrence Boadt, *Reading the Old Testament: An Introduction* (Mahwah, NJ: Paulist Press, 1984), 444.

28. NJBC, 346.

has anointed him. He is the messenger of the Lord "to bring good news to the afflicted, to bind up the brokenhearted, to proclaim liberty to the captives, release to the prisoners, To announce a year of favor from the LORD and a day of vindication by our God; To comfort all who mourn; to place on those who mourn in Zion a diadem instead of ashes, To give them oil of gladness instead of mourning, a glorious mantle instead of a faint spirit" (Is 61:1b–3).

This passage predicts the complete salvation of God's people.[29] The reference to the spirit "signals the special action of God (Jgs 3:10; 11:19; 1 Sm 10:5–13)." While other Old Testament prophecies spoke of the spirit with reference to the messianic king (Is 11:1–2) and promised it to the messianic people (Jl 3; Zec 12:10), here the spirit is given to anoint prophecy. The term *anointed* "is linked with preaching and hearing; it designates an interior enlightening to know God's word and a strengthening to follow it." The phrase "release to prisoners" can also be translated as "light to prisoners." In either case, "prisoners are led out of dark dungeons to full daylight." This passage "looks to the total salvation of God's people—bodily and spiritually, individually and socially." Finally, the reference to "the day of vindication of the Lord" is almost always used to describe God "repairing the injured or weakened force of salvation (34:8; 59:17)."[30]

This Old Testament prophecy is definitively fulfilled in the earthly ministry of Jesus. In the Gospel of Luke, Jesus inaugurates his public ministry by reading this passage in the synagogue on the Sabbath. After proclaiming this passage, Jesus announces that he is the one about whom Isaiah prophesied: "Today this scripture passage is fulfilled in your hearing" (Lk 4:21). "With these words Jesus announced that the messianic era had come."[31] In his words and deeds Christ brought good news to the poor and oppressed, comforted the brokenhearted, brought freedom to those oppressed by the enemy, and freed those imprisoned by illness—the blind saw the salvation of the Lord, the deaf heard the good news, and the mute praised the Lord. God's saving action, hindered by the corruption and self-interest of the religious establishment of Jesus' day, was fully and definitively realized in Christ.

---

29. The following analysis is taken from NJBC, 346.

30. Ibid.

31. Ibid.

This passage, with its emphasis on the gift of the spirit for prophecy, anticipates the Sacrament of Confirmation, which strengthens the Christian's participation in Christ's prophetic ministry. The seven gifts of the Holy Spirit conferred in Confirmation make the recipients "witnesses before the world to the Gospel of our Lord Jesus Christ" (RM, Ritual Masses I, 4A, Collect) and enable them "by the holiness of their lives" to "exercise the prophetic mission of your people" (OC, 59).

"I Will Put a New Spirit within You"

Ezekiel, a younger contemporary of Jeremiah, was among those taken into exile to Babylon, where he "became the first prophet to be commissioned outside Judah or Israel."[32] His early prophecies contended that the destruction of Jerusalem and the Temple and the exile to Babylon were punishment for the nation's sin and idolatry. In his later prophecies he "argues that the Judahites who embrace his preaching are the people whom the Lord has chosen as a new Israel, enlivened by a new heart, imbued with new breath (chaps. 36–37), and restored to a re-created land, Temple, and covenant relationship (chaps. 40–48)."[33] One of the Old Testament options for the Sacrament of Confirmation is Ezekiel 36:23–28, God's promise that he will give his people a new heart and a new spirit.

This passage begins with the assertion that God will vindicate his name—his glory and honor—among the nations who saw Judah's defeat as a sign of God's weakness. "I will prove the holiness of my great name," says the Lord, "profaned among the nations, in whose midst you have profaned it"; then they "shall know that I am the LORD, says the Lord GOD" (v. 23). He then promises to restore them to their own land. He will cleanse his people from their impurities and from their idols, giving them "a new heart," "natural hearts" in place of their "stony hearts" (v. 26). The promise of a new heart points to a complete transformation: "The heart is the seat of thinking and loving, so it will be a way of looking at life from God's point of view."[34] God is creating a new people. "God's initiative to cleanse Israel (cf. 24:13–14) is the first

32. NABRE, 1013.

33. Ibid.

34. NJBC, 325.

act in the creation of a new people, no longer disposed to repeating Israel's wicked past (chap. 20)." [35]

The Lord also promises to give his rebellious people a new spirit. The spirit or breath of God (ruah), "creates and gives life (Gn 1:2; 2:7e; 6:17f), lays hold of people to endow them with superhuman power (Gn 41:38; Ex 31:2; 1 Sm 16:13), particularly the prophets (Jgs 3:10)."[36] This promised spirit has both a communal and an individual effect. On the one hand it is "the power to live as an entire nation, not just as individuals."[37] But this does not preclude the transformation of the individual recipient, for "more mysteriously, for each recipient the Spirit will be the principle of an inward renewal making possible a faithful observance of the law of God . . . ; thus the Spirit will be the principle inspiring the new covenant . . . ; like life-giving water it will nourish fruits of integrity and holiness, which in turn will guarantee the favor and protection of God for humanity. . . . This effusion of the Spirit will be effected through the Messiah who will be the first recipient of it, to be able to accomplish his saving work."[38] God, in order to bring about a permanent restoration, "replaces Israel's rebellious and obdurate interiority ('heart of stone') with an interiority ('heart of flesh') susceptible to and animated by God's intentions ('my spirit')."[39] Only God's gift of a new spirit and a new heart can transform a rebellious and disobedient people into "a chosen race, a royal priesthood, a holy nation . . . to proclaim everywhere your mighty deeds" (RM, Preface I of the Sundays in Ordinary Time).

Ezekiel's prophecy is one of the prophetic proclamations of "a radical redemption of the People of God, purification from all their infidelities, a salvation which will include all the nations" (CCC, 64). It acknowledges the reality of the human heart which "is heavy and hardened. God must give man a new heart (Ez 36:26–27), and so it recognizes that conversion is first of all a work of the grace of God who makes our hearts return to him: 'Restore us to thyself, O LORD, that we may be restored!' (Lam 5:21)" (CCC, 1432). The promise of a new spirit also anticipates the gift of the Holy Spirit to all of God's people, for it is

35. NABRE, n. 36:25–26.
36. NJB, 1451, note f.
37. NJBC, 325.
38. NJB, 1451, note f.
39. NABRE, n. 36:25–26.

one "the prophetic texts that directly concern[s] the sending of the Holy Spirit . . . by which God speaks to the heart of his people in the language of promise, with the accents of 'love and fidelity'" (CCC, 715).[40] Ezekiel's prophecy anticipates the Sacrament of Confirmation in its promise of a transforming gift of the Spirit that will enable the people of God to serve him with love and fidelity.

Digging into the Bible

In its commentary on Ezekiel 36 (quoted above, footnote 38), the *New Jerusalem Bible* cites a number of biblical passages illustrating each point. Look up the following references in support of each of the following points:

1. The Spirit makes it possible for each recipient to faithfully observe God's law: Ezekiel 11:19; 37:14, Psalm 51:12–15; Isaiah 32:15–19.
2. The Spirit inspires the new covenant: Jeremiah 31:31–34.
3. The Spirit nourishes the fruits of integrity and holiness, which guarantee God's favor and protection: Isaiah 44:3; Ezekiel 37:24; 39:29.
4. The Messiah will distribute the Spirit to accomplish his saving work: Isaiah 11:1–3; 42:1; 61:1.

"I Will Pour Out My Spirit upon the Servants and Handmaids"

The book of Joel was written following Israel's return from exile in Babylon, sometime "between the last half of 5th and the first half of 4th century."[41] Joel writes in response to two devastating natural disasters. The first is a spring invasion of locusts that "has stripped bare my vines, splintered my fig tree, shearing off its bark and throwing it away, until its branches turn white" (1:7). The second is a drought: "The seed lies shriveled beneath clods of dirt; the storehouses are broken down, for

40. Other prophetic texts cited in this passage are Ez 11:19; 37:1–14; Jer 31:31–34; and Jl 3:1–5.

41. NJBC, 400.

the grain is dried up" (1:17). In a poignant lament he concludes, "Joy itself has dried up among the people" (1:12).

Joel uses these two events to develop "a theme of reversal of fortunes."[42] The first two chapters focus on the crisis precipitated by these two events. The turning point comes in the midst of the people's despair: "Then the LORD grew jealous of his land and took pity on his people. In response the LORD said to his people: I am sending you grain, new wine, and oil, and you will be satisfied by them; Never again will I make you a disgrace among the nations" (2:18–19). God promises a dramatic restoration: "I will repay you double what the swarming locust has eaten" (2:25). The passage for the Rite of Confirmation comes from the second half of the book, the reversal of Israel's fortunes.

The people's despair is palpable: "Before our very eyes has not food been cut off? And from the house of our God, joy and gladness" (1:16). However, although the drought has dried up the people's joy (1:12), God urges them to take heart: "Children of Zion, delight and rejoice in the LORD, your God!" (2:23a). The deprivation brought on by these disasters will be miraculously reversed. "You will eat until you are fully satisfied," he promises, "then you will praise the name of the LORD, your God, who acts so wondrously on your behalf!" (2:26). The suffering, deprivation and despair brought on by these disasters will give way to consolation, abundance and joy.

In addition, God promises a marvelous outpouring of his spirit: "I will pour out my spirit upon all flesh" (3:1). The children will prophesy, the elderly "will dream dreams" and the young men "will see visions" (3:1). Even the servants will be recipients of the Lord's spirit (3:2). "God's spirit will be poured out on all, regardless of social standing. It is both spirit of prophecy, characterized here by dreams and visions . . . and cause of inward renewal."[43] St. Peter cites this passage from Joel in his sermon on the day of Pentecost (see Acts 2:17–21) "to suggest that the newly constituted Christian community, filled with divine life and power, inaugurates the Lord's Day, understood as salvation for all who believe that Jesus of Nazareth is the Christ."[44] If Pentecost is the New Testament fulfillment of Joel's prophecy, Confirmation is its sacramental continuation, as we will see in chapter 9.

---

42. Ibid.

43. NJB, 1521, note b.

44. NABRE, 1101, n. 3:1–5.

Conclusion

The Old Testament passages for the celebration of the Sacrament of Confirmation are all passages from the prophetic books that predict a future gift of God's Spirit to his anointed one, the Messiah, and to the People of God. Each sheds light on important aspects of the Sacrament of Confirmation. Isaiah 11 enumerates the gifts of the Spirit given especially to bring justice to the poor and afflicted, Isaiah 42 describes the peaceful servant, and Isaiah 61 the prophetic and merciful servant. Ezekiel 36 looks ahead to a Spirit-renewed mind and heart enabling Israel to live a life of obedience and fidelity to God. Joel predicts an outpouring of the Spirit, renewing the whole people of God and making them prophets of his mercy. These prophecies all point to the power and fruits of Confirmation, bestowing the gifts of the Spirit, enabling the confirmed to be peaceful, prophetic, and merciful servants of Christ, transformed in heart and mind.

Chapter 8

Confirmation: Signs and Symbols

The Second Vatican Council called for the reform of the Sacrament of Confirmation so that "the rite and words of this Sacrament" would "express more clearly the holy things which they signify and the Christian people, so far as possible, should be enabled to understand them with ease and take part in them fully, actively, and as befits a community" (SC, 21). In this chapter we will look at the different elements of the Rite of Confirmation and how they express the holy things which they signify. We will begin by looking at the conferral of the sacrament within Mass and the participants, especially the bishop, parents, and sponsor. We will examine the language of the rite, especially the essential words, the Renewal of Baptismal Promises, the Sign of Peace, and the Lord's Prayer. We will give special attention to the sacred chrism. And we will also consider the different gestures—imposing hands over the candidates and on the candidates, as well as the sign of the cross made on the forehead. Because of the close connection between the Sacraments of Baptism and Confirmation, we will also highlight the connection between the sacramental signs of these two sacraments. Our goal is to enable the readers to understand readily the sacramental signs of Confirmation so that they can participate in the sacramental celebration "fully, actively, and as befits a community" (SC, 21).

Conferral within Mass

The first sign of the Sacrament of Confirmation is its celebration within Mass: "As a rule, Confirmation takes place within Mass" (OC, 13). Why? So that "the fundamental connection" of Confirmation "with all of Christian Initiation, which reaches its culmination in the Communion of the Body and Blood of Christ, may stand out in a clearer light" (OC, 13). This fundamental connection is most clearly manifested in the adult catechumens, who normally receive the sacraments of initiation in one continuous rite. "Confirmation is so closely linked with the Holy Eucharist [PO, 5] that the faithful, after being signed by Holy Baptism and Confirmation, are incorporated fully into the Body of Christ through participation in the Eucharist" (DCN). This is also the assumption of the OC: "The newly confirmed therefore participate in the Eucharist, which completes their Christian Initiation" (OC, 13).

Activity

The Mass for the Conferral of Confirmation can be celebrated with red or white vestments, "or a festive color" (RM, Ritual Masses I, 4, For the Conferral of Confirmation). What do these different colors signify (cf. chapter 2, "Liturgical Colors")?

The Participants

The participants in the Sacrament of Confirmation—the bishop, family and friends, and the sponsor—signify different aspects of the sacrament. The presence and participation of the parents in the celebration of the Sacrament of Confirmation are signs of their duty as Christian parents. They—above all others—are called "to show concern for the initiation of their children to the sacramental life both by forming and gradually increasing a spirit of faith in the children and, sometimes with the help of their instructors who are responsible for catechetical formation, by preparing them for the fruitful reception of the Sacraments of Confirmation and the Eucharist" (OC, 3).

The bishop—successor to the Apostles, recipient of the fullness of the Sacrament of Holy Orders, and the normal minister of this sacrament—provides "a clearer reference to the first outpouring of the Holy Spirit on the day of Pentecost. For after the Apostles were filled with the Holy Spirit, they themselves gave the Spirit to the faithful through the laying on of hands" (OC, 7). Indeed, the essential actions of Confirmation "had been associated from the beginning, in all liturgical traditions, with the ministry of the bishop. It was he who normally presided at the ceremonies of initiation. Even though presbyters and deacons did many of the baptismal rites, the laying on of hands and anointing for the giving of the Spirit was to be done by the bishop. And it was he who was to preside at the Eucharist that completed initiation.

It was obviously fitting that he, as head of the Church into which people were being initiated, should be the one to complete the process."[1] Conferral by the bishop has a twofold significance: first, "the close bond that joins the confirmed to the Church," and second, "the mandate received from Christ to bear witness to him before all" (OC, 7). We will explore these two aspects in more detail in the following chapter.

The family and friends of the one to be confirmed constitute a sign that complements the sacramental reality signified by the bishop—they signify and in a certain way make present the Body of Christ, the Church. "The whole People of God, represented by the families and friends of the candidates for Confirmation and by members of the local community, will be invited to take part in such a celebration and will endeavor to express their faith by means of the fruits the Holy Spirit has produced in them" (OC, 4). As this passage indicates, family and friends are signs not only of "the whole People of God," but in a sense are also signs *to those being confirmed* of the fruits of the sacrament, since their participation expresses their faith through the gifts and power of the Holy Spirit conferred through the Sacrament of Confirmation.

The sponsor of the one being confirmed is another sign. Whenever possible, "it is desirable that the godparent at Baptism, if available, also be the sponsor at Confirmation" (OC, 5). Having the same person serve as the godparent at Baptism and the sponsor at Confirmation "more clearly" expresses "the link between Baptism and Confirmation" (OC, 5); when this is the case "the function and responsibility of the sponsor are exercised more effectively" (OC, 5). To better appreciate the responsibility of the sponsor for Confirmation it will be helpful to briefly recall the signification and role of the baptismal godparent. The baptismal godparent is a sign of "both the expanded spiritual family of the one to be baptized and the role of the Church as mother" (GICI, 8). He or she "helps the baptized person to lead a Christian life in keeping with baptism and to fulfill faithfully the obligations inherent in it" (CIC, 874) and so helps the newly baptized "on the road of Christian life" (CCC, 1255). The Confirmation sponsor's responsibility, as we noted in the previous chapter, is to help the newly confirmed "to fulfill their baptismal promises faithfully in accordance with the Holy Spirit whom they have received" (OC, 5). Choosing the baptismal

1. Walsh, *The Sacraments of Initiation*, 150.

godparent as the Confirmation sponsor manifests the responsibility he or she accepted at Baptism and the integral relationship between Baptism and Confirmation.

The Renewal of Baptismal Promises

The close connection between Baptism and Confirmation is signified in ways that we have just noted—by celebration within the Eucharist and by having the same the same person serve as the sponsor for both sacraments. This connection is further signified by the structure of the Rite of Confirmation, in particular the Renewal of Baptismal Promises. "When Confirmation is celebrated separately from Baptism . . . the Liturgy of Confirmation begins with the renewal of baptismal promises and the profession of faith by the confirmands. This clearly shows that Confirmation follows Baptism" (CCC, 1298).[2]

The renewal of the baptismal promises takes the form of a dialogue between the bishop and the candidates. He first asks them if they "renounce Satan, and all his works and empty promises" (OC, 23). He then asks them to affirm their belief in the Trinity, beginning with the Father, "the Creator of heaven and earth" (OC, 23). He next asks if they believe in Jesus Christ, summarizing his incarnation and Paschal Mystery. The following question concerns the Holy Spirit, and is expanded to focus on the sacrament: "the Lord, the giver of life, who today through the Sacrament of Confirmation is given to you in a special way just as he was given to the Apostles on the day of Pentecost?" (OC, 23). Finally, the candidates affirm their belief "in the holy Catholic Church, the communion of saints, the forgiveness of sins, the resurrection of the body, and life everlasting?" (OC, 23). The bishop concludes with a formula found also in the RBC n. 96: "This is our faith. This is the faith of the Church. We are proud to profess it in Christ Jesus our Lord" (OC, 23).

The Imposition of Hands "On" and "Over"

The imposition of hands, a gesture that signifies the gift of the Holy Spirit, occurs at two points in the conferral of the Sacrament of

2. As noted previously, "When adults are baptized, they immediately receive Confirmation and participate in the Eucharist" (CCC, 1298).

Confirmation. The bishop first lays hands "over" the candidates and says the prayer invoking the seven gifts of the Holy Spirit upon the candidates. In the OC this is titled "The Laying on of Hands" (OC, 24). The bishop then lays hands "on" the candidates as he anoints them with chrism and says the essential words: "N., be sealed with the gift of the Holy Spirit," which constitute the essential elements of the Sacrament of Confirmation. The OC calls this liturgical unit "The Anointing with Chrism." In this section we will follow the order of the rite and look first at "The Laying on of Hands," and then "The Anointing with Chrism," including a detailed look at the sacred chrism.

This part of the rite follows the Renewal of Baptismal Promises and begins with an invitation to the assembly to pray that "God the almighty Father" would "gracious pour out the Holy Spirit" on the candidates "to confirm them with his abundant gifts, and through his anointing conform them more fully to Christ, the Son of God" (OC, 24). The petition "to confirm them with his abundant gifts" is a reference to "The Laying on of Hands," the prayer for the seven gifts of the Holy Spirit. The second petition, to "conform them more fully to Christ" through the anointing of the Spirit is a reference to "The Anointing with Chrism." This is, then, both an invitation to prayer and a preparation for the elements to follow.

The bishop then "lays hands over all those to be confirmed (as do the Priests who are associated with him)" (OC, 25). This gesture, the hands extended over a thing, person, or group, has "since the time of the apostles . . . signified the gift of the Spirit" (CCC, 1299). The bishop alone proclaims the prayer, as follows:

> Almighty God, Father of our Lord Jesus Christ,
> who brought these your servants to new birth
> by water and the Holy Spirit,
> freeing them from sin:
> send upon them, O Lord, the Holy Spirit, the Paraclete;
> give them the spirit of wisdom and understanding,
> the spirit of counsel and fortitude,
> the spirit of knowledge and piety;
> fill them with the spirit of the fear of the Lord.
> Through Christ our Lord.
> R. Amen. (OC, 25)

This prayer begins by expressing the close connection between Baptism and Confirmation, describing Baptism as a "new birth by water and the Holy Spirit" that brings freedom from sin.

The prayer next invokes the Holy Spirit: "send upon them, O Lord, the Holy Spirit, the Paraclete." The reference to the Holy Spirit as the Paraclete is a title used by Jesus in John 14:16, 26; 15:26 and 16:7. The Greek word that is translated *Paraclete* "can mean spokesman, mediator, intercessor, comforter, consoler, although no one of these terms encompasses the meaning in John."[3] Didymus the Blind explained one aspect of this title of the Holy Spirit thus: "He calls the Holy Spirit the Comforter, a name taken from his office, which is not only to relieve the sadness of the faithful but also to fill them with unspeakable joy. Everlasting gladness is in those hearts in which the Spirit dwells."[4] This prayer and gesture, although it is not one of the essential elements of the sacrament, nevertheless "contributes to the complete perfection of the rite and to a more thorough understanding of the Sacrament" (DCN).

The Spirit's presence is a mystery, both intensely personal and pervasively universal. St. Basil the Great, who authored the first treatise devoted exclusively to the Holy Spirit, explained the mystery of the Spirit's simultaneous personal and cosmic presence. "The Spirit . . . is shared yet remains whole. Consider the analogy of the sunbeam: each person on whom its kindly light falls rejoices as if the sun existed for him alone, yet it illumines land and sea and is master of the atmosphere. In the same way, the Spirit is given to each one who receives him as if he were the possession of that person alone, yet he sends forth sufficient grace to fill the entire universe. Everything that partakes of his grace is filled with joy according to its capacity—the capacity of its nature, not of his power."[5]

The prayer for the seven gifts of the Holy Spirit is immediately followed by the essential elements of the sacrament: the laying on of the hand and the anointing with chrism accompanied by the essential words, "N., be sealed with the gift of the Holy Spirit." In promulgating the reformed Order of Confirmation in 1971 according to the mandate of the Second Vatican Council, Pope Blessed Paul VI affirmed that this act "in a certain way represents the apostolic laying on of hands. Since

3. NABRE, 168, n. 14:16.

4. Elowsky, *John 11–21*, 186.

5. Ibid., 150.

this anointing with Chrism aptly signifies the spiritual anointing of the Holy Spirit, who is given to the faithful, We wish to confirm its existence and importance" (DCN). This, however, was not an innovation, but a preservation of an ancient tradition. "Very early, the better to signify the gift of the Holy Spirit, an anointing with perfumed oil (*chrism*) was added to the laying on of hands. This anointing highlights the name 'Christian,' which means 'anointed' and derives from that of Christ himself whom God 'anointed with the Holy Spirit [Acts 10:38]'" (CCC, 1289).

Both the laying on of hands and anointing with oil are biblical signs. There are a number of Old Testament examples of the laying on of hands as a liturgical sign. Israel blessed the two sons of Joseph, Ephraim and Manasseh, by laying his hand on their heads and pronouncing a blessing (Gn 48:13–16). In the desert, the rite that prepared the Levites for liturgical service in the tent of meeting included the laying on of hands (Nm 8:10). Moses prepared Joshua to succeed him as the leader of Israel in part by laying his hand upon him (Nm 27:18–23). We read in Deuteronomy that "Joshua, son of Nun, was filled with the spirit of wisdom, since Moses had laid his hands upon him; and so the Israelites gave him their obedience, just as the LORD had commanded Moses" (Dt 34:9).

The Gospels tell us that Jesus used this gesture to bless children (Mk 10:16) and to heal the sick (Lk 13:13), as did the Apostles (Mk 16:18). In the Acts of the Apostles, the Holy Spirit is given "by the Apostles' imposition of hands" (CCC, 699). In addition, it was used to set people apart for Church ministry (Acts 6:6; 13:3; 2 Tm 1:6), and the Letter to the Hebrews calls "laying on of hands" one the basic teachings of the faith (Heb 6:2). Anointing with oil is also a symbol "rich in meaning: oil is a sign of abundance and joy [Dt 11:14; Ps 23:5 and 104:15]; it cleanses (anointing before and after a bath) and limbers (the anointing of athletes and wrestlers); oil is a sign of healing, since it is soothing to bruises and wounds [Is 1:6; Lk 10:34]; and it makes radiant with beauty, health, and strength" (CCC, 1293). Anointing with oil is part of several sacraments, Baptism, Anointing of the Sick, Holy Orders, and Confirmation, and it retains its varied "meanings in the sacramental life. The pre-baptismal anointing with the oil of catechumens signifies cleansing and strengthening; the anointing of the sick expresses healing and comfort. The post-baptismal anointing with sacred chrism in Confirmation and ordination is the sign of consecration. By Confirmation Christians, that is, those who are anointed, share more completely in the mission of Jesus Christ and the fullness of the Holy Spirit with which he is filled, so that their lives may give off 'the aroma of Christ' [2 Cor 2:15]" (CCC, 1294).

Chrism is made from olive oil or another plant oil mixed with an aromatic substance such as balsam and is consecrated only by a bishop. In addition to the Sacrament of Confirmation, it is used in the Sacraments of Baptism and Holy Orders and in the dedication of churches and altars. Chrism "is a sign that Christians, incorporated by Baptism into the Paschal Mystery of Christ, dying, buried, and rising with him, are sharers in his kingly and prophetic Priesthood and that by Confirmation they receive the spiritual anointing of the Spirit who is given to them."[6]

The *Rite for the Blessing of Oils and the Consecration of Chrism* explains the meaning of chrism. The bishop begins by inviting the people to ask God to "bless this oil so that all who are anointed with it may be inwardly transformed and come to share in eternal salvation."[7] Chrism, in all of its sacramental uses, is a sign and means of inner transformation through the Holy Spirit and so contributes to our salvation. At the conclusion of the invitation, "the bishop may breathe over the opening of the vessel of Chrism."[8] As we have already seen, chrism is a sign of the Holy Spirit. The bishop breathing on the chrism recalls the Spirit of God "moving over the face of the waters" at creation (Gn 1:2, RSVCE) and Jesus' resurrection appearance to the disciples in which "he breathed on them and said to them, 'Receive the holy Spirit'" (Jn 20:22). The bishop now says the prayer of consecration. He can choose between two consecratory prayers. Each reveals different aspects of the meaning and power of the chrism. The first prayer asks the Father to "fill it with the power of your Holy Spirit through Christ your Son."[9] This prayer also explains that the name chrism is derived from Christ: "It is from him that Chrism takes its name and with Chrism you have anointed for yourself Priests and kings, Prophets and Martyrs."[10] This

6. RPont, *The Rite for the Blessing of Oils and the Consecration of Chrism*, 2.
7. Ibid., 24.
8. Ibid., 25.
9. Ibid.
10. Ibid.

prayer emphasizes its use in the Sacrament of Baptism: "Make this Chrism sign of life and salvation for those who are to be born again in the waters of Baptism."[11]The second prayer explains how in the Old Testament God "gave your people a glimpse of the power of this holy oil" and then "brought that mystery to perfection in the life of our Lord Jesus Christ."[12] Henceforth, "through the sign of holy Chrism, you dispense your life and love to men." The prayer then asks, "Father, by the power of your love, make this mixture of oil and perfume a sign and source ✠ of your blessing. . . . Above all, Father, we pray that through this sign of your anointing you will grant increase to your Church until it reaches the eternal glory."[13] Each of the sacraments that includes anointing with chrism gives increase to the Church: Baptism, which incorporates new members into the Body of Christ; Confirmation, which equips believers with the gifts of the Spirit to participate fully in the mission of the Church; and Holy Orders, through which the faithful are instructed in the authentic faith of the apostles and sanctified chiefly through the Eucharist and Penance. This prayer of consecration offers a beautiful summary of the power of this liturgical sign: "Let the splendor of holiness shine on the world from every place and thing signed with this oil."[14]

In each prayer, just before the invocation of the Holy Spirit, the priests concelebrating with the bishop "extend their right hands towards the Chrism, without saying anything, until the end of the prayer."[15] In the first prayer, they do so beginning at the words: "And so, Father, we ask you to bless ✠ this oil you have created. Fill it with the power of your Holy Spirit through Christ your Son," until the conclusion of the prayer. This gesture signifies that the priests "assist their bishop 'as witnesses and cooperators in the consecration of Chrism,' thereby affirming how they share in his sacred office of building up, sanctifying and governing the Church."[16]

---

11. Ibid.

12. Ibid.

13. Ibid.

14. Ibid.

15. Ibid.

16. Peter J. Elliott, *Ceremonies of the Liturgical Year according to the Modern Roman Rite: A Manual for Clergy and All Involved in Liturgical Ministries* (San Francisco: Ignatius, 2002), 155.

The consecration effects a profound change in the scented oil, which is now sacred chrism. St. Cyril of Alexandria compares this change with the transubstantiated bread of the Eucharist. "But be sure not to regard the *myron* [chrism] merely as ointment. Just as the bread of the Eucharist after the invocation of the Holy Spirit is no longer just bread, but the body of Christ, so the holy *myron* after the invocation is no longer ordinary ointment but Christ's grace, which through the presence of the Holy Spirit instils his divinity into us."[17] The chrism is another example of how God communicates his presence to us through material substances that have been transformed by his word and Spirit.

The Sign of the Cross on the Forehead

Why is the chrism applied to the forehead? What is the significance of the forehead? It was considered by some Church Fathers the place of shame. St. Cyril of Jerusalem explained to the catechumens the anointing on the forehead: "First you were anointed on the forehead so that you might lose the shame which Adam, the first transgressor, everywhere bore with him, and so that you might 'with unveiled face behold the glory of the Lord' [2 Cor 3:18]."[18] St. Augustine called the forehead "the home of shame": "Do not hesitate, do not be ashamed. When you first believed, you received the sign of Christ on your forehead, the home of shame. Remember your forehead and do not be afraid of another man's tongue."[19] One suggested explanation for this interpretation is the mark that Cain received from God (Gn 4:15).[20]

St. John Chrysostom saw the forehead as the frontline of spiritual battle—the catechumen is anointed on the forehead "to make the devil turn away his eyes. He does not dare to look at you directly because he sees the light blazing from your head and blinding his eyes. From that day onwards you will confront him in battle, and this is why the bishop anoints you as athletes of Christ before leading you to the spiritual arena."[21] Theodore of Mopsuestia described the forehead as "the

17. Yarnold, *The Awe-Inspiring Rites*, 82–83.

18. Yarnold, *The Awe-Inspiring Rites*, 83.

19. Ibid., 4.

20. Ibid., 83.

21. Ibid., 160. Although Chrysostom is here referring to a prebaptismal anointing, the symbolism of the forehead applies also to the postbaptismal anointing that became the Sacrament of Confirmation.

highest and noblest part of the body. . . . So you receive this mark on the forehead to show what a great privilege you are receiving."[22] Like St. Cyril, Theodore also cites 2 Cor 3:18: "For now we see in a mirror dimly, but then face to face."[23] He agrees with Chrysostom in relating it to spiritual warfare. By receiving the seal "on the upper part of the face . . . the demons can see it a long way off and are deterred from coming close to harm us in the future."[24] At the same time, it is a sign to God "that we are members of his household and soldiers of Christ our Lord."[25]

The Spiritual Seal

The anointing with chrism on the forehead is accompanied by the essential words of this sacrament: "N., be sealed with the gift of the Holy Spirit" (OC, 27). These words indicate the twofold meaning of this action: the gift of the Holy Spirit and the imprinting of a spiritual seal. The OC explains these two meanings: "Signed with the perfumed oil by the hand of the bishop, the baptized received the indelible character, the seal of the Lord, together with the gift of the Spirit that conforms them more perfectly to Christ and gives them the grace of spreading among men and women 'the sweet odor of Christ'" (OC, 9). The candidate says "Amen" to the essential words of the sacrament, the exterior sign of her or his interior assent to all that the sacrament confers.

We have already discussed the first meaning of the anointing, the gift of the Holy Spirit. Here we will discuss the second, the spiritual seal or indelible character, a sign we also encountered in the Sacrament of Baptism. The *Catechism* combines both meanings in introducing a discussion of the seal in the Sacrament of Confirmation: "By this anointing the confirmand receives the 'mark,' the seal of the Holy Spirit" (CCC, 1295). A seal has several meanings. It can be "a symbol of a person (cf. Gn 38:18), a sign of personal authority (cf. Gn 41:42), or ownership of an object (cf. Dt 32:34)" (CCC, 1295). In his Bread of Life discourse, "Christ himself declared that he was marked with his Father's seal" (CCC, 1296; cf. Jn 6:27). Christians are also marked with

22. Ibid., 178.

23. Ibid.

24. Ibid., 178–179.

25. Ibid., 179.

a seal (see the discussion in chapter 6, pp. 107–110). Confirmation "imprints on the soul an indelible spiritual mark, the 'character,' which is the sign that Jesus Christ has marked a Christian with the seal of his Spirit by clothing him with power from on high so that he may be his witness" (CCC, 1304). The seal of Confirmation "evokes the completion of gifting that comes with Pentecost. The Holy Spirit is the ultimate gift of God, of which God does not repent and after which God has nothing else to give. . . . The gift of the Spirit puts the identifying stamp of Christ on the person being initiated, as it was the Spirit who identified Christ as the Son of God at his baptism. Christ will be recognizable henceforth in the Christian through the presence in him or her of the Spirit. . . . The Spirit given in confirmation may be grieved and the gifts left unused, but the Spirit once given is there forever. Once sealed with this gift one is forever signed, sealed, and delivered for Christ and the Spirit."[26]

The OC summarizes the meaning of these two liturgical units: first, the imposition of hands over the candidates accompanied by the prayer for the seven gifts of the Holy Spirit; and second, the anointing with chrism and the essential words. "The whole rite presents a two-fold symbolism. Through the laying of hands on the candidates by the Bishop and the concelebrating Priests, the biblical gesture, by which the gift of the Holy Spirit is invoked, is expressed in a manner well suited to the understanding of the Christian people. In the anointing with Chrism and the accompanying words, the effect of the giving of the Holy Spirit is clearly signified. Signed with the perfumed oil by the hand of the Bishop, the baptized received the indelible character, the seal of the Lord, together with the gift of the Spirit that conforms them more perfectly to Christ and gives them the grace of spreading among men and women 'the sweet odor of Christ'" (OC, 9).

The Sign of Peace

After anointing each candidate with chrism and sealing him or her with the gift of the Spirit, the bishop concludes the sacramental rite with the sign of peace. He says, "Peace be with you," and the newly confirmed answers, "And with your spirit" (OC, 27). This "signifies and

26. Walsh, *The Sacraments of Initiation*, 159.

demonstrates ecclesial communion with the bishop and with all the faithful" (CCC, 1301). The greeting "Peace be with you" comes from one of Jesus' resurrection appearances—his appearance to the disciples who have locked themselves in a room. They rejoice to see him, and he says to them, "Peace be with you" (Jn 20:21). This greeting is reserved to the bishop, reflecting the fullness of his sacramental configuration to Christ, for through episcopal ordination "bishops, in an eminent and visible manner, take the place of Christ himself, teacher, shepherd, and priest, and act as his representative" (CCC, 1558). This is also the greeting reserved to the bishop when he celebrates the Eucharist, so it is the greeting with which he begins the Mass for the Conferral of Confirmation. The Sign of Peace highlights the communal dimension of Confirmation, strengthening the recipients' union with Christ's Body, the Church through his visible, sacramental representative, the bishop.

The Lord's Prayer

Finally, the OC emphasizes the first time the newly confirmed—now endowed with "the fullness of the God's Spirit" (RBC, 68)—pray the Lord's Prayer in the Mass. For those baptized as infants, the Lord's Prayer was said by the assembly at the conclusion of the baptismal rite before the altar "in their name, in the Spirit of our common sonship" (RBC, 68). Now, in the second sacrament of initiation, praying the Lord's Prayer in the Eucharistic liturgy is again an event of singular significance. "Great importance is likewise to be attached to the saying of the Lord's Prayer, which those to be confirmed recite together with the congregation—either during Mass before Communion or outside Mass before the blessing—because it is the Spirit who prays in us and in the Spirit the Christian says, 'Abba, Father'" (OC, 1).

This reference to "the Spirit who prays in us and the in the Spirit the Christian says, 'Abba, Father,'" alludes to several New Testament passages that speak of prayer as the work of the Holy Spirit. We will look at the reference to "Abba, Father" in chapter 9. Here we will reflect on the reference to "the Spirit who prays in us," which suggests the essential role the Holy Spirit plays in prayer. It is an allusion to Romans 8:26: "we do not know how to pray as we ought, but the Spirit himself intercedes with sighs too deep for words." This is a challenging verse, asking us to look into our heart. "Are we convinced that 'we do not know how to pray as we ought?'" asks the *Catechism* (CCC, 2736). "Only when we humbly acknowledge that 'we do not know how to pray as we ought,' are we ready to receive freely the gift of prayer" (CCC, 2559) from the Holy Spirit, for he, "the artisan of God's works, is the master of prayer" (CCC, 741). Prayer is God's gift and can only be received with the open and empty hands of humility.

Conclusion

The different signs—words, actions, and sacred chrism—that make up the Sacrament of Confirmation clearly express the holy things that they signify (SC, 71; DCN). The imposition of hands *over* the candidates and the accompanying prayer effectively express the impartation of the seven gifts of the Holy Spirit. The imposition of the hand *on* the candidate, the anointing with sacred chrism, the sign of the cross made on the forehead, and the essential words together signify and bring about the seal or character of the sacrament. These elements are examples of the inseparability of "the liturgical word and action . . . both insofar as they are signs and instruction and insofar as they accomplish what they signify" (CCC, 1155). The Renewal of Baptismal Promises, the recitation of the Lord's Prayer and the use of chrism also manifest the sacrament's connection with the Sacrament of Baptism. The dialogic character of the sacrament is expressed through the Renewal of Baptism Promises and the Sign of Peace. The signs of the Sacrament of Confirmation remind us that through sacramental "words, actions, and symbols . . . the Spirit puts both the faithful and the ministers into a living relationship with Christ, the Word and Image of the Father, so that they can live out the meaning of what they hear, contemplate, and do in the celebration" (CCC, 1101). We will now reflect on how we live out the meaning of what we "hear, contemplate, and do in the celebration" of the Sacrament of Confirmation.

Chapter 9

Confirmation: Living the Sacrament

Confirmation, said Pope Francis, "must be understood in continuity with Baptism, to which it is inseparably linked."[1] Thus, we cannot speak of the transforming effects of Confirmation without referring to the sacramental effects of Baptism. The Church likens Confirmation to the outpouring of the Spirit at Pentecost (CCC, 1302), as a result of which "Confirmation brings an increase and deepening of baptismal grace" (CCC, 1303). We will begin by looking at Confirmation as a personal Pentecost. We will then consider the specific ways in which it increases and deepens baptismal grace. First, like Baptism, Confirmation imparts an indelible seal or character. It also conforms us more fully to Christ, rooting "us more deeply in the divine filiation which makes us cry, 'Abba, Father' (Rom 8:15)" (CCC, 1303). Confirmation also binds us more perfectly to the Body of Christ, a union begun at Baptism, and it strengthens us to bear witness to the Gospel, a duty first received at Baptism. Finally, Confirmation increases in us the Spirit's gifts, whose temple we became at Baptism. While we will discuss each effect separately, it is good to remember that they are integrally related.

A Personal Pentecost

In the Sacrament of Confirmation "those who have been baptized . . . receive the outpouring of the Holy Spirit whom the Lord sent upon the Apostles at Pentecost" (OC, 1). According to the *Catechism*, the connection between Confirmation and Pentecost is expressed by the sacramental celebration: "It is evident from its celebration that the effect of the sacrament of Confirmation is the full outpouring of the Holy Spirit as once granted to the apostles on the day of Pentecost" (CCC, 1302). That this connection is "evident from its celebration" recalls, for example,

1. Francis, General Audience, January 29, 2014, http://w2.vatican.va/content/francesco/en/audiences/2014/documents/papa-francesco_20140129_udienza-generale.html.

the article on the Holy Spirit in the Renewal of Baptismal Promises in which the candidates are asked:

> Do you believe in the Holy Spirit,
> the Lord, the giver of life,
> who today through the Sacrament of Confirmation
> is given to you in a special way
> just as he was given to the Apostles on the day of Pentecost?
> (OC, 23)

We also hear an allusion to Pentecost in the bishop's invitation to the people before the prayer for the seven gifts of the Spirit that God would "graciously pour out the Holy Spirit upon them [the candidates]" (OC, 24).

Confirmation as a personal experience of Pentecost is developed in the model homily for the celebration of Confirmation. "The Apostles, who had received the Holy Spirit on the day of Pentecost in fulfillment of the Lord's promise, had the power to complete the work of Baptism by the giving of the Holy Spirit, as we read in the Acts of the Apostles. . . . The Bishops, as successors of the Apostles, possess the same power and, either in their own right or through Priests lawfully appointed to fulfill this ministry, they confer the Holy Spirit on those who have already been born again in Baptism" (OC, 22; homily). The Holy Spirit is given at Confirmation "to complete the work of Baptism" by perfecting Baptismal grace (CCC, 1316) and strengthening the baptized (CIC, c. 879).

This completion and perfecting of Baptismal grace has also been described using the image of marriage. Honorius of Autun called the anointing with chrism at Confirmation "the nuptial garment" and explained the two anointings with chrism, first at Baptism, then at Confirmation. "The baptized are twice anointed with chrism: once by the priest at baptism, and on the head; second, by the bishop at confirmation, and on the forehead. . . . By the priest's unction their souls are espoused to Christ; by the bishop's confirmation they are endowed with the kingdom of Christ."[2] The twentieth-century Orthodox theologian Alexander Schmemann describes the perfecting aspect of Confirmation as both Pentecost and ordination: "Confirmation is thus the personal Pentecost of man, his entrance into the new life in the Holy Spirit, which is the true life of the Church. It is his ordination as

2. Monti, *A Sense of the Sacred*, 126.

truly and fully man, for to be fully man is precisely to belong to the Kingdom of God."[3]

Imparts a Character or Seal

Confirmation, along with Baptism and Holy Orders, is one of the sacraments that marks the recipient "with the character or seal of the Lord" (OC, 2). The Church understands this seal as "the sign that Jesus Christ has marked a Christian with the seal of his Spirit by clothing him with power form on high so that he may be his witness" (CCC, 1304). It also "perfects the common priesthood of the faithful, received in Baptism" (CCC, 1305). St. John Paul II affirmed the apostolic origin of this effect. "And so we Christians, having been incorporated into the Body of Christ our Lord by faith and Baptism, are marked by the seal of the Spirit when we receive this anointing. The Apostle Paul explicitly teaches this in speaking to the Christians of Corinth: 'It is God who establishes us with you in Christ, and has commissioned us; he has put his seal upon us and given us his Spirit in our hearts as a guarantee' (2 Cor 1:21–22; cf. Eph 1:13–14; 4:30)."[4]

St. Cyprian of Carthage in the third century also taught that the seal was of apostolic origin. "Peter and John made good only what they lacked: after prayers had been said for them and hands were laid upon them, the Holy Spirit was invoked and poured out upon them. And this same practice we observe today ourselves: those who are baptized in the Church are presented to the appointed leaders of the Church, and by our prayer and the imposition of our hands they receive the Holy Spirit and are made perfect with the Lord's seal."[5] St. Ambrose, writing about a century after St. Cyprian, explained the meaning of the seal in terms of the seven gifts of the Holy Spirit. "Recall then that you have received the spiritual seal, the spirit of wisdom and understanding, the spirit of right judgment and courage, the spirit of knowledge and reverence, the spirit of holy fear in God's presence. Guard what you have received. God the Father has marked you with his sign; Christ the Lord

3. Alexander Schmemann, *For the Life of the World: Sacraments and Orthodoxy*, 2nd revised and expanded ed. (Crestwood, NY: St. Vladimir's Seminary Press, 1973), 75.

4. John Paul II, General Audience, October 14, 1998, http://w2.vatican.va/content/john-paul-ii/en/audiences/1998/documents/hf_jp-ii_aud_14101998.html.

5. Cyprian of Carthage, *The Letters of Cyprian*, vol. 4 (New York: Newman Press, 1989), 58–59.

has confirmed you and has placed his pledge, the Spirit, in your hearts" (CCC, 1303).

The seal of Confirmation differs from the seal of Baptism in this respect: "the character received in Confirmation entrusts the person with the public nature of his or her being Christian. While Baptism focuses more on the individual life of the member of the Church, Confirmation places a stress on the communal aspect."[6] This character is a guarantee of a relationship strengthened by the seven gifts of the Holy Spirit by which the recipient receives God's power to be his witness. If we may revisit Pentecost one more time, "Confirmation puts the seal on Baptism as Pentecost completes Easter."[7]

St. John Paul II explained "the salvific value and spiritual effect" of this seal, which effects an enduring reciprocal relationship between the believer and the Blessed Trinity.[8] "The seal of the Holy Spirit therefore signifies and brings about the disciple's total belonging to Jesus Christ, his being always at the latter's service in the Church, and at the same time it implies the promise of divine protection in the trials he will have to endure to witness to his faith in the world."[9] The phrase "signifies and brings about" is a reminder of the dual nature of liturgical signs, which both instruct and "accomplish what they signify" (CCC, 1155).

The relationship that the seal creates in turn leads to mission. St. John Paul II explains: "The baptized who receive the sacrament of Confirmation with full and mature awareness solemnly declare before the Church, with the support of God's grace, their readiness to let themselves be grasped by the Spirit of God in an ever new and ever deeper way, to become witnesses to Christ the Lord."[10] The stipulation of receiving the sacrament "with full and mature awareness" is a reminder of the importance of the recipient's disposition (see chapter 3, p. 51), which is an important factor in determining the fruits of the sacrament (CCC, 1128). Thus, the seal or character conferred at Confirmation is both mutual gift and mutual commitment. It is the candidate's gift of his life to God and God's gift of a new and deeper

6. Haffner, *The Sacramental Mystery*, 83.

7. Ibid., 84.

8. John Paul II, General Audience, October 14, 1998, http://w2.vatican.va/content/john-paul-ii/en/audiences/1998/documents/hf_jp-ii_aud_14101998.html.

9. Ibid.

10. Ibid.

participation in the divine life. And it is the candidate's commitment to serve the Lord with the totality of his or her being, resting in the Lord's commitment of abiding presence and protection.

Conforms Us More Fully to Christ

Confirmation also conforms us more fully to Christ (OC, 2), which the Church understands as being more deeply rooted in the divine filiation, a deeper experience that we are sons and daughters of God (CCC, 1316). This fuller conformity to Christ is manifested in a simple, Spirit-inspired prayer—"Abba, Father" (CCC, 1303), a prayer that occurs three times in the New Testament. We hear it first on the lips of Jesus in the Garden of Gethsemane: "Abba, Father, all things are possible to you. Take this cup away from me, but not what I will but what you will" (Mk 14:36). "Abba" is an Aramaic term that apparently was not used during the time of Jesus as an address to God without being qualified in some way.[11] However, it was "Jesus' special way of addressing God with filial intimacy,"[12] the prayer "used by Jesus in the moment of his supreme earthly confidence in God."[13]

This prayer occurs twice in the letters of St. Paul: Romans and Galatians. He reminded the Christians in Rome that they did not receive "a spirit of slavery to fall back into fear, but . . . a spirit of adoption, through which we cry, 'Abba, Father'" (Rom 8:15). In describing our fuller conformity to Christ through Confirmation, it is worth noting that this is the verse cited by the *Catechism* (cf. n. 1303). Under the action of the Holy Spirit this prayer expresses the Christian's intimacy with God. "The vivifying Spirit of the risen Son is the dynamic principle of adoptive sonship. It empowers the Christian's inmost conviction, as one exclaims of God, 'Father!' Without the Spirit the Christian would never be able to utter this cry."[14] The Apostle wrote in similar language to the Galatians. "As proof that you are children, God sent the spirit of his Son into our hearts, crying out, 'Abba, Father!'" (Gal 4:6). For

---

11. NABRE, n. on Mk 14:36, p. 91.
12. Ibid.
13. NJBC, 853.
14. Ibid., 788.

St. Paul, this cry was, "even in Gentile communities the mode of address distinctive of Christians."[15]

The prayers of the Confirmation liturgy petition God for this fuller conformity to his Son. It is part of the bishop's invitation to the community to pray for the outpouring of the gifts of the Holy Spirit on the candidates: "Let us pray to God the almighty Father . . . that he will graciously pour out the Holy Spirit upon them . . . and through his anointing conform them more fully to Christ, the Son of God" (OC, 24). The Prayer over the Offerings reveals the unity between deeper conformity to Christ, participation in his mission, and the strength received from the Sacraments of Confirmation and the Eucharist, asking the Lord to "grant that, being conformed more perfectly to your Son, they may grow steadily in bearing witness to him, as they share in the memorial of his redemption" (RM, Ritual Masses I, 4A).

One of the collects for the Ritual Mass for Confirmation asks for the radical transformation toward which the sacrament is directed—conformity to "the full stature of Christ": "Graciously pour out your Holy Spirit upon us, we pray, O Lord, so that, walking in oneness of faith and strengthened by the power of his love, we may come to the measure of the full stature of Christ" (Collect B). This prayer paraphrases a passage from the Letter to the Ephesians in which the members of the Church are urged to work "for building up the body of Christ, until we all attain to the unity of faith and knowledge of the Son of God, to mature manhood, to the extent of the full stature of Christ" (Eph 4:12–13). In this prayer and its scriptural basis we see again the communal, ecclesial dimension of the Sacrament of Confirmation.

Strengthens Us to Bear Witness to the Gospel

The grace of Confirmation unites us more closely to the Church and equips us to be effective witnesses to the Gospel. According to Vatican Council II's *Dogmatic Constitution on the Church*, "By the sacrament of confirmation they [the faithful] are more perfectly bound to the Church and are endowed with the special strength of the Holy Spirit. Hence they are, as true witnesses of Christ, more strictly obliged to spread the

15. Ibid., 853.

faith by word and deed" (LG, 11). Through the impartation of the character or seal of this sacrament, wrote St. Thomas Aquinas, "the confirmed person receives the power to profess faith in Christ publicly and as it were officially" (CCC, 1305), a point we discussed above. The confirmed Christian is empowered "to confess the name of Christ boldly, and never to be ashamed of the Cross (CCC, 1303)." This particular grace is given "for the building up of his Body in faith and charity" (OC, 2).

This grace is the subject of a number of petitions made throughout the liturgy for Confirmation. We hear it in the Collect that begins the ritual Mass:

> Fulfill for us your gracious promise, O Lord, we pray,
> so that by his coming
> the Holy Spirit may make us witnesses before the world
> to the Gospel of our Lord Jesus Christ.
> (RM, Ritual Masses I, 4A, Collect)

One of the suggested intercessions that concludes the celebration of the sacrament is for the newly confirmed:

> For these his servants,
> whom the gift of the Holy Spirit has confirmed:
> that, rooted in faith and grounded in love,
> they may bear witness to Christ the Lord by their way of life.
> (OC, 30, Universal Prayer)

Next, the Prayer over the Offerings at the start of the Liturgy of the Eucharist (following the celebration of the sacrament) asks that the newly confirmed "may grow steadily in bearing witness to him" (RM, Ritual Masses I, 4A). Finally, the Ritual Mass for Confirmation may conclude with a Prayer over the People that includes this invocation for the newly confirmed:

> May they never be ashamed
> to confess Christ crucified before the world.
> (Prayer over the People)

This grace of the Sacrament of Confirmation is beautifully summed up in the Prayer after Communion:

> Instruct, O Lord, in the fullness of the Law
> those you have endowed with the gifts of your Spirit
> and nourished by the Body of your Only Begotten Son,

> that they may constantly show to the world
> the freedom of your adopted children
> and, by the holiness of their lives,
> exercise the prophetic mission of your people.
> (RM, Ritual Masses I, 4B, Prayer after Communion)

The outpouring of the gifts of the Spirit will continually deepen the recipient's understanding of the faith, so that the confirmed may be a sign of Christ to the world by prophetic word and personal holiness.

Increases the Gifts of the Spirit within Us

The Sacrament of Confirmation also increases the seven gifts of the Holy Spirit within us (CCC, 1303): wisdom, understanding, counsel, fortitude, knowledge, piety, and fear of the Lord. These gifts are invoked in the prayer before the anointing with chrism, a prayer based on Isaiah 11:2–3.[16] St. Ambrose described these gifts as "the cardinal, the fundamental, virtues. What is more fundamental than piety, what is more fundamental than the knowledge of God, what is more fundamental than strength, than God's counsel, than the fear of God? Just as the fear of the world is weakness, so fear of God is great strength."[17] We are fortunate to have catecheses on these seven gifts by St. John Paul II and Pope Francis, to which we will now turn, listening in, as it were, on two popes, one a saint, discussing the gifts of the Holy Spirit.

Wisdom

The first spiritual gift we will consider is wisdom. This is not, says Pope Francis, wisdom "in the sense that he has an answer for everything, that he knows everything."[18] Rather, it means that one "'*knows' about God*, he knows how God acts, he knows when something is of God and when it is not of God." St. John Paul II describes it as "a light which we receive from on high . . . a special sharing in that mysterious

16. See chapter 7 for a discussion of Isaiah 11:2–3 and chapter 8 for a discussion of the prayer invoking these seven gifts.

17. Yarnold, *The Awe-Inspiring Rites*, 124.

18. Quotations from Pope Francis in this section are from his General Audience on April 9, 2014, https://w2.vatican.va/content/francesco/en/audiences/2014/documents/papa-francesco_20140409_udienza-generale.html.

and highest knowledge which is that of God himself."[19] St. Thomas Aquinas spoke of having "a certain taste of God," a sense to which both popes refer. Commenting on this, St. John Paul II explains that through this taste of God "the truly wise person is not simply the one who knows the things of God but rather the one who experiences and lives them." In a similar vein, Pope Francis says that "The heart of the wise man in this sense has a *taste and savor* for God." This spiritual gift gives rise to a new perception of reality, "a new awareness," says St. John Paul II, "a knowledge permeated by charity, by means of which the soul becomes familiar, so to say, with divine things, and tastes them." It is, says Pope Francis, "the grace of being able *to see everything with the eyes of God*. It is simply this: it is to see the world, to see situations, circumstances, problems, everything through God's eyes." This gift, he says, "teaches us to see with God's eyes, to feel with God's heart, to speak with God's words."

According to St. John Paul II, through this gift of wisdom, "the entire life of the individual Christian, with all its events, hopes, plans, and achievements, is caught up in the breath of the Spirit, who permeates it with Light 'from on high.'" Pope Francis emphasizes that it is nothing less than "seeing with God's eyes, hearing with God's ears, loving with God's heart, directing things with God's judgment." The truly wise person not only knows the things of God but also "experiences and lives them," concludes St. John Paul II.

Understanding

The second spiritual gift is the gift of understanding, a gift that Pope Francis says "is *closely connected to faith*. When the *Holy Spirit* dwells in our hearts and enlightens our minds, he makes us grow day by day in the *understanding of what the Lord has said and accomplished*. Jesus himself told his disciples: I will send you the Holy Spirit and he will enable you to understand all that I have taught you."[20] Through this gift the Spirit implants in our hearts a desire to comprehend the faith more deeply.

---

19. Quotations from Pope John Paul II in this section are from his Regina Coeli Address on April 9, 1989, http://www.vatican.va/liturgical_year/pentecost/documents/hf_jp-ii_reg_19890409_en.html.

20. Quotations from Pope Francis in this section are from his General Audience on April 30, 2014, https://w2.vatican.va/content/francesco/en/audiences/2014/documents/papa-francesco_20140430_udienza-generale.html.

Faith, says St. John Paul II, is a desire to understand more deeply what we believe: "an interior urge comes to us from the Holy Spirit who, with faith, gives us precisely this special gift of intelligence and, as it were, intuition of the divine truth."[21] Through this gift the Spirit gives us both the desire and the ability to know our faith more deeply.

This spiritual gift touches and elevates our natural intellect. St. John Paul II explains that the word *intellect* "derives from the Latin 'intus legere', which means 'to read within,' to penetrate, to understand thoroughly. Through this gift the Holy Spirit who 'sees into the depths of God' (1 Cor 2:10), communicates to the believer a glint of such a penetrating capacity, opening the heart to the joyous understanding of God's loving plan."[22] Pope Francis contrasts the natural operation of our intellect with its supernatural operation when directed by the gift of understanding: "one can understand a situation with human understanding, with prudence, and this is good. But to understand a situation in depth, as God understands it is the effect of this gift."

As an illustration of this gift, both Pope Francis and St. John Paul II cite Jesus' encounter with the two disciples on the road to Emmaus (Lk 24:13–32). This episode, says Pope Francis, "aptly expresses the depths and power of this gift." Having witnessed the suffering, death and burial Jesus, these two disciples, "disappointed and grief stricken, leave Jerusalem and return to their village called Emmaus. As they are on their way, the risen Jesus draws near and begins talking with them, but their eyes, veiled with sadness and despair, are unable to recognize him. Jesus walks with them, but they are so sad, in such deep despair, that they do not recognize him. When, however, the Lord explains the Scriptures to them so that they might understand that he had to suffer and die in order then to rise again, *their minds are opened and hope is rekindled in their hearts* (cf. Lk 24:13–27)." According to St. John Paul II, it is the gift of understanding that enables every disciple to experience what these two disciples experienced. "Once again the experience of the disciples of Emmaus is renewed; having recognized the Risen Lord in the breaking of the bread, they said to one another: 'Were not our hearts burning within us while he spoke to us on the way and opened the

---

21. Quotations from Pope John Paul II in this section are from his Regina Coeli Address on April 16, 1989, http://www.vatican.va/liturgical_year/pentecost/documents/hf_jp-ii_reg_19890416_en.html.

22. Pope Francis repeats this point in his catechesis.

scriptures to us?' (Lk 24:32)." This gift, says Pope Francis, is particularly operative when we read the Sacred Scriptures. "One can read the Gospel and understand something, but if we read the Gospel with this gift of the Holy Spirit, we can understand the depths of God's words. And this is a great gift, a great gift for which we all must ask and ask together: Give us, Lord, the gift of understanding."

St. John Paul II says that the gift of understanding, "while it sharpens the understanding of divine things, renders ever more clear and penetrating the understanding of human things. Thanks to it one sees better the many signs of God which are written in creation. Thus is discovered the not merely earthly dimension of events of which human history is woven. One can even arrive at prophetically interpreting the present and the future: signs of the times, signs of God!" Just as our natural world is interwoven with the glory of God, so through the gift of understanding our natural comprehension is interwoven with the light of the Spirit.

The gift of understanding transforms our natural intellect, enabling us to grasp things both human and divine, events past, present, and future, and to penetrate ever more deeply into the meaning of God's Word. Pope Francis stresses our need for this gift: "The gift of understanding is important for our Christian life. Let us ask it of the Lord, that he may give us, that he may give us all this gift to understand the things that happen as he understands them, and to understand, above all, the Word of God in the Gospel."

Counsel

Counsel is the third gift of the Spirit. We saw above that the gift of understanding enlightens our intellect; the gift of counsel, says St. John Paul II, enlightens "the conscience in moral choices which daily life presents."[23] In the words of Pope Francis, through the gift of counsel the Spirit "enables our conscience to make a concrete choice in communion with God, according to the logic of Jesus and his Gospel."[24] This gift,

23. Quotations from Pope John Paul II in this section are from his Regina Coeli Address on May 7, 1989, http://www.vatican.va/liturgical_year/pentecost/documents/hf_jp-ii_reg_19890507_en.html.

24. Quotations from Pope Francis in this section are from his General Audience on May 7, 2014, http://w2.vatican.va/content/francesco/en/audiences/2014/documents/papa-francesco_20140507_udienza-generale.html.

continues St. John Paul II, "enriches and perfects the virtue of prudence," which is the cardinal virtue that directs us "to discern our true good in every circumstance and to choose the right means of achieving it" (CCC, 1806). Through counsel, he says, the Spirit directs the soul, "especially when it is a matter of important choices (for example, of responding to a vocation), or about a path to be followed among difficulties and obstacles."

St. John Paul II stresses that the gift of counsel is particularly necessary in the present time. "A need that is keenly felt in our days, disturbed by not a few crises and by a widespread uncertainty about true values, is that which is called 'reconstructing consciences.' That is to say, one is aware of the necessity of neutralizing certain destructive factors which easily find their way into the human spirit when it is agitated by passions, and of introducing healthy positive elements into it." St. John Paul II calls the gift of counsel "a new breath in the conscience, suggesting to it what is licit, what is becoming, what is more fitting for the soul." Similarly, Pope Francis teaches that through the gift of counsel "the Spirit makes us grow interiorly, he makes us grow positively, he makes us grow in the community and he helps us not to fall prey to self-centeredness and one's own way of seeing things."

Our choices can strengthen or weaken the Spirit's ministry of counsel in our life. In this regard Pope Francis stresses the importance of prayer. "The essential condition for preserving this gift is prayer. . . . To pray with the prayers that we all learned as children, but also to pray in our own words. To ask the Lord: 'Lord, help me, give me counsel, what must I do now?' Prayer, says Pope Francis, creates a "space so that the Spirit may come and help us in that moment, that he may counsel us on what we all must do. . . . No one, no one realizes when we pray on the bus, on the road: we pray in the silence of our heart. Let us take advantage of these moments to pray, pray that the Spirit gives us the gift of counsel." Pope Francis also emphasizes the importance of encountering God in his Word. "In intimacy with God and in listening to his Word, little by little we put aside our own way of thinking, which is most often dictated by our closures, by our prejudice and by our ambitions, and we learn instead to ask the Lord: what is your desire? What is your will?"

St. John Paul II likens the conscience enlightened by the gift of counsel to "the 'healthy eye' of which the Gospel speaks (Mt 6:21), an eye which acquires, as it were, a new pupil, by means of which it is able to see better what to do in a given situation, no matter how intricate and difficult. Aided by this gift, the Christian penetrates the true meaning of gospel values, in particular those expressed in the Sermon on the Mount (cf. Mt 5:7)." According to Pope Francis, the ultimate fruit of this gift of counsel, preserved and nourished by prayer and the prayerful reading of Scripture is that "a *deep, almost connatural harmony* in the Spirit grows and develops within us."

Fortitude

St. John Paul II describes the fourth spiritual gift, fortitude, as "a supernatural impulse which gives strength to the soul, not only on exceptional occasions such as that of martyrdom, but also in normal difficulties: in the struggle to remain consistent with one's principles; in putting up with insults and unjust attacks; in courageous perseverance on the path of truth and uprightness, in spite of lack of understanding and hostility."[25] The spiritual *gift* of fortitude supports and strengthens the cardinal *virtue* of fortitude, the virtue that enables us to persevere through difficulties, consistently pursue the good, resist temptations, overcome obstacles, and conquer fear (CCC, 1808). Pope Francis uses the parable of the sower (Mt 13:1–9, 18–23) to explain this gift: "through the gift of fortitude, the Holy Spirit *liberates the soil of our heart,* he frees it from sluggishness, from uncertainty and from all the fears that can hinder it, so that Lord's Word may be put into practice authentically and with joy."[26]

St. John Paul II acknowledges the urgent need today for this spiritual gift: "Perhaps today as never before the moral virtue of fortitude needs the support of the corresponding gift of the Holy Spirit." He notes two contrary tendencies that are both opposed to fortitude: timidity and domination. "This virtue finds little room in a society in which surrender and accommodation on the one hand, and domination and toughness on the other, are widespread in economic, social and political

25. Quotations from Pope John Paul II in this section are from his Regina Coeli Address on May 14, 1989, http://www.vatican.va/liturgical_year/pentecost/documents/hf_jp-ii_reg_19890514_en.html.

26. Quotations from Pope Francis in this section are from his General Audience on May 14, 2014, http://w2.vatican.va/content/francesco/en/audiences/2014/documents/papa-francesco_20140514_udienza-generale.html.

relations. Timidity and aggressiveness are two forms of lack of fortitude which are often found in human behavior; they result repeatedly in the distressing sight of one who is weak and cowardly towards the powerful, or of one who is arrogant and overbearing towards the defenseless." In timidity we see a lack of fortitude, in aggressiveness and domination its counterfeit. The gift of fortitude supplies what nature lacks and corrects what the Fall has deformed.

Fortitude is particularly evident, says Pope Francis, in "*difficult moments* and *extreme situations* . . . This is the case with those who are facing particularly harsh and painful situations that disrupt their lives and those of their loved ones." As an example, he cites "those men, of those women who have a difficult life, who fight to feed their family, to educate their children: they do all of this because the spirit of fortitude is helping them." But he notes that fortitude is not reserved for emergencies; rather, it "must constitute the tenor of our Christian life, in the *ordinary daily routine*. As I said, we need to be strong every day of our lives, to carry forward our life, our family, our faith."

Both St. John Paul II and Pope Francis stress this point. St. John Paul II advises that when we experience the weakness of "human nature subject to physical and psychological infirmities, we should ask the Holy Spirit for the gift of Fortitude to remain firm and decisive on the path of goodness." Pope Francis offers similar advice. "Dear friends, sometimes we may be tempted to give in to laziness, or worse, to discouragement, especially when faced with the hardships and trials of life. In these cases, let us not lose heart, let us invoke the Holy Spirit so that through the gift of fortitude he may lift our heart and communicate new strength and enthusiasm to our life and to our following of Jesus."

Knowledge

St. John Paul II defines the gift of knowledge as the gift that enables us "to know the true value of creatures in their relationship to the Creator."[27] "It is a special gift," says Pope Francis, "which leads us to grasp, through creation, the greatness and love of God and his profound

---

27. Quotations from Pope John Paul II in this section are from his Regina Coeli Address on April 23, 1989, http://www.vatican.va/liturgical_year/pentecost/documents/hf_jp-ii_reg_19890423_en.html.

relationship with every creature."[28] When the Spirit illumines our eyes through the gift of knowledge, he says, we are able "to contemplate God, in the beauty of nature and in the grandeur of the cosmos . . . *to discover how everything speaks to us about Him and His love*. All of this arouses in us great wonder and a profound sense of gratitude!"

The development of science and technology has brought with it "the temptation to give a naturalistic interpretation to the world," says St. John Paul II. In the face of "the manifold magnificence of created things, their complexity, variety and beauty," one can be tempted to divinize them "to the extent of making them the supreme purpose of his very life. This happens especially when it is a matter of riches, pleasure and power, which indeed can be drawn from material things." "These are the principal idols," concludes St. John Paul II, "before which the world too often prostrates." The gift of knowledge helps us resist these temptations and idols by helping us "to value things correctly in their essential dependence on the Creator."

Like St. John Paul II, Pope Francis recognizes the tendency to divinize the world, "the temptation to stop at creatures, as if these could provide the answer to all our expectations." And consistent with the thought of his sainted predecessor, he describes an "attitude of excess" that views man as the master of creation. "Creation is not some possession that we can lord over for our own pleasure; nor, even less, is it the property of only some people, the few: creation is a gift, it is the marvelous gift that God has given us, *so that we will take care of it and harness it for the benefit of all, always with great respect and gratitude*." The gift of knowledge helps us overcome these temptations and erroneous attitudes, explains St. John Paul II, by discovering "the theological meaning of creation, seeing things as true and real, although limited, manifestations of the Truth, Beauty, and infinite Love which is God, and consequently he feels impelled to translate this discovery into praise, song, prayer, and thanksgiving." The gift of knowledge becomes for the believer "a source of serenity and peace and makes the Christian a joyful witness of God," says Pope Francis, "in the footsteps of St. Francis of Assisi and so many saints who knew how to praise and laud his love through the contemplation of creation."

---

28. Quotations from Pope Francis in this section are from his General Audience on May 21, 2014, http://w2.vatican.va/content/francesco/en/audiences/2014/documents/papa-francesco_20140521_udienza-generale.html.

Let us conclude with the words of Pope Francis. "The gift of knowledge sets us in profound *harmony with the Creator* and allows us to participate in the clarity of his vision and his judgement. And it is in this perspective that we manage to accept man and woman as the summit of creation, as the fulfillment of a plan of love that is impressed in each one of us and that allows us to recognize one another as brothers and sisters."

Piety

Pope Francis says that the sixth gift, piety, "touches the very heart of our Christian life and identity."[29] He explains that it is the gift that "indicates our belonging to God and our profound relationship with Him, a bond that gives meaning to our life and keeps us sound, in communion with Him, even during the most difficult and tormenting moments." The relationship granted by the gift of piety is not an obligation or requirement, it "is not intended as a duty or an imposition. It is a bond that comes from within. It is *a relationship lived with the heart*: it is our friendship with God, granted to us by Jesus, a friendship that changes our life and fills us with passion, with joy. Thus, the gift of piety stirs in us above all gratitude and praise." The sentiments stirred by this gift constitute "the reason and *the most authentic meaning of our worship and our adoration*."

St. John Paul II describes the abundant effects of this gift. Through the gift of piety "the Spirit heals our hearts of every form of hardness, and opens them to tenderness towards God and our brothers and sisters."[30] The awareness of our spiritual poverty and weakness reveals our need for God's "grace, help and pardon. The gift of piety directs and nourishes such need, enriching it with sentiments of profound confidence in God; trusted as a good and generous Father." It also transforms our feelings for others. Piety "extinguishes in the heart those fires of tension and division which are bitterness, anger and impatience, and nourishes feelings of understanding, tolerance, and pardon." The

29. Quotations from Pope Francis in this section are from his General Audience on June 4, 2014, http://w2.vatican.va/content/francesco/en/audiences/2014/documents/papa-francesco_20140604_udienza-generale.html.

30. Quotations from Pope John Paul II in this section are from his Angelus Address on May 28, 1989, http://www.vatican.va/liturgical_year/pentecost/documents/hf_jp-ii_ang_19890528_en.html.

Christian infused with the gift of piety "always sees others as children of the same Father, called to be part of the family of God which is the Church. He feels urged to treat them with the kindness and friendliness which are proper to a frank and fraternal relationship." This transfigured attitude towards others is an expression of spiritual gentleness, as Pope Francis explains: "The gift of piety which the Holy Spirit gives us makes us gentle, makes us calm, patient, at peace with God, at the service of others with gentleness." This gift, concludes St. John Paul II, "is, therefore, at the root of that new human community which is based on the civilization of love."

The gift of piety, says Pope Francis, is the Spirit's gift that enables us "to conquer our fear, our uncertainty, and our restless, impatient spirit, and to make of us joyful witnesses of God and of his love, by worshipping the Lord in truth and in service to our neighbor with gentleness and with a smile, which the Holy Spirit always gives us in joy."

Fear of the Lord

The seventh and final gift of the Spirit is the fear of the Lord. Given the negative connotations of the word "fear," this gift is easily misunderstood, which both St. John Paul II and Pope Francis recognize. "It certainly is not that 'fear of God' which causes people to flee from every thought and memory of him as something or someone who disturbs and upsets," says St. John Paul II.[31] Pope Francis concurs: "It does not mean being afraid of God: we know well that God is Father, that he loves us and wants our salvation, and he always forgives, always; thus, there is no reason to be scared of him!"[32] Rather, St. John Paul II says that the spiritual gift of the fear of the Lord "is a sincere and reverential feeling that a person experiences before the tremendous majesty of God, especially when he reflects upon his own infidelity and the danger of being 'found wanting' (Dn 5:27) at the eternal judgement which no one can escape."

---

31. Quotations from Pope John Paul II in this section are from his Angelus Address on June 11, 1989, http://www.vatican.va/liturgical_year/pentecost/documents/hf_jp-ii_ang_19890611_en.html.

32. Quotations from Pope Francis in this section are from his General Audience on June 11, 2014, http://w2.vatican.va/content/francesco/en/audiences/2014/documents/papa-francesco_20140611_udienza-generale.html.

Referring to the awareness of our sinfulness and God's holiness and justice, Pope Francis calls this gift "an 'alarm' against the obstinacy of sin. When a person lives in evil, when one blasphemes against God, when one exploits others, when he tyrannizes them, when he lives only for money, for vanity, or power, or pride, then the holy fear of God sends us a warning: be careful! With all this power, with all this money, with all of your pride, with all your vanity, you will not be happy." However, this gift combines a proper trepidation "with faith in the divine mercy and with the certitude of the fatherly concern of God who wills the eternal salvation of each one." Through this gift "the Holy Spirit instils in the soul most of all a filial love which is a sentiment rooted in love of God. The soul is now concerned not to displease God, whom he loves as a Father, not to offend him in anything, to 'abide in him and grow in charity' (cf. Jn 15:4–7)." The fear of the Lord nourishes our growth in the virtues: "the practice of the Christian virtues and especially of humility, temperance, chastity and mortification of the senses, depends on this holy and just fear, united in the soul with love for God."

The experience of our own frailty, indeed, creates an opening for the Holy Spirit, who "comforts us and lets us perceive that the only important thing is to allow ourselves to be led by Jesus into the Father's arms," continues Pope Francis. This is what the Holy Spirit accomplishes in us through the fear of the Lord. "Fear of the Lord allows us to be aware that everything comes from grace and that our true strength lies solely in following the Lord Jesus and in allowing the Father to bestow upon us his goodness and his mercy. To open the heart, so that the goodness and mercy of God may come to us. This is what the Holy Spirit does through the gift of fear of the Lord: he opens hearts. The heart opens so that forgiveness, mercy, goodness and the caress of the Father may come to us, for as children we are infinitely loved."

In his commentary on Isaiah 11:2–3, St. Ambrose helps us understand the integral relationship among these seven gifts, which he says all flow from the fear of the Lord. Isaiah, says St. Ambrose, "elevates fear that he might possess what can follow from it, for holy fear is shaped by wisdom, instructed by understanding, directed by counsel, empowered by strength, ruled by knowledge and adorned with piety."[33] "Take up," he exhorts his listeners—and us, "the fear of the Lord."[34]

Activity

Identify the spiritual gift defined below:

1. A special sharing in that mysterious and highest knowledge which is that of God himself.
2. A bond that gives meaning to our life and keeps us sound, in communion with Him.
3. A transformation of our natural intellect, enabling us to grasp things both human and divine events past, present and future, and to penetrate ever more deeply into the meaning of God's Word.
4. A sincere and reverential feeling that a person experiences before the tremendous majesty of God.
5. Lifts our heart and communicates new strength and enthusiasm to our life and to our following of Jesus.
6. Enables us to know the true value of creatures in their relationship to the Creator.
7. Enables our conscience to make a concrete choice in communion with God.

Key: 1. Wisdom; 2. Piety; 3. Understanding; 4. Fear of the Lord; 5. Fortitude; 6. Knowledge; 7. Counsel.

Conclusion

The Sacrament of Confirmation deepens our relationship with the Most Holy Trinity by enriching us with the gifts of the Holy Spirit, conforming us more closely to the Son, uniting us more perfectly to his Body, the Church, and drawing us more deeply into his messianic program. At the same time, it makes each recipient more fully who God intended

33. McKinion, *Isaiah 1–39*, 99.
34. Ibid.

him or her to be from eternity (Eph 1:4). "To be truly man means to be fully oneself. The confirmation is the confirmation of man in his own, unique 'personality.' It is, to use again the same image, his ordination to be himself, to become what God wants him to be, what He has loved in me from all eternity. It is the gift of vocation."[35] And becoming our true selves does not mean turning in on our own selfish wants and desires. Rather, becoming our true selves means opening ourselves to others, becoming men and women "for others," "just as Christ is 'the man for others.'"[36] It is no exaggeration to say that "Confirmation is the opening of man to the wholeness of divine creation, to the true catholicity of life. This is the 'wind,' the *ruah* of God entering our life, embracing it with fire and love, making us available for divine action, filling everything with joy and hope" [37] so that "we may come to the measure of the full stature of Christ" (RM, Ritual Masses I, 4B, Collect).

35. Schmemann, *For the Life of the World*, 76.
36. *Dominus Iesus* (Congregation for the Doctrine of the Faith, 2000), no. 19.
37. Schmemann, *For the Life of the World*, 76.

PART IV

The Sacrament of the Eucharist

"The Holy Eucharist . . . brings Christian initiation to completion and represents the center and goal of all sacramental life" (SacCar 17). While the seven sacraments together "form an organic whole in which each particular sacrament has its own vital place . . . the Eucharist occupies a unique place as the 'Sacrament of sacraments': 'all the other sacraments are ordered to it as to their end'" (CCC, 1211). This is because Christ is "*truly, really, and substantially*" present (CCC, 1374) under the appearances of bread and wine, a presence we discussed in chapter 1. For this reason, Christ's presence in the Eucharist "raises the Eucharist above all the sacraments as 'the perfection of the spiritual life and the end to which all the sacraments tend'" (CCC, 1374).

We will begin our study of the Eucharist in chapter 10 with an overview of the sacrament before we consider in detail its Old Testament roots. The first Old Testament event we will look at is Israel's celebration of the Passover in preparation for their Exodus from Egypt. Next, we will look at God's miraculous provision of manna during Israel's wilderness wanderings, a sign that Christ said he himself fulfilled (Jn 6:51). The third event that prefigures the Eucharist is the ratification of Israel's covenant with the Lord on Mt. Sinai. We will conclude this chapter by looking at three Old Testament figures mentioned in Eucharistic Prayer I (the Roman Canon): Abel, Abraham, and Melchizedek. As we will see, these events and figures are recalled in the readings and prayers of the eucharistic liturgy.

After looking at the Old Testament types of the Eucharist, we are ready in chapter 11 to look carefully at the signs that comprise the Sacrament of sacraments. We will begin by looking at the church building and its furnishings, which the Second Vatican Council called "signs and symbols of heavenly realities" (SC, 122). We will next introduce the gestures and postures that are part of the Mass. We will then walk carefully and prayerfully through the liturgical signs of the celebration of the Eucharist, beginning with the Introductory Rites, followed by the Liturgy of the Word, the Liturgy of the Eucharist, and finally the Concluding Rites. We will also note liturgical signs which we have already discussed in the introductory chapters. The Mass is a dynamic dialogue woven from words, actions, and objects that engage the whole person, drawing us into the eternal Trinitarian dialogue of love.

This examination of the signs of the Eucharist—bearers of the saving and sanctifying power of Christ (CCC, 1189)—will lead us to reflect on the transforming power of the Eucharist. We will organize our presentation around a quote from St. Augustine and cited by Pope Benedict XVI. St. Augustine, writes the pope, "imagines the Lord saying to him: 'I am the food of grown men; grow, and you shall feed upon me; nor shall you change me, like the food of your flesh, into yourself, but you shall be changed into me.' It is not the eucharistic food that is changed into us, but rather we who are mysteriously transformed by it. Christ nourishes us by uniting us to himself; 'he draws us into himself'" (SacCar 70). Receiving the Body and Blood of Christ deepens our union with the Blessed Trinity, Father, Son, and Holy Spirit. This deeper union strengthens us in our struggle against sin. Our reception of the Body and Blood of Christ also builds up his Body, the Church, and strengthens our commitment to the unity of Christ's Body for which he prayed (Jn 17:21, 23). In addition, it draws us into his compassion for the world. Finally, receiving the glorified Body and Blood of Christ (EE, 18) is the pledge of the eternal glory that awaits us. The divine life received in Baptism and perfected in Confirmation is completed in the Eucharistic sacrifice which we offer in union with Christ and in the Eucharistic banquet in which we receive him and abide in him.

Chapter 10

The Eucharist: Overview and Old Testament Roots

The prophet Malachi prophesied following Israel's return from exile in Babylon, possibly during the time of Nehemiah, ca. 445 BC. The initial enthusiasm and zeal that accompanied Israel's return to its homeland had waned, and Malachi now rebukes the priests for offering blind, lame, or sick animals to God, sacrifices forbidden by the Law (Lv 22:17–25 and Dt 17:1). God's judgment through the prophet is harsh: "Oh, that one of you would just shut the temple gates to keep from kindling fire on my altar in vain! I take no pleasure in you, says the LORD of hosts; and I will not accept any offering from your hands!" (Mal 1:10). He then proclaims a stunning comparison: "From the rising of the sun to its setting, my name is great among the nations; Incense offerings are made in my name everywhere, and a pure offering; For my name is great among the nations, says the Lord of hosts" (v. 11). He praises the offerings made to deities throughout the world—"from the rising of the sun to its setting"—over "the offensive sacrificial abuse (involving animals) in Jerusalem."[1] The intent is not to praise pagan worship but to shame the priests of Judah, for the pagans at least exhibit the right disposition while the Judean priests cheat the Lord.[2]

By the middle of the second century this prophecy of a pure offering being made everywhere in the name of Lord was interpreted as pointing to the Eucharistic sacrifice. St. Justin Martyr (d. 155) in his *Dialogue with Trypho* refers several times to this verse from Malachi. "This prophecy is about the bread which Christ handed down to us to do for remembrance of his incarnation for the sake of those who believe in him, for whom he suffered; and about the cup, which he handed

1. NJBC, 360.
2. Ibid.

down for us to do, giving thanks, for remembrance of his blood."[3] In another passage he explains that this prophecy affirms the sacrificial character of the Eucharist: "He is prophesying about the sacrifices which are offered in every place by us, the nations, that is the bread of thanksgiving and likewise the cup of thanksgiving, saying that we glorify his name, but you profane it."[4]

Through Malachi God is preparing the messianic people for the sacrament of Christ's Passion: "So God bears witness in advance that he is well pleased with all the sacrifices in his name, which Jesus the Christ handed down to be done, namely in the eucharist of the bread and the cup, and are done in every place in the world by the Christians."[5] So important is this prefigurement of the Eucharist that it has been included in Eucharistic Prayer III: "You are indeed, Holy, O Lord . . . and you never cease to gather a people to yourself, *so that from the rising of the sun to its setting a pure sacrifice may be offered to your name.*"

Instituted by Christ

When the two disciples encountered Jesus on the road to Emmaus, they were profoundly moved by his presence, even though they did not recognize him (Lk 24:13–35; see chapter 1, p. 9). "But they urged him, 'Stay with us, for it is nearly evening and the day is almost over'" (Lk 24:29). Commenting on this encounter, St. John Paul II wrote, "Amid the shadows of the passing day and the darkness that clouded their spirit, the Wayfarer brought a ray of light which rekindled their hope and led their hearts to yearn for the fullness of light" (MND, 1). Although he did stay with them, "Soon afterwards, Jesus' face would disappear, yet the Master would 'stay' with them, hidden in the 'breaking of the bread' which had opened their eyes to recognize him" (MND, 1). Later, just before his Ascension, Jesus promised the eleven, "I am with you always, until the end of the age" (Mt 28:20). Christ fulfilled the promise of his abiding presence in a preeminent way, wrote

3. Justin Martyr, *Dialogue with Trypho* 70.4, quoted in R. C. D. Jasper and G. J. Cuming, *Prayers of the Eucharist: Early and Reformed*, 3rd rev. and enlarged ed. (Collegeville, MN: The Liturgical Press, 1990), 27–28.

4. Justin Martyr, *Dialogue with Trypho* 3, in Jasper and Cuming, *Prayers of the Eucharist*, 27–28.

5. Justin Martyr, *Dialogue with Trypho*, 117.1, in Jasper and Cuming, *Prayers of the Eucharist*, 28.

St. John Paul II, in the Eucharist. "The Eucharist is a mystery of presence, the perfect fulfillment of Jesus' promise to remain with us until the end of the world" (MND, 16). The Eucharist fulfills both Christ's desire to remain with us and his response to our urgent appeal for his abiding presence.

The New Testament contains four accounts of Christ's institution of the Eucharist: Matthew 26:17–29; Mark 14:12–25; Luke 22:7–20; and 1 Corinthians 11:23–26. Jesus prepared his disciples for this event in the Bread of Life discourse in John 6 in which he "calls himself the bread of life" (CCC, 1338). Below is the *Catechism*'s synthesis of the institution accounts:

> Then came the day of Unleavened Bread, on which the passover lamb had to be sacrificed. So Jesus sent Peter and John, saying, "Go and prepare the passover meal for us, that we may eat it. . . . " They went . . . and prepared the passover. And when the hour came, he sat at table, and the apostles with him, and he said to them, "I have earnestly desired to eat this passover with you before I suffer; for I tell you I shall not eat it again until it is fulfilled in the kingdom of God." . . . And he took bread, and when he had given thanks he broke it and gave it to them, saying, "This is my body which is given for you. Do this in remembrance of me." and likewise the cup after supper, saying, "This cup which is poured out for you is the New Covenant in my blood." (CCC, 1339)

The Lord's command to do this in remembrance of him is not only a request to remember his words and actions. "It is directed at the liturgical celebration, by the apostles and their successors, of the memorial of Christ, of his life, of his death, of his Resurrection, and of his intercession in the presence of the Father [1 Cor 11:26]" (CCC, 1341).

In the Eucharist, Christ the Lord left his Church "a memorial of his death and resurrection: a sacrament of love, a sign of unity, a bond of charity, a Paschal banquet 'in which Christ is consumed, the mind is filled with grace, and a pledge of future glory is given to us'" (SC, 47). Furthermore, it is the consummation of Christian initiation: "The holy Eucharist completes Christian initiation. Those who have been raised to the dignity of the royal priesthood by Baptism and configured more deeply to Christ by Confirmation participate with the whole community in the Lord's own sacrifice by means of the Eucharist" (CCC, 1322).

The Names of the Sacrament

This sacrament, "the source and summit of the Christian life" (LG, 11), is known by a number of different names that express its "inexhaustible richness. . . . Each name evokes certain aspects of it" (CCC, 1328). The name *Eucharist* comes from the Greek work *eucharistein,* which means "to give thanks." At the Last Supper, Jesus took the bread and gave thanks (1 Cor 11:24) and likewise the chalice (Lk 22:17), words repeated in the Institution Narrative of the Mass: "he himself took bread, and, giving you thanks . . ."; "he took the chalice, and giving you thanks . . ." (RM, Eucharistic Prayer III). It also recalls "the Jewish blessings that proclaim—especially during a meal—God's works: creation, redemption, and sanctification" (CCC, 1328).

It is also called the *Lord's Supper* due to "its connection with the supper which the Lord took with his disciples on the eve of his Passion" (CCC, 1329), a term found in St. Paul's first letter to the church at Corinth (1 Cor 11:20). It is also called the Lord's Supper because it is an anticipation of "the wedding feast of the Lamb" (Rev 19:9) celebrated "in the heavenly Jerusalem" (CCC, 1329). These two aspects—the Last Supper celebrated in the Upper Room and the eschatological banquet celebrated in heaven—are contained in the invitation to Communion: "Behold the Lamb of God. . . . Blessed are those called to the supper of the Lamb" (RM, Order of Mass, 132). It is a reminder, too, that we are guests at his banquet, not he at ours.

The early Christians referred to their Eucharistic assemblies as the *Breaking of Bread.* The Acts of the Apostles tells us that "they devoted themselves to the teaching of the apostles and to the communal life, to the breaking of the bread and to prayers" (Acts 2:42; also in Acts 2:46; 20:7, 11). It was something that they saw Jesus do many times. When he miraculously fed the four thousand (Mt 14:19) and the five thousand (Mt 15:36) he "broke the loaves" and distributed them. At the Last Supper he took the bread and after blessing it "broke it" (Mt 26:26; 1 Cor 11:24). After the Resurrection, the disciples on the road to Emmaus only recognized him when he broke the bread (Lk 24:30–31). Finally, as St. Paul told the Corinthians, the bread broken is communion with the Lord and with one another: "The bread that we break, is it not a participation in the body of Christ? Because the loaf of bread is one, we, though many, are one body, for we all partake of the one loaf" (1 Cor 11:16–17). This passage is also the source of another name, *Holy Communion*, since the sacrament unites us to Christ, and "union with Christ is also union with all those to whom he gives himself" (DCE, 14).

Several names express the sacrificial character of the Eucharist. It is called the "*Holy Sacrifice* because it makes present the one sacrifice of Christ the Savior and includes the Church's offering" (CCC, 1330). The term *sacrifice of praise* is found in both Testaments. The psalmist says, "I will offer a sacrifice of praise and call on the name of the Lord" (Ps 116:17). The author of the Letter to the Hebrews encourages his readers thus: "Through him [then] let us continually offer God a sacrifice of praise, that is, the fruit of lips that confess his name" (Heb 13:15). The writer of 1 Peter speaks of *spiritual sacrifice*, exhorting believers to let themselves "be built into a spiritual house to be a holy priesthood to offer spiritual sacrifices acceptable to God through Jesus Christ" (1 Pt 2:5). Lastly, as we discussed in the introduction, Malachi speaks of a "pure offering" (Mal 1:11). These terms emphasize that the Eucharist "completes and surpasses all the sacrifices of the Old Covenant" (CCC, 1330).

Another name for the Eucharist—*Peace*—comes from one of the priest's greetings at the beginning of Mass: "Grace to you and peace from God our Father and the Lord Jesus Christ" (RM, Order of Mass, 2). "The early Church understood the mystery of the Eucharist as underlying the expression 'peace,'" and so very quickly it "became one of the names of the eucharistic sacrament."[6] It is there that we experience union and communion with the Lord and with one another—"The Eucharist is peace from the Lord."[7] In the Eucharist the early Christians—slaves and free, barbarians and Greeks, Gentiles and Jews—"met with the new sphere of peace that faith had opened up."[8] For this reason they often referred to it simply as "peace." In the Eucharist they experienced a new peace, one "that transcended all boundaries and limits, in which everyone was at home everywhere."[9] In their celebration of the Eucharist, they "did something politically most significant: they created

---

6. Joseph Ratzinger, *God Is Near Us: The Eucharist, the Heart of Life* (San Francisco: Ignatius, 2003), 117.

7. Ibid.

8. Ibid.

9. Ibid., 118.

spheres of peace and built, as it were, highroads of peace through a world of strife."[10]

Lastly, perhaps the most familiar name, *Holy Mass* (*Missa*), comes from the Latin dismissal, *Ite, missa est*, translated as "Go forth, the Mass is ended" (RM, Order of mass, 144). "In antiquity," explains Pope Benedict XVI, "*missa* simply meant 'dismissal.' However in Christian usage it gradually took on a deeper meaning. The word dismissal has come to imply a 'mission.' These few words succinctly express the missionary nature of the Church" (SacCar, 51). The *Holy Mass* tells us that "the liturgy in which the mystery of salvation is accomplished concludes with the sending forth (mission) of the faithful, so that they may fulfill God's will in their daily lives" (CCC, 1332).

Digging into the Catechism

The *Catechism of the Catholic Church* gives several other names for the Eucharist. What aspects of the Eucharist do these names reveal?

Eucharistic assembly or synaxis (CCC, 1329)

Holy and Divine Liturgy (CCC, 1330)

Sacred Mysteries (CCC, 1330)

Most Blessed Sacrament (CCC, 1330)

Holy Things (CCC, 1331)

Memorial (CCC, 1330)

The Minister and the Recipient

The proper minister for this sacrament is a validly ordained priest—only he "can preside at the Eucharist and consecrate the bread and the wine so that they become the Body and Blood of the Lord" (CCC, 1411). The intimate relationship between the Eucharist and the priesthood is expressed in the liturgy of the Chrism Mass, celebrated by the bishop during Holy Week at which the priests renew the promises they made at ordination. The Preface recalls Christ's institution of the priesthood:

10. Ibid.

"For Christ . . . with a brother's kindness . . . chooses men to become sharers in his sacred ministry through the laying on of hands. They are to renew in his name the sacrifice of human redemption, to set before your children the paschal banquet, to lead your holy people in charity, to nourish them with the word and strengthen them with the Sacraments" (RM, Preface for Chrism Mass, 12). These liturgical words make "clear how the conferral of Priestly power is accomplished through the laying on of hands; and, by the listing one by one of its duties, that power is described which is the continuation of the power of Christ, the High Priest of the New Testament" (GIRM, 4).

A correct understanding of the ministerial priesthood also puts something else "in its proper light, something certainly to be held in great esteem, namely, the royal Priesthood of the faithful, whose spiritual sacrifice is brought to completion through the ministry of the Bishop and the Priests, in union with the Sacrifice of Christ, the sole Mediator. For the celebration of the Eucharist is the action of the whole Church" (GIRM, 5; cf. PO, 2). The priesthood of the faithful, as we have explained in previous chapters, is first conferred in the Sacrament of Baptism and strengthened in the Sacrament of Confirmation.

The proper recipient of the Sacrament of the Eucharist is any baptized Catholic. Children may receive the Eucharist when they "have sufficient knowledge and careful preparation so that they understand the mystery of Christ according to their capacity and are able to receive the body of Christ with faith and devotion" (CIC, c. 913 §1). It can be given "to children in danger of death if they can distinguish the body of Christ from ordinary food and receive communion reverently" (CIC, c. 913 §2). Following the reception of First Communion, the faithful are obliged to receive the Eucharist at least once a year, and this if at all possible during the Easter season (CIC, c. 920). Further, they are obliged to participate in the Mass on Sundays and feast days, even if they cannot receive sacramental communion (CCC, 1389).

Sacrifice, Meal, Pledge, and Presence

There are four distinct but inseparable aspects of the Eucharist. It is at one and the same time a true sacrifice, a meal, a pledge and foretaste of the eternal glory that awaits us, and Christ's substantial presence—body and blood, soul and divinity.

When the Church speaks of the Eucharist as a sacrifice, she means three things. First, it is the memorial of Christ's once for all sacrifice on Calvary. As we explained in chapter 1, when the Church celebrates the memorial of Christ's Paschal Mystery, the event becomes "in a certain way present and real"—Christ's Passion, Death, and Resurrection "is made present" (CCC, 1362–1366). In 1562, the Council of Trent, the Catholic Church's response to the Protestant Reformation, formulated what has become the classic explanation of the Eucharist as the memorial of Christ's sacrifice. "The victim is one and the same: the same now offers through the ministry of priests, who then offered himself on the cross; only the manner of offering is different. . . . The same Christ who offered himself once in a bloody manner on the altar of the cross is contained and offered in an unbloody manner" (CCC, 1367). Thus, Christ's sacrifice of Calvary and the sacrifice of the Mass "are *one single sacrifice*" (CCC, 1367, italics original). Because it recalls and makes present Christ's saving work, it continues to bear fruit and to advance the redemption of the world.

Second, the Church, as the Body of Christ, also "participates in the offering of her Head" (CCC, 1368). One with Christ, "she herself is offered whole and entire" and unites herself to Christ's unceasing intercession for the world (CCC, 1368; cf. Heb 7:25). In this way, the Holy Sacrifice of the Mass "becomes also the sacrifice of the members of his Body. The lives of the faithful, their praise, sufferings, prayer, and work, are united with those of Christ and with his total offering, and so acquire a new value. Christ's sacrifice present on the altar makes it possible for all generations of Christians to be united with his offering" (CCC, 1368). The words of the Mass make this aspect explicit in the priest's invitation to the assembly before the Prayer over the Gifts: "Pray, brethren, that my sacrifice and yours may be acceptable to God, the almighty Father" (RM, Order of Mass, 29).

Finally, the Eucharist is also a sacrifice of praise and thanksgiving to the Father. As we saw above, the name *eucharist* comes from the Greek word meaning "to give thanks." We hear this, for example, in the introduction to the preface:

> It is truly right and just, our duty and our salvation,
> always and everywhere to give you thanks,
> Lord, holy Father, almighty and eternal God,
> through Christ our Lord.
> (RM, Order of Mass, 33 and following)

We hear it also at the beginning of Eucharistic Prayer IV:

> We give you praise, Father most holy,
> for you are great,
> and you have fashioned all your works
> in wisdom and in love.
> (RM, Order of Mass, 117)

The Eucharist is a sacrifice of praise and thanksgiving because "the whole of creation loved by God is presented to the Father through the death and the Resurrection of Christ. Through Christ the Church can offer the sacrifice of praise in thanksgiving for all that God has made good, beautiful, and just in creation and in humanity" (CCC 1359).

In addition to being a sacrifice, the Eucharist is also a meal, "the sacred banquet of communion with the Lord's body and blood" (CCC, 1382). When we receive the Body and Blood of Christ we experience the most intimate union possible with him. The words of consecration over the bread include the command to "eat of it," and the words of consecration over the wine likewise include Christ's command to "drink from it" (RM, Order of Mass, 89–90). But the words of consecration also express the sacrificial character of the meal, for we are to eat of the Body "which will be given up for you" and to drink the Blood "which will be poured out for you and for many for the forgiveness of sins" (RM, Order of Mass, 89–90). As Christ's own words make clear, "the celebration of the Eucharistic sacrifice is wholly directed toward the intimate union of the faithful with Christ through communion" (CCC 1382). The unity of these two aspects is also symbolized by the altar, for it is "the altar of the sacrifice and the table of the Lord. . . . The Christian altar is the symbol of Christ himself, present in the midst of the assembly of his faithful, both as the victim offered for our reconciliation and as food from heaven who is giving himself to us" (CCC, 1383).

So far, we have considered the Eucharist as sacrifice and meal. But we must also recognize that it is the "Pledge of the Glory to Come" (CCC, 1402). This is expressed in one of the petitions from Eucharistic Prayer IV, a request

> that we may enter into a heavenly an inheritance
> with the Blessed Virgin Mary, Mother of God,
> with blessed Joseph, her Spouse,
> and with your Apostles and Saints in your kingdom.
> (RM, Order of Mass, 122)

This means, then, that "the Eucharist is also an anticipation of the heavenly glory" (CCC, 1402). "While the Eucharist makes present what occurred in the past," writes St. John Paul II, "it also impels us towards the future, when Christ will come again at the end of history" (MND, 15). The Memorial Acclamation expresses the future dimension of eucharistic communion:

> When we eat this bread and drink this Cup,
> we proclaim your Death, O Lord,
> until you come again.
> (RM, Order of Mass, 91)

This anticipation of our promised glory makes the Mass "a straining toward the goal, a foretaste of the fullness of joy promised by Christ (cf. Jn 15:11)" (EE, 18). And this, in turn, draws us more deeply into the Eucharist "and fills our Christian journey with hope" (MND, 15).

Finally, in addition to being a sacrifice, a meal, and a pledge of eternal glory, the Eucharist is a mystery of presence. Through the power of Christ's word (the words of consecration) and the work of the Holy Spirit (the epiclesis) Christ becomes substantially present on the altar, a mystery we explored in chapter 1. Here it will suffice to listen to the teaching of St. John Paul II. "With the entire tradition of the Church, we believe that Jesus is truly present under the Eucharistic species . . . whole and entire, in the reality of his body and blood. Faith demands that we approach the Eucharist fully aware that *we are approaching Christ himself*. . . . The Eucharist is a mystery of presence, the perfect fulfillment of Jesus' promise to remain with us until the end of the world" (MND, 16; italics added).

St. John Paul II says that this fourth aspect of the Eucharist, Christ's presence, forms the ground for the other dimensions—sacrifice, meal, and pledge. "It is precisely his presence which gives the other aspects of the Eucharist—as meal, as memorial of the Paschal Mystery, as eschatological anticipation—a significance which goes far beyond mere symbolism" (MND, 16). The Eucharist makes real and present the saving events of Christ's Paschal Mystery, a re-presentation of his sacrifice ordered to sacramental communion in which we "come to share in the divine nature" (2 Pt 1:4) and so experience through the presence of the risen, ascended and glorified Christ a foretaste of the glory of heaven, when he will be for all eternity "all in all" (1 Cor 15:28).

Structure

The Mass "unfolds according to a fundamental structure which has been preserved throughout the centuries down to our own day" (CCC, 1346). It begins with the Introductory Rites: the Greeting, Penitential Rite, Gloria, and the Collect (opening prayer). This leads into the Liturgy of the Word, with readings, homily, Creed, and Universal Prayer. This is followed by the Liturgy of the Eucharist, with the presentation of the bread and wine, the Eucharistic Prayer, sacramental Communion, and the Prayer after Communion. The celebration closes with the Concluding Rites, which may include announcements, followed by the final blessing and the dismissal. These different elements, however, constitute a higher unity. The Liturgy of the Word and the Liturgy of the Eucharist "form a fundamental unity" and "one single act of worship" (CCC, 1346). "The Eucharistic table set for us is the table both of the Word of God and of the Body of the Lord" (CCC, 1346; DV 21).

Digging Into the Catechism

Read a description of the Mass from about the year 155 in CCC, 1345. Which of the parts described above do you recognize?

Old Testament Sources

There are a number of Old Testament events that prefigured the Eucharist. In this section we will look at three. We will begin with the celebration of the Passover in preparation for Israel's exodus from Egypt. We will next consider God's miraculous provision of manna in the wilderness, and then the ratification of Israel's covenant on Mt. Sinai. In addition to these three events, we will also look at three Old Testament figures named in Eucharistic Prayer I, a prayer used by the Church continuously since the fourth century: Abel, Abraham, and Melchizedek. These events and personages prefigure many aspects of the Eucharist that can enrich our experience of and deepen our participation in the Mass.

Passover and Exodus

The most important Old Testament type of the Eucharist is the Israelites' observance of the Passover prior to the tenth and final plague—the death of all of the firstborn Egyptians—and their hasty departure from Egypt and slavery. Its importance is signaled in part by the fact that "Jesus chose the time of the Passover" to institute the Eucharist (CCC, 1339), and it was his earnest desire to do so, as he told his disciples: "I have eagerly desired to eat this Passover with you before I suffer" (Lk 22:15). In addition, St. Paul refers to Christ as the paschal lamb in his First Letter to the Corinthians: "For our paschal lamb, Christ, has been sacrificed" (1 Cor 5:7). Finally, the account of the Passover is the Old Testament reading for Holy Thursday, the Evening Mass of the Lord's Supper. It is also one of the Old Testament options for the Votive Mass of the Mystery of the Holy Cross, the Votive Mass of the Most Holy Eucharist, and the Votive Mass of the Most Precious Blood of Our Lord Jesus Christ. The words and actions of Jesus, the apostolic teaching, and the liturgy confirm the significance of the Passover for understanding the Holy Sacrifice of the Mass.

The celebration of the Passover is recounted in Exodus 12. Following the ninth plague, the Darkness, Pharaoh is still unwilling to let the Israelites leave (Ex 10:27), so the Lord tells Moses he will bring one final plague on the Egyptians: "Every firstborn of the land of Egypt will die," even "all the firstborn of the animals," but the Israelites will be spared—"not even a dog will growl" (Ex 11:5–7). "As if to affirm victory over Pharaoh and sovereignty over the Israelites, the Lord proclaims a new calendar for Israel."[11] Moses instructs each household to get a year-old male lamb, either a sheep or a goat, without blemish (Ex 12:3–6). At the appointed time each household is then to slaughter the lamb "during the evening twilight" (Ex 12:6). They are then to apply the blood "to the two doorposts and the lintel of the houses in which they eat it . . . roasted with unleavened bread and bitter herbs" (Ex 12:8). Furthermore, they are to "eat it in a hurry," dressed for travel —"It is the LORD's Passover" (Ex 12:11). For on that night, says the Lord, "I will go through Egypt, striking down every firstborn of the land, human being and beast alike, and executing judgment on all the gods of Egypt" (Ex 12:12). But the houses marked with blood will be spared:

11. NABRE, 77, n. 12:2.

"Seeing the blood," says the Lord, "I will pass over you; thereby, when I strike the land of Egypt, no destructive blow will come upon you" (Ex 12:13). This section concludes with instructions for the annual celebration of this "day of remembrance . . . as a statue forever" (Ex 12:14–20).

Moses then instructs the people as the Lord has commanded him. "Then the people knelt and bowed down, and the Israelites went and did exactly as the LORD had commanded Moses and Aaron" (Ex 12:27–28). And so it happened. "Pharaoh arose in the night, he and all his servants and all the Egyptians; and there was loud wailing throughout Egypt, for there was not a house without its dead" (Ex 12:30). Pharaoh summons Moses and Aaron and says "Leave my people at once, you and the Israelites! Go and serve the LORD as you said" (Ex 12:31). The Israelites depart in haste, taking with them articles of silver, gold, and clothing from the Egyptians. "Indeed, the Lord had made the Egyptians so well-disposed toward the people that they let them have whatever they asked for. And so they despoiled the Egyptians" (Ex 12:35–36). Henceforth, when they celebrated the Passover and people asked the meaning of the rite, they would reply, "It is the Passover sacrifice for the LORD, who passed over the houses of the Israelites in Egypt; when he struck down the Egyptians, he delivered our houses" (Ex 12:27).

The Church Fathers explained how this event prefigured Christ. In his Paschal Homily, St. Melito of Sardis said, "O new and inexpressible mystery! The slaying of the lamb became the salvation of Israel, the death of the lamb became life for the people and its blood frightened the angel (cf. Ex 12:23). Angel, answer me: What was it that filled you with fear: the slaying of the lamb or the Lord's life? The lamb's death or the Lord's life? The lamb's blood or the Lord's Spirit? What you feared is clear: you saw the Lord's mystery fulfilled in the lamb, the Lord's life in the slaying of the lamb, the figure of the Lord in the lamb's death and for this you did not destroy Israel."[12] Another ancient author wondered, "What must the power of the reality be (i.e., the Christian Passover), if a simple figure of it caused salvation?"[13]

12. Raniero Cantalamessa, *The Eucharist: Our Sanctification*, rev. ed., trans. Frances Longergan Villa (Collegeville, MN: The Liturgical Press, 1993), 7.

13. Cantalamessa, *The Eucharist*, 7.

St. Justin Martyr has left us with this explanation.

> Those who were saved in Egypt, were saved by the blood of the Pasch, with which they anointed doorposts and lintels. For the Pasch was Christ, Who was later immolated. And, as the blood of the Pasch saved those who were in Egypt, so the blood of Christ was to preserve from death those who have believed in Him. Does this mean that God would have made a mistake if this sign . . . was not found on the doors? No, but it announced in advance the salvation that was to come by the blood of Christ, by Whom are saved (the sinners) of all nations, when, having received pardon for their sins, they sin no more."[14]

For St. Justin, the "sign" means the sign of the cross, for the Church fathers noted that "the anointing of the lintels and doorposts formed a kind of cross."[15] Finally, let us listen to St. Bede's interpretation: "The lamb in the law of Passover rightly shows us a type of him, since, having once liberated the people from their Egyptian servitude, it sanctified the people every year by being immolated in memory of their liberation, until he came, to whom such a sacrificial offering gave testimony."[16] The fulfillment of this event is proclaimed at the Easter Vigil in the Easter Proclamation, the Exsultet:

> These, then, are the feasts of Passover,
> in which is slain the Lamb, the one true Lamb,
> whose Blood anoints the doorposts of believers.
> (RM, Easter Vigil, 19)

Manna

A second Old Testament type of the Eucharist is the manna which fed the Israelites in the desert (CCC, 1094). Jesus himself taught that this sign pointed to and was fulfilled by him. In Capernaum the crowd asked Jesus to perform a sign—citing the example of the manna in the desert—so that they might believe in him (Jn 6:31). He answered them, "Amen, amen, I say to you, it was not Moses who gave the bread from heaven; my Father gives you the true bread from heaven. . . . I am the bread of life" (Jn 6:32, 35). He then developed this teaching and made it more explicit: "For my flesh is true food, and my blood is true drink. . . . This is the bread that came down from heaven. Unlike your ancestors

14. Daniélou, *The Bible and the Liturgy*, 164.

15. Ibid.

16. Heen and Krey, *Hebrews*, 115.

who ate and still died, whoever eats this bread will live forever" (Jn 6:55, 58).

The Apostle Paul refers to this event in his First Letter to the Corinthians. All those who left Egypt, he writes, "ate the same spiritual food" (1 Cor 10:3). Commenting of this St. Ambrose wrote, "All those who ate the bread [manna] died in the desert, but this food which you receive, this 'living bread which came down from heaven,' furnishes the energy of eternal life. Whoever eats this bread 'will not die forever,' for it is the body of Christ."[17] The liturgical use of this Old Testament event, recounted in Exodus 16 and Deuteronomy 8,[18] also affirms its relationship to the Eucharist. Both versions are Old Testament options for the Votive Mass of the Most Holy Eucharist, and the Deuteronomic account is also one of the options for the Most Holy Body and Blood of Christ (Corpus Christi).

The event in the wilderness took place "just one full month after their departure from Egypt."[19] The people began to grumble about the hardships in the desert and to long for the days in Egypt when "we sat by our kettles of meat and ate our fill of bread! But you have led us into this wilderness to make this whole assembly die of famine!" (Ex 16:3). The Lord told Moses, "I am going to rain down bread from heaven for you" (Ex 16:40). The glory of the Lord then appeared in a cloud, and he told Moses that he would feed the people with meat at twilight and give them their fill of bread in the morning (Ex 16:11). That evening "quail came up and covered the camp. In the morning there was a layer of dew all about the camp, and when the layer of dew evaporated, fine flakes like hoarfrost on the ground" (Ex 16:14). They were then given specific instructions on gathering the manna—only "as much of it as each needs to eat," and not to "leave any of it over until morning" (Ex 16:16, 19). "The people here are tested on their willingness to follow the instruction regarding the manna; sacred food must be gathered according to divine rubrics."[20] Some, however, "kept a part of it over until morning, and it became wormy and stank" (Ex 16:20). A warning to all those tempted to disregard rubrics!

17. Bray, *1–2 Corinthians*, 90.

18. Other Old Testament accounts are found in Numbers 11 and Psalms 105:40 and 78:17–31.

19. NABRE, 83, n. on 16:1.

20. NJBC, 50.

In the account in Deuteronomy, Moses gives a spiritual explanation for the people's hunger in the wilderness and God's miraculous provision. God, he says, was directing "all your journeying in the wilderness, so as to test you by affliction, to know what was in your heart: to keep his commandments or not" (Dt 8:2). The lesson of the manna, "a food unknown to you and your ancestors," was given "so you might know that it is not by bread alone that people live, but by all the comes forth from the mouth of the LORD" (Dt 8:3). The Lord's ultimate purpose in this, though, was to "make you prosperous in the end" (Dt 8:16). These lessons find their fulfillment in the Eucharist. God is still the author of our days and ways, and he still wants to purify our hearts so that we might receive the freedom and joy he promises and so make us "prosperous in the end."

The type—manna—and its fulfillment—the Body of Christ—are sacramentally recalled in the words of the epiclesis of Eucharistic Prayer II:

> Make holy, therefore, these gifts, we pray,
> by sending down your Spirit upon them like the dewfall.
> (RM, Order of Mass, 101)

The coming of the Spirit "like the dewfall" recalls "the dew that fell upon the camp of the Chosen People on their way to the Promised Land which, when evaporated, revealed the heavenly manna (Ex 16:13–17)."[21] But the dew of the Holy Spirit gives us the bread of eternal life, the Body of Christ.

Covenant

A third Old Testament event that foreshadows the Eucharist is the ratification of the covenant in the wilderness "in a blood rite"[22] described in Exodus 24. When Moses explains to the people "all the words and ordinances of the LORD," they all answer, "We will do everything that the LORD has told us" (Ex 24:3). Then, "a solemn ritual is prepared."[23] Moses records God's words and builds "an altar and twelve sacred stones for the twelve tribes of Israel" at the foot of the mountain (Ex 24:4). After the altar is completed, the young men "offer burnt offerings and sacrifice

21. Carstens and Martis, *Mystical Body, Mystical Voice*, 182.

22. NJBC, 55.

23. Ibid.

young bulls as communion offerings to the LORD" (Ex 24:5). Moses puts half of the blood in large bowls and splashes the other half on the altar. He reads aloud the book of the covenant to which the people assent, and then splashes the people with the blood saying, "This is the blood of the covenant which the LORD has made with you according to all these words" (Ex 24:8). Why are the people splashed with blood? "Moses, being the mediator between God and the people, symbolically unites them by sprinkling the blood of the same victims first on the altar, which represents Yahweh, and then on the people. The covenant is thus ratified in blood."[24] "Word and rite," concludes one scholar, "are inseparably united."[25]

Christ fulfills not only the Passover and manna but also the covenant. At the Last Supper Jesus offers his disciples the cup saying, "This is my blood of the covenant" (Mk 14:24 and Mt 26:28).[26] Citing Exodus 24:8, the *Catechism of the Catholic Church* says that Christ's Death is "the sacrifice of the New Covenant [Jer 31], which restores man to communion with God by reconciling him to God through the 'blood of the covenant, which was poured out for many for the forgiveness of sins'" (CCC, 613). The Letter to the Hebrews develops the theme of "the blood of Christ . . . through which atonement was made and the new covenant inaugurated."[27] In doing so, the author describes how Moses inaugurated the covenant by the sprinkling of blood saying, "This is 'the blood of the covenant which God has enjoined upon you'" (9:20). A contemporary scholar explains this reference to Exodus 24:3–8: "Since the new is the fulfillment of the old, the author seeks a parallel in the inauguration of the two and finds it in the account of the sacrifice related in Ex 24:5–8."[28] Finally, the Church has made this passage one of the Old Testament readings for Corpus Christi, the Votive Mass of the Most Holy Eucharist, and the Votive Mass off the Most Precious Blood. In the latter we hear an allusion in the Prayer over the Offerings in

24. NJB, 113, N. C.

25. NJBC, 55.

26. The reference to the covenant in the accounts of Matthew and Mark are understood as references to Exodus 24:3–8. The Pauline (1 Cor 11:25) and Lucan (Lk 22:20) accounts refer to the "new covenant," a reference to Jeremiah 31:31. See Carstens and Martis, *Mystical Body, Mystical Voice,* 190.

27. NJBC, 937.

28. Ibid.

the petition that we may "celebrate anew the sprinkling of his [Christ's] Blood, in which lies all our salvation" (RM, Votive Mass, no. 7).

Abel, Abraham, and Melchizedek

The final Old Testament source for the Eucharist that we will consider is the three Old Testament figures named in Eucharistic Prayer I, the Roman Canon: Abel, Abraham, and Melchizedek. Following the consecration there is a prayer asking God to

> Be pleased to look upon these offerings
> with a serene and kindly countenance,
> and to accept them,
> as once you were pleased to accept
> the gifts of your servant Abel the just,
> the sacrifice of Abraham, our father in faith,
> and the offering of your high priest Melchizedek,
> a holy sacrifice, a spotless victim. (RM, Order of Mass, 94)

This particular text dates from at least the fourth century since St. Ambrose (d. 389) quotes it.[29] All three figures are found in Genesis.

The account of Abel and his older brother Cain, the sons of Adam and Eve, is recorded in Genesis 4. Abel was "a herder of flocks, and Cain a tiller of the ground" (Gn 4:2). Each brings an offering to the Lord. Cain's offering is "from the fruit of the ground," while Abel's is "the fatty portion of the firstlings of his flock" (Gn 4:4). The Lord looks "with favor on Abel and his offering" but not on Cain and his offering, but the text does not explain why Abel's is accepted and Cain's is not. Cain, "very angry and dejected," kills Abel, and when God asks him where Abel is, he replies, "I do not know. Am I my brother's keeper?" (Gn 4:9). In punishment, Cain is banished from the Lord's presence.

Why God accepted Abel's offering and not Cain's is not clear. "Most commentators believe Abel's offering was the choice part and Cain's was not, but the emphasis falls on Yhwh's inscrutable acceptance of one and not the other."[30] But it is not hard to see why, for the early Church, Abel prefigured the Passion of Christ, "innocent Abel, who made a sacrifice of the firstlings of his flock (Gn 4:4) and himself succumbed to his brother's hate—our gift is 'the Lamb of God,' the first-born of all creation [Heb 1:6;

29. Yarnold, *The Awe-Inspiring Rites*, 139.

30. NJBC, 13.

Col 1:18; Rom 8:20], who turned His death, suffered at the hands of His own people, into a sacrifice of redemption."[31]

The second reference in the Roman Canon is to "the sacrifice of Abraham, our father in faith." God tells Abraham that he will make him "a great nation. . . . All the families of the earth will find blessing in you" (Gn 12:2–3), a promise that he repeats in Genesis 13:16 and 15:5. In response, Abraham "put his faith in the LORD, he attributed it to him as an act of righteousness" (Gn 15:6). However, after the birth of his only son with his wife Sarah—he previously had a son, Ishmael, with Hagar, Sarah's servant (Gn 16)—God puts him to the test, telling him to take his son Isaac, "your only one, whom you love," and offer him as a burnt offering (Gn 22:2). In this command "God emphasizes in every word the value Abraham attaches to this son."[32] Abraham obeys God's command and sets out to sacrifice Isaac, his only son and thus the heir to the promises the Lord has made to him. When Isaac sees the preparations for the sacrifice but no sheep, he questions his father, "Here are the fire and the wood, but where is the sheep for the burnt offering?" (Gn 22:7). "God will provide the sheep for the burnt offering," answers Abraham (Gn 22:8). His response is "not a ruse but evidence of Abraham's handing everything over to God."[33]

Only when Abraham has bound Isaac, placed him on the altar, and taken the knife does the Lord intervene to stay his hand through an angel: "Abraham, Abraham! . . . Do not lay your hand on the boy. . . . For now I know that you fear God, since you did not withhold from me your son, your only one" (Gn 22:11–12). Abraham looks up, sees a ram caught in a thicket, and offers it to the Lord. He has revealed that he "truly fears God, for he has not withheld his favored son. He has finally learned to give up control over his own life that he might receive it as grace."[34]

This compelling event has been called "a masterpiece, presenting God as the Lord whose demands are absolute, whose will is inscrutable, and whose final word is grace. Abraham shows the moral grandeur of the founder of Israel, facing God, willing to obey God's word in all

31. Joseph A. Jungmann, SJ, *The Mass of the Roman Rite: Its Origins and Development,* 2 vols. (Dublin: Four Courts/Christian Classics, 1986), 2:228.

32. NJBC, 25.

33. Ibid.

34. Ibid.

its mysterious harshness."[35] For this reason he has been described as "the hero of obedience to God, ready to make a sacrifice of his very son, but receiving him back alive (cf. Heb, 11:19)," prefiguring the Passion of Christ, God's only-begotten Son, who as "our sacrifice, too, the most perfect expression of obedience unto death, has risen again and returned to life."[36] The importance of this passage as a type of the Paschal Mystery is indicated liturgically by its placement as the second reading for the Easter Vigil (RM, Easter Vigil, 25).

The final Old Testament reference in Eucharistic Prayer I is "the offering of your high priest Melchizedek." This event is recounted in Genesis 14:17–20. Melchizedek, the king of Salem, meets Abraham as he is returning victorious from battle. Melchizedek is described as a priest, and he brings bread and wine and blesses Abraham, who then gives Melchizedek a tenth of the spoils. The parallel with Christ is clear: Melchizedek, "as priest of the most high God, offers up bread and wine—our oblation also is taken from bread and wine."[37] St. Cyprian saw in Melchizedek's gifts a foreshadowing of Christ's offering of himself, and in his priesthood a prefiguring of Jesus Christ, the eternal high priest: "For who is more a priest of the most high God," he asks, "than our Lord Jesus Christ, who offered sacrifice to God the Father and offered the very same thing that Melchizedek had offered, bread and wine, that is, actually, his body and blood?"[38]

Over the centuries, the Church has affirmed and deepened its understanding of this mystery of Christ's offering and priesthood. "The church sees in the gesture of the king-priest Melchizedek who 'brought out bread and wine,' a prefiguring of her own offering" (CCC, 1333). Similarly, "the Christian tradition considers Melchizedek, 'priest of God Most High,' as a prefiguration of the priesthood of Christ, the unique 'high priest after the order of Melchizedek' [Heb 5:10]; 'holy, blameless, unstained' [Heb 7:26], 'by a single offering he has perfected for all time those who are sanctified' [Heb 10:14], that is, by the unique sacrifice of the cross" (CCC, 1544). The importance of this event is further signaled by its inclusion as one of the Old Testament readings for

35. NJBC, 25.

36. Jungmann, *The Mass*, vol. 2, 228.

37. Ibid.

38. Mark Sheridan, ed., *Genesis 12–50*, vol. OT 2 of *Ancient Christian Commentary on Scripture* (Downers Grove, IL: InterVarsity Press, 2002), 26.

the Solemnity of the Most Holy Body and Blood of Christ (Corpus Christi) and the Votive Mass of the Most Holy Eucharist.

These three figures—Abel, Abraham, and Melchizedek— prefigure different aspects of the Mass. Abel's sacrifice "represents the Sacrifice of the Cross, with which the Mass forms but one and the same Sacrifice"; Abraham's sacrifice, "in which the immolation takes place in an unbloody manner," anticipates the unbloody Sacrifice of the Mass; and Melchizedek's sacrifice, "which represents the Sacrifice of the Mass, in which Bread and Wine are used upon the Altar; but, after Consecration, there remains neither Bread nor Wine, but only the species or appearances, serving but to veil the Divine Victim."[39] In addition to revealing different aspects of the Eucharist, their invocation in the great prayer of the Church strengthens our faith. "The outstanding types from the Old Dispensation are reviewed to encourage the soul, and a certain pride takes possession of our hearts as we link our action with the action of these biblical saints."[40]

Conclusion

The Old Testament types of the Eucharist that we have considered are the work of the God of whom Isaiah wrote, "You have carried out your wonderful plans of old, faithful and true" (Is 25:1). The Passover celebrated in Egypt received its "definitive meaning" in the Upper Room, in the Last Supper that Jesus celebrated with his disciples and which he commanded them to continue in memory of him. The bread from heaven that nourished Israel in the wilderness anticipated Jesus, the true bread from heaven (Jn 6:51). The covenant that was ratified in the desert with the blood of animals points to the chalice of Christ's blood, "the blood of the new and eternal covenant, which will be poured out . . . for the forgiveness of sins" (RM, Order of Mass, 90). Finally, Abel, Abraham, and Melchizedek foreshadow different aspects of the Eucharistic sacrifice: the innocent man slain for his pleasing gift, the father willing to sacrifice his beloved and only son, and the priest-king bringing gifts of bread and wine. We turn now to consider in detail the signs of the Eucharist.

39. Prosper Guéranger, *Explanation of the Prayers and Ceremonies of Holy Mass* (Chicago: Biretta Books, 2007), 41.

40. Jungmann, *The Mass*, vol. 2, 228.

Chapter 11

The Eucharist: Signs and Symbols

The Eucharist, "the source and summit of the Christian life" (LG, 11), that contains the whole good of the Church, Christ himself (PO, 5), is the most complex of all the sacraments.[1] The substantial presence of Christ himself, body and blood, soul and divinity, under the signs of bread and wine, merits and demands a celebration of profound depth and reverence. It is composed of two fundamental parts—the Liturgy of the Word and the Liturgy of the Eucharist—that form a unity. Each part unfolds through dynamic and ancient liturgical elements, each element building on what has gone before and propelling the celebration forward to the high point of sacramental Communion. We will need to begin our exploration of the signs and symbols of the Eucharist at the beginning—the place where the Eucharist is celebrated. The church building is a sacrament with a lowercase *s*, *sacramental* but not *a* sacramental. To say that the church building is sacramental means that "the edifice is itself a part of the liturgy, a sacred thing, made holy by a divine presence through solemn consecration; it is a sacramental object, an outward sign of an invisible spiritual reality."[2] As stated in chapter 5, sacramentals are sacred signs instituted by the Church which "signify effects, particularly of a spiritual nature, which are obtained through the intercession of the Church" (CCC, 1667). "They always include a prayer, often accompanied by a specific sign, such as the laying on of hands, the sign of the cross, or the sprinkling of holy water (which recalls Baptism)" (CCC, 1668). We will now look at the church building itself and its furnishings.

1. We have already looked at a number of these signs in chapters 1 and 2: the gesture of invoking the Holy Spirit (the epiclesis), images, song, the sign of the cross, silence, movement, incense, and color.

2. William Busch, "Secularism in Church Architecture," *Church Property Administration* 19, no. 6 (November–December 1955): 32.

The Church Building and Its Furnishings

As an orderly array of signs and symbols of heavenly realities, the church building itself is sacramental, signifying and symbolizing the heavenly Jerusalem that makes present spiritual realities and that participates in the liturgy. It is a visible expression of the New Jerusalem, heaven itself,[3] the sacramental dwelling place of God, a place in which Christ himself is present and active in the sacred liturgy, glorifying the Father in the Spirit and sanctifying his people. In its mystagogical catechesis, the rite of the *Dedication of a Church and an Altar* explains that the twelve anointings of the church are "a symbol that the church is an image of the holy city of Jerusalem."[4] The sanctuary of the church building is a fulfillment of the holy of holies of the Temple and an image of the dwelling place of God in heaven. It is the place from which God's word is proclaimed and where His future kingdom becomes present now through the Eucharistic sacrifice offered on the altar. It is the goal of liturgical procession, pointing God's people to the eschatological fulfillment of human life and the entire cosmos. These spiritual realities are signified by marking it "off from the body of the church by elevation or by structure and ornamentation" (GIRM, 295).

The altar and ambo are the preeminent symbols of Christ's presence. The spiritual and liturgical center of the church building is the altar, for the church building exists for the altar. The symbolism of the altar is fourfold: Christ himself; the altar of sacrifice; the table of the paschal banquet; and the center of the thanksgiving made present through the Eucharist. It is because "the altar is Christ" (DCA, 4) that the priest begins and concludes the Mass by reverencing it with a kiss. The ambo is "the 'table of God's word' and is therefore a symbol of the surpassing dignity of that word" (IOM, 53). From it are proclaimed "readings, the Responsorial Psalm, and the Easter Proclamation (Exsultet); likewise it may be used for giving the Homily and for announcing the intentions of the Universal Prayer. The dignity of the ambo requires that only a minister of the word should stand at it" (GIRM, 309).

The altar and the ambo are the two tables of the Lord, the table of his Word and of his Body.

3. CCC, 1180.

4. DCA, II.16.

> From listening to the word of God, faith is born or strengthened (cf. Rom 10:17); in the Eucharist the Word made flesh gives himself to us as our spiritual food. Thus, "from the two tables of the word of God and the Body of Christ, the Church receives and gives to the faithful the bread of life." Consequently it must constantly be kept in mind that the word of God, read and proclaimed by the Church in the liturgy, leads to the Eucharist as to its own connatural end. (SacCar, 44)

This integral relationship between altar and ambo, word of God and Body of Christ, should be visually expressed in the design of these furnishings. "Great pains must therefore be taken, in keeping with the design of each church, over the harmonious and close relationship of the ambo with the altar" (LM, 32).

The chair of the priest celebrant is another liturgical sign. "Christ is present in the person of the Bishop or priest who presides at the liturgy. The chair stands as a sign of his office, especially with regard to the Bishop. It symbolizes unity, leadership, and service to the gathered assembly" (IOM, 54). The choice of materials, design and placement should express its dignity and make manifest its intimate relationship with the altar, the symbol of Christ himself, and the ambo, the symbol of Christ's Word. Movement from one of these elements to the other—altar, ambo, and chair—are also signs of the movement of the celebration. "When the priest and ministers move from chair to ambo or to altar, the different parts of the Mass are more clearly distinguished, and the presence of the Lord in word and sacrament is more effectively conveyed" (IOM, 54).

The altar, ambo, and chair signify different aspects of Christ's presence among us, but the fullness of his presence is signified by the tabernacle in which the Most Blessed Sacrament is reserved. The tabernacle "is the place where Emmanuel, 'God-with-us' dwells on earth in our earthly image of heaven: the church sanctuary. Here the golden box of the Old Testament's Ark of the Covenant finds its fulfillment in sacramental life of the church: God's presence abides with us even as it dwells within each and every Christian who takes that presence out to the world in evangelization, caring for the sick, the homeless, and even in the ordinary tasks of employment and raising a family."[5]

---

5. Denis R. McNamara, *Catholic Church Architecture and the Spirit of the Liturgy* (Chicago: Hillenbrand Books, 2009), 220.

The tabernacle should "be made of solid and inviolable material that is not transparent," not moveable, and locked (GIRM, 314). In addition, "a special lamp, fueled by oil or wax, should shine permanently to indicate the presence of Christ and honor it" (GIRM, 316). The tabernacle should be located either in the sanctuary "apart from the altar of celebration," or in a chapel that is "organically connected to the church and readily noticeable by the Christian faithful" (GIRM, 315). According to St. John Paul II, "The presence of Jesus in the tabernacle must be a kind of *magnetic pole* attracting an ever greater number of souls enamored of him, ready to wait patiently to hear his voice and, as it were, to sense the beating of his heart" (MND, 18, italics original).

Two other liturgical symbols within the sanctuary are a crucifix and candles. Either on or near the altar "there is to be a cross, with the figure of Christ crucified upon it, a cross clearly visible to the assembled people" (GIRM, 308). Since the cross is "a constant reminder of the cost of salvation and the symbol of Christian hope" (IOM, 55) it is preferable that the cross "remain near the altar even outside of liturgical celebrations so as to call to mind for the faithful the saving Passion of the Lord" (GIRM, 308). Candles are signs of the presence of Christ who is the light of the world (Jn 8:12). They are also a reminder of the Christian's Baptism by which the Father has granted us a "share in the inheritance of the holy ones in light" (Col 1:12). Because they are signs of reverence and festivity, "candles are to be used at every liturgical service" (GIRM, 307), placed either "on or next to the altar" (GIRM, 117). A minimum of two are to be used in any celebration, "or even four or six, especially for a Sunday Mass or a holy day of obligation. If the diocesan Bishop celebrates, then seven candles should be used" (GIRM, 117). Altar, ambo, chair, crucifix, and candles signify the presence of Christ, the light of the world, in the person of the priest and in word and sacrament, making present under sacramental signs his Paschal Mystery.

Gestures and Postures

As we noted in chapter 3, active participation in the liturgy is both interior and exterior. We participate "interiorly" when our hearts and minds are attuned to what we "outwardly hear, do and say during the Liturgy" (IOM, 26). We participate "exteriorly" when we express through gesture and demeanor our "inner participation in the Liturgy. This ritual interplay between these elements points to the transcendence and the immanence of the living God" (IOM, 26). In liturgical worship we worship God with every aspect of our being, not only our minds and spirits but also our bodies, hands, and feet. Because "the Lord gives himself to us in bodily form . . . we must likewise respond to him bodily."[6] In the Eucharist every spiritual use of the body is utilized: "singing, speaking, keeping silence, sitting, standing, kneeling."[7] "The non-verbal elements of the Liturgy can express what cannot be articulated in words and, at times, can reinforce the spoken word" (IOM, 27).

The common postures prescribed for the Eucharist signify a number of different things. Adopting the same bodily posture is first of all "a sign of the unity of the members of the Christian community gathered together for the Sacred Liturgy" (GIRM, 42). Not only does it express "the intentions and spiritual attitude of the participants," it also "fosters them" (GIRM, 42). Just as our spirit "instructs" our body, so also our body can "instruct" our spirit. For example, we sit "to concentrate on listening to the word of God"; standing is "a sign of readiness . . . [and] an expression of the victory of Christ"; kneeling "is an expression of faith . . . the bodily expression of our positive response to the real presence of Jesus Christ, who as God and man, with body and soul, flesh and blood is present among us."[8] In addition, common postures and gestures (bowing, making the sign of the cross), contribute "to making the entire celebration resplendent with beauty and noble simplicity" (GIRM, 42). They also help to clarify "the true and full meaning of its different parts"—standing or kneeling for prayer, sitting to listen (GIRM, 43). Finally, they assist in "fostering the participation of all" (GIRM, 42). The common gestures and postures of the Mass illustrate an important principle that informs every liturgical celebration, that what matters is not "private inclination or arbitrary choice"—what "I" or "we" want, or what seems fashionable today—but rather "what serves the common spiritual good of the People of God" (GIRM, 42).

---

6. Ratzinger, *God Is Near Us*, 91.

7. Ibid.

8. Ibid., 92–93.

Activity

Note the posture appropriate to the following parts of Mass:

1. The Responsorial Psalm
2. The Gospel
3. The Homily
4. The profession of faith (the Creed)
5. The Sanctus (Holy, Holy, Holy)
6. The Institution Narrative
7. After the Lamb of God (Agnus Dei)

The Introductory Rites

As we noted in chapter 1, the introductory dialogue between the priest, the sacramental sign of Christ the Head, and the assembly, the sacramental sign of the Body of Christ, makes manifest "the mystery of the Church gathered together" (GIRM, 50). This is followed by the Penitential Act by which the community prepares itself "to celebrate the sacred mysteries" (RM, Order of Mass, 4). This signifies the penitential character the Church who "is at the same time holy and in need of cleansing, and so is unceasingly intent on repentance and reform" (RP, 3). This penitential character is manifested "in [the] liturgy when the faithful confess that they are sinners and ask pardon of God and of their brothers and sisters" (RP, 4). It concludes with the priest's prayer for mercy, forgiveness, and everlasting life, "which, however, lacks the efficacy of the Sacrament of Penance" (GIRM, 51).

This may be followed by the Gloria, "a most ancient and venerable hymn by which the Church, gathered in the Holy Spirit, glorifies and entreats God the Father and the Lamb" (GIRM, 53). It is said or sung on Sundays outside Advent and Lent, on Solemnities and Feasts, and other celebrations "of a more solemn character" (GIRM, 53). The text of the Gloria, it should be noted, "may not be replaced by any other" (GIRM, 53).

The Introductory Rites conclude with the opening prayer, known as the Collect. Following the priest's invitation to pray, all are directed to "pray in silence with the Priest for a while" (RM, Order of Mass, 9) "so that they may become aware of being in God's presence and may call to mind their intentions" (GIRM, 54). The priest then pronounces the prayer, "through which the character of the celebration finds expression" (GIRM, 54). It is usually called the Collect because in addition to expressing the character of the particular celebration, it also "gathers up, as it were, all the petitions that the faithful have expressed privately."[9] The priest proclaims the presidential prayers—Collect, Prayer over the Offerings, the Eucharistic Prayer, and the Prayer after Communion (GIRM, 30)—"while standing and with hands slightly raised and outstretched. This practice appears already in the tradition of the Old Testament (Ex 9:29; Ps 28:2; 63:5, 134:2, Is 1:15), and was taken over by Christians in memory of the Lord's passion: "Not only do we raise our hands, but also hold them outstretched, so that by imitating the Lord in his passion, we bear witness to him as we pray' [Tertullian]" (CB, 104). The presidential prayers are addressed to God "in the person of Christ, in the name of the entire holy people and all present" (GIRM, 30).

The Eucharist as a dialogue between God and his children in Christ and the Holy Spirit is clearly expressed by the Introductory Rites: the Greeting by the priest and the people's response, the dialogic nature of the different forms of the Penitential Act, and the dialogic elements of the Collect. The local community, constituted as the Body of Christ, Head and members, prepared through the Penitential Act to "celebrate the sacred mysteries," having praised the Most Holy Trinity in the Gloria, and offering their individual and common prayer to the Father through Christ in the Holy Spirit, is now ready to enter into dialogue with God in the Liturgy of the Word, to hear and respond to the word of life and love.

The Liturgy of the Word

The Liturgy of the Word, as St. John Paul II has emphasized, is above all a dialogue. "It should also be borne in mind," writes the Saint, "that *the*

9. Cabié, *The Eucharist*, 53.

liturgical proclamation of the word of God, especially in the Eucharistic assembly, is not so much a time for meditation and catechesis as *a dialogue between God and his People,* a dialogue in which the wonders of salvation are proclaimed and the demands of the Covenant are continually restated. On their part, the People of God are drawn to respond to this dialogue of love by giving thanks and praise, also by demonstrating their fidelity to the task of continual 'conversion'" (DD, 4; italics original). The Liturgy of the Word is comprised of several elements. At its heart are the readings from Sacred Scripture, which are developed and concluded by the Homily, the Creed, and the Universal Prayer. The Liturgy of the Word proclaims the power and love of God. "The word of God constantly proclaimed in the Liturgy is always . . . a living and effective word through the power of the Holy Spirit. It expresses the Father's love that never fails in its effectiveness toward us" (LM, 4).

The Readings

On Sundays and festive days, the Liturgy of the Word consists of three readings plus the responsorial psalm. The first reading is from the Old Testament, the second from one of the New Testament letters or the Book of Revelation, and the Gospel. The purpose behind this arrangement is to bring "out the unity of the Old and New Testaments and of the history of salvation, in which Christ is the central figure, commemorated in his paschal mystery" (LM, 66.1). To provide "a more varied and richer reading of Sacred Scripture on Sundays and festive days," there is a three-year cycle of readings (LM, 66.2). Two principles govern the Order of Reading for Sundays and festive days, the principle of harmony, and the principle of semicontinuous reading. "One or the other applies according to the different seasons of the year and the distinctive character of the particular liturgical season" (LM, 66.3).

The principle of harmony acknowledges two kinds of harmony. The first kind of harmony recognizes and highlights the correlation between the doctrine and events of the Old and New Testaments. "The present Order of Readings selects Old Testament texts mainly because of their correlation with New Testament texts read in the same Mass, and particularly with the Gospel text" (LM, 67). A second kind of harmony "exists between texts of the readings for each Mass during Advent, Lent, and Easter, the seasons that have a distinctive importance or character" (LM, 67). The readings for the Sundays in Ordinary Time are arranged according to the principle of semicontinuous reading since these Sundays "do not have a distinctive character. Thus the text of both the apostolic and Gospel readings are arranged in order of semicontinuous reading, whereas the Old Testament reading is harmonized with the Gospel" (LM, 67).[10]

The "high point of the liturgy of the word" is the reading of the Gospel, for which "the other readings, in their established sequence from the Old to the New Testament, prepare the assembly" (LM, 13). Every element signals the importance of this rite, beginning with the Book of the Gospels, which is "a visible sign of Jesus Christ, the Word of God."[11] From the early centuries of the Church this sacramental sign has been accorded special honor, from manuscripts "prepared in gold or silver script upon a purple background, or . . . richly decorated with miniatures" to bindings of "ivory or pure gold or silver."[12] "The Liturgy itself teaches the great reverence that is to be shown this reading by setting it off from the other readings with special marks of honor" (GIRM, 60). These marks of honor include standing for the reading, the minister who proclaims it—either a deacon or a priest—the blessing (given to the deacon) or prayer (said by the priest) of preparation, the procession from the altar to the ambo with incense and candles, the dialogue between the minister and the assembly, incensing the Book, and the Sign of the Cross made on the book and then on the forehead, mouth, and breast. This triple signing means that, "For the word which Christ brought and which is set down in this book we are willing to stand up with a mind that is open; we are ready to confess it with our mouth; and above all we are determined to safeguard it faithfully in our hearts."[13] Through word, posture, gesture, movement, light and smell, "the faithful acknowledge and confess that Christ is present and is speaking to them" (GIRM, 60).

---

10. The same principles govern the readings for weekdays, for which there are two readings, the first from the Old Testament, an Apostle, or during Easter, the Acts of the Apostles, arranged in a two-year cycle, and a Gospel, "arranged in a single cycle, repeated each year" (LM, 69).

11. Elliott, *Ceremonies of the Modern Roman Rite*, 39.

12. Jungmann, *The Mass*, vol. 1, 442.

13. Ibid., 454.

St. Jerome speaks eloquently of Christ's presence in the Gospel.

> We are reading the sacred Scriptures. For me, the Gospel is the Body of Christ; for me, the holy Scriptures are his teaching. And when he says: *whoever does not eat my flesh and drink my blood* (Jn 6:53), even though these words can also be understood of the [Eucharistic] Mystery, Christ's body and blood are really the word of Scripture, God's teaching. When we approach the [Eucharistic] Mystery, if a crumb falls to the ground we are troubled. Yet when we are listening to the word of God, and God's Word and Christ's flesh and blood are being poured into our ears yet we pay no heed, what great peril should we not feel? (VD, 56)

The proclamation of the Gospel is a real and powerful encounter between the faithful and the Great Shepherd who nourishes his sheep with his living Word.

The Homily

The reading of the Gospel is followed by the homily, "which extends its proclamation" (CCC, 1154). Pope Francis reminds us that the homily, because of its liturgical, eucharistic context, is "a distinctive genre" (EG, 137–138). For this reason, "it surpasses all forms of catechesis as the supreme moment in the dialogue between God and his people which lead up to sacramental communion. The homily takes up once more the dialogue which the Lord has already established with his people" (EG, 137). As a dialogue between a Father and his children, it should relate closely to "the life of the community" (SacCar, 46), "lead to an understanding of the mystery being celebrated, serve as a summons to mission, and prepare the assembly for the profession of faith, the universal prayer, and the Eucharistic liturgy" (VD, 59). The primary purpose of the homily, then, is to "lead the community of the faithful to celebrate the Eucharist actively, so that they may hold fast in their lives to what they have grasped by faith" (LM, 24).

Creed

The dialogue between the Blessed Trinity and the people of God continues with the Profession of Faith, also known as the Creed. When the faithful recite the Creed they are making their personal response "to the Word of God proclaimed in the readings taken from Sacred Scripture and explained in the Homily" while also honoring and confessing "the great mysteries of the faith" (GIRM, 67). It is, however, much more than our assent "to a body of abstract truths; rather, when it is recited the whole of life is drawn into a journey towards full communion with the living God. We can say that in the creed *believers are invited to enter into the mystery which they profess and to be transformed by it*" (LF, 45; italics added).

Pope Francis emphasizes the personal and dynamic character of this liturgical sign. "The believer who professes his or her faith is taken up, as it were, into the truth being professed. *He or she cannot truthfully recite the words of the creed without being changed, without becoming part of that history of love which embraces us and expands our being,* making it part of a great fellowship, the ultimate subject which recites the creed, namely, the Church. All the truths in which we believe point to the mystery of the new life of faith as a journey of communion with the living God" (LF, 45; italics added).

Finally, the recitation of the Creed is a sign of the close relationship between Baptism and the Eucharist, for the Creed recalls the promises made at Baptism, as St. John Paul II explains. "The Sunday assembly commits us therefore to an *inner renewal of our baptismal promises*, which are in a sense implicit in the recitation of the Creed, and are an explicit part of the liturgy of the Easter Vigil and whenever Baptism is celebrated during Mass" (DD, 41; italics added). The Creed is just one way the celebration of the Eucharist nourishes and strengthens the grace of Baptism and conforms us more closely to Christ.

The Universal Prayer

The Liturgy of the Word concludes with the Universal Prayer, also referred to as the Prayer of the Faithful. It is the people's response to "the Word of God which they have received in faith" and an exercise of "the office of their baptismal priesthood" (GIRM, 69), by which they share in Christ's ministry of intercession according to Hebrews 7:25: "Enlightened and moved by God's word, all the baptized, gathered for worship by Christ the High Priest, share in his priestly intercession for all humanity" (IOM, 96). The recommended series of intentions is as follows: "a) for the needs of the Church; b) for public authorities and the salvation of the whole world; c) for those burdened by any kind of difficulty; d) for the local community" (GIRM, 70). However, for special celebrations such as Marriage or a funeral, the petitions "may be concerned more closely with the particular occasion" (GIRM, 70). This too normally takes the form of a dialogue, with the deacon or lay reader announcing the petitions and the assembly standing and expressing their prayer "by an invocation said in common" (GIRM, 71). The result is that "as the liturgy of the word has its full effects in the faithful, they are better prepared to proceed to the liturgy of the Eucharist" (LM, 30).

Conclusion

We noted above that in the Mass Christ nourishes us from two tables, the table of his word and the table of his Body. The two are so intrinsically related that the Church in fact speaks of "the twofold table," one "table" that nourishes us in distinct but complementary ways, as the following passage explains: "The Church is nourished spiritually at the twofold table of God's word and of the Eucharist: from the one it grows in wisdom and from the other in holiness. In the word of God the divine covenant is announced; in the Eucharist the new and everlasting covenant is renewed. On the one hand the history of salvation is brought to mind by means of human sounds; on the other it is made manifest in the sacramental signs of the Liturgy" (LM, 10). Having grown in wisdom, we are now ready to grow in holiness; having heard the divine covenant proclaimed, we are ready to enter into its renewal; having listened to the history of our salvation, we are now ready for its manifestation. "It can never be forgotten, therefore, that the divine word read and proclaimed by the Church in the Liturgy has as its one purpose the sacrifice of the New Covenant and the banquet of grace, that is, the Eucharist" (LM, 10).

The Liturgy of the Eucharist

At the Last Supper "Christ took the bread and the chalice, gave thanks, broke the bread and gave it to his disciples, saying: Take, eat and drink: this is my Body; this is the chalice of my Blood. Do this in memory of me" (GIRM, 72). The Liturgy of the Eucharist takes its fundamental structure from these words and actions. Just as Christ took the bread and the chalice, so "At the Preparation of the Gifts, bread and wine with water are brought to the altar, the same elements, that is to say, which Christ took into his hands" (GIRM, 72a). Then, just as Christ gave thanks over them, "In the Eucharistic Prayer, thanks is given to

God for the whole work of salvation, and the offerings become the Body and Blood of Christ" (GIRM, 72b). Finally, just as Christ broke the bread and gave it to his disciples, and likewise gave them the chalice of his Blood, so "through the fraction and through Communion, the faithful, though many, receive from the one bread the Lord's Body and from the one chalice the Lord's Blood in the same way that the Apostles received them from the hands of Christ himself" (GIRM, 72c).

The Presentation of the Gifts

The Liturgy of the Eucharist begins with the preparation of the altar, "which is the center of the whole Liturgy of the Eucharist" (GIRM, 73). The corporal, purificator, Missal, and chalice (unless it is prepared at the credence table) are placed on the altar. Once the altar is prepared, bread and wine are brought forward, "and perhaps other gifts to relieve the needs of the Church and of the poor" (RM, Order of Mass, 22). "It is desirable" that these gifts be brought in procession by members of the faithful to "express their participation" (RM, Order of Mass, 22). Bringing gifts to help those in need has been the Church's practice "from the very beginning . . . inspired by the example of Christ who became poor to make us rich" (CCC, 1351, citing 2 Cor 8:9). St. Justin Martyr has left us a description of this custom from the mid-second century: "Those who are well off, and who are also willing, give as each chooses. What is gathered is given to him who presides to assist orphans and widows, those whom illness or any other cause has deprived of resources, prisoners, immigrants and, in a word, all who are in need" (CCC, 1351).

As we noted in chapter 2, in the section "Movement," the presentation of the gifts is also a silent intercession for the needs of the world in which "*we also bring to the altar all the pain and suffering of the world,* in the certainty that everything has value in God's eyes" (SacCar, 47). A proper understanding of this liturgical element "enables us to appreciate how God invites man to participate in bringing to fulfilment his handiwork, and in so doing, gives human labor its authentic meaning, since, through the celebration of the Eucharist, it is united to the redemptive sacrifice of Christ" (SacCar, 47).

The priest receives the gifts of bread and wine. He first blesses God for the gift of bread, "fruit of the earth and work of human hands" which, through the power of God's word and Spirit, "will become for us the bread of life" (RM, Order of Mass, 23), and then places it on the altar. Next, the wine is poured into the chalice along with a little water, a mingling that signifies the marvelous exchange by which "we come to share in the divinity of Christ who humbled himself to share in our humanity" (RM, Order of Mass, 24). The priest then blesses the Lord for the wine, "fruit of the vine and work of human hands, it will become our spiritual drink" (RM, Order of Mass, 25). These gifts—"fruit of the earth" and "fruit of the vine"—"continue to signify the goodness of creation" (CCC, 1333). Only after the bread and wine have been presented to God are they placed on the altar.

These words and actions recall one of the Old Testament figures we discussed in chapter 10: Melchizedek. "The presentation of the offerings at the altar takes up the gesture of Melchizedek and commits the Creator's gifts into the hands of Christ who, in his sacrifice, brings to perfection all human attempts to offer sacrifices" (CCC, 1350). This rite may conclude by incensing the gifts, the cross and altar, the priest and the people, an action to "honor the elements and the altar and to acknowledge the presence and action of Christ in the priest celebrant and other members of the liturgical assembly" (IOM, 58; see also the section in chapter 2, "Incense").

The priest then bows and, in a quiet voice, prays, "With humble spirit and contrite heart may we be accepted by you, O lord, and may our sacrifice in your sight this day be pleasing to you, Lord God" (RM, 26). This is a prayer that all "who participate may offer a genuine sacrifice, and, imitating the sacrifice of Christ, they may be one with the gift offered."[14] This prayer is taken from Daniel, the prayer of Azariah offered on behalf of himself and his friends Shadrach and Meshach in the midst of the fiery furnace: "But with contrite heart and humble spirit let us be received; as through it were burnt offerings of rams and bulls, or tens of thousands of lambs, so let our sacrifice be in your presence today and find favor before you; for those who trust in you cannot be put to shame" (Dn 3:39–40). The Lord answered their prayer by making "the inside of the furnace as though a dew-laden breeze were blowing through it" (Dn 3:50). So too will he answer our prayer and accept our sacrifice when it is offered with true humility and contrition.

14. Carstens and Martis, *Mystical Body, Mystical Voice,* 164.

This is followed by "a rite in which the desire for inner purification finds expression" (GIRM, 76). The priest washes his hands as he prays quietly for his own sanctity, "Wash me, O Lord, from my iniquity and cleanse me from my sin" (RM, Order of Mass, 28), a prayer taken from Psalm 51:4. "While originating with a former need for the priest to wash his hands after assembling and arranging the elements of bread and wine and incensing them, the washing of hands was also well known in early Christianity, as in Judaism, as a symbolic expression of the need for inner purity at the beginning of a religious action" (IOM, 109).

The priest then invites the people to pray "that my sacrifice and yours may be acceptable to God, the almighty Father" (RM, Order of Mass, 29). In the previous chapter we recalled this invitation in our explanation of how the Church participates in Christ's offering that is sacramentally re-presented in the Mass. Here we will develop that by listening to the words of St. John Paul II: "Yet the faithful must realize that, because of the common priesthood received in Baptism, 'they participate in the offering of the Eucharist.' Although there is a distinction of roles, they still 'offer to God the divine victim and themselves with him'" (DD, 51). Here we encounter one of the ways that the baptized exercise their participation in the priesthood of Christ.

The people stand (GIRM, 146), the posture of readiness for action, and respond to the priest's invitation by asking the Lord to accept the sacrifice at his hands "for the praise and glory" of God's name, "for our good and the good of all his holy Church" (RM, Order of Mass, 29). Why do we celebrate the Mass? To give praise and glory to God, to be spiritually nourished so that we may grow in holiness and effectively proclaim the Gospel, and so that the Church may be an ever more effective "sign of unity and an instrument of your peace among all people" (RM, Eucharistic Prayer for Reconciliation II). The priest then says the Prayer over the Offerings that is proper to the particular celebration.

Especially noteworthy in these preparatory rites of the Liturgy of the Eucharist are the references to sacrifice. First there is the priest's prayer: "may our sacrifice in your sight this day be pleasing to you, Lord God" (RM, Order of Mass, 26). Then his invitation to the assembly to pray "that my sacrifice and yours may be acceptable to God, the almighty Father" (RM, Order of Mass, 29). And finally, the people's invocation for the Lord "to accept the sacrifice" at his hands (RM, Order of Mass, 29). These references help us recall the different aspects of the sacrifice of the Mass: a memorial sacrifice in which the one sacrifice of Christ is sacramentally re-presented in an unbloody manner; the Church's union with Christ in presenting his sacrifice to the Father in the Holy Spirit; and a sacrifice of praise and thanksgiving to God.

The Eucharistic Prayer

We now come to "the center and high point of the entire celebration . . . the Eucharistic Prayer itself, that is, the prayer of thanksgiving and sanctification" (GIRM, 78). In this prayer the priest, "in the name of the entire community," addresses "God the Father through Jesus Christ in the Holy Spirit," and "the whole congregation of the faithful joins with Christ in confessing the great deeds of God and in the offering of Sacrifice. The Eucharistic Prayer requires that everybody listens to it with reverence and in silence" (GIRM, 78).

Every Eucharistic Prayer—Eucharistic Prayers I–IV, the two for reconciliation, the four for various needs and occasions, and the three for Masses with children (in a supplement)—has the same structural elements. It begins with thanksgiving, "expressed especially in the Preface" (GIRM, 79), followed by the acclamation or Sanctus (Holy, Holy, Holy). Then follows the epiclesis (remember this from chapter 1), the account of Christ's institution of the Eucharist and the Consecration of the bread and wine, the *anamnesis* that recalls and makes present the Paschal Mystery (see chapter 1), and the offering (oblation) of the sacrifice to the Father. It concludes with intercessions for the living and the dead, the concluding doxology, and the people's "Amen." All of the Eucharistic Prayers "have been handed down to us by the Church's living Tradition and are noteworthy for their inexhaustible theological richness," says Pope Benedict XVI. For this reason, "the faithful need to be enabled to appreciate that richness" (SacCar, 48).

The Preface

The Preface begins with a dialogue between the priest and people that echoes the Greeting that begins the Mass: "The Lord be with you/And with your spirit" (RM, Order of Mass, 33ff.). Then the priest invites the people to lift up their hearts, to which they give their assent. This is an invitation to the assembly "to raise and place in God's presence their entire being, thoughts, memories, emotions, and expectations, in grateful attention and anticipation" (IOM, 115). However, St. Cyril of Jerusalem was realistic about our frailty: "We must be mindful of God at all times, but if human weakness makes this impossible we should try especially hard at this time."[15] St. John Chrysostom explained the meaning of "lift up your hearts": "Let no one have any thought of earthly, but let him lose himself of every earthly thing and transport himself whole and entire into heaven."[16] This invitation expresses the participation of the earthly liturgy in the heavenly liturgy (see chapter 2). The dialogue concludes with an exhortation to "give thanks to the Lord our God" (RM, Order of Mass, 33) and the people's assent that thanksgiving "is right and just" (RM, Order of Mass, 33). This dialogue is a sign of the liturgy's communal character: "Since the celebration of Mass is a communal action, the dialogue between priest celebrant and the congregation is of special value. It is not only an external sign of communal celebration, but also the means of greater interchange between priest and people" (IOM, 115).

The body of the Preface continues the theme of thanksgiving to the Father "for all his works: creation, redemption, and sanctification" (CCC, 1352), "or for some particular aspect of it, according to the varying day, festivity, or time of year" (GIRM, 79). Let us look at a few examples. Preface I of Advent speaks of how Christ "assumed at his first coming the lowliness of human flesh," fulfilling God's design "formed long ago" and opening "for us the way to eternal salvation" (RM, Order of Mass, 33). On the feasts of saints Preface I of Saints praises God for the gift of the saints: "By their way of life you offer us an example, by communion with them you give us companionship, by their intercession, sure support" (RM, Order of Mass, 66). Preface III of Easter praises Christ who "never ceases to offer himself for us but defends us and ever pleads our cause before you" (RM, Order of Mass, 47). The Preface of the Immaculate Conception of the Blessed Virgin Mary, the patronal feast day of the United States, recalls that God preserved Mary "from all stain of original sin" in order to "prepare a worthy Mother for your Son, . . . signify the beginning of the Church" and "be for your people an advocate of grace and a model of holiness" (RM, Proper of Saints,

15. Yarnold, *The Awe-Inspiring Rites*, 91.

16. Daniélou, *Angels*, 64.

December 8.). The Preface summarizes the meaning of the particular liturgical celebration and gives voice to our praise and thanksgiving.

The Sanctus Acclamation

The Preface concludes with the Sanctus—"Holy, holy, holy"—sung (preferably) or said by the priest and people. It is based on several biblical texts. The Old Testament prophet Isaiah saw a vision of the Lord and heard the seraphim cry out, "Holy, holy, holy is the LORD of hosts! All the earth is filled with his glory!" (Is 6:3). The Apostle John also saw of vision of heaven and heard the four living creatures continually exclaim: "Holy, holy, holy is the Lord God almighty, who was, and who is, and who is to come" (Rev 4:8). To this is added the praise of the crowd that welcomed Jesus as he entered Jerusalem (itself taken from Ps 118:25–26): "Hosanna to the Son of David; blessed is he who comes in the name of the Lord; hosanna in the highest" (Mt 21:9). Here again the earthly liturgy joins the heavenly liturgy and we are invited, in the words of St. John Chrysostom, to "abide there beside the very throne of glory, hovering with the Seraphim, and singing the most holy song of the God of glory and majesty."[17] Theodore of Mopsuestia has left us a fifth century description of this angelic praise:

> This is the praise which we all assemble together to sing at the top of our voices, so that we sing the same hymns as the invisible natures. . . . By this means we show the greatness of the mercy He has bestowed freely upon us. A religious fear fills our conscience, either before or after we have cried out, "Holy!"[18]

Every time the Mass is celebrated, the earthly Church joins the heavenly liturgy so that together "the entire communion of saints, the heavenly powers, and all of creation give praise to the God of the universe" (IOM, 117).

The Consecratory Epiclesis

The Eucharistic Prayer continues with an introductory section that extends the praise of God's holiness—"You are indeed Holy, O Lord, the fount of all holiness" (RM, EP II, 100)—that leads into the epiclesis. As we discussed in chapter 1 (see p. 18), in the consecratory epiclesis

17. Daniélou, *Angels*, 64.

18. Ibid., 65.

"the Church implores the power of the Holy Spirit that the gifts offered by human hands be consecrated, that is, become Christ's Body and Blood and that the unblemished sacrificial Victim to be consumed in Communion may be for the salvation of those who will partake of it" (GIRM, 79c). St. Cyril of Jerusalem has left us with a description of the epiclesis from the mid-fourth century: "we call upon the merciful God to send the Holy Spirit on our offerings, so that he may make the bread Christ's body, and the wine Christ's blood; for clearly whatever the Holy Spirit touches is sanctified and transformed."[19] Compare this with the epiclesis from Eucharistic Prayer III:

> Therefore, O Lord, we humbly implore you:
> by the same Spirit graciously make holy
> these gifts we have brought to you for consecration,
> [and makes the Sign of the Cross once over the bread and
> chalice together, saying:]
> that they may become the Body ✠ and Blood
> of your Son our Lord Jesus Christ,
> at whose command we celebrate these mysteries.
> (RM, Order of Mass, 109)

It is accompanied by a gesture dating back to the Apostles: "The life giving power of the Spirit, who moved over the waters in the first days of creation and overshadowed Mary in the moment of the incarnation, is vividly expressed by the ancient gesture of bringing together the hands with the palms downward and extended over the elements to be consecrated" (IOM, 118). Word and gesture together signify the transforming power of the Holy Spirit.

The Institution Narrative

"At the heart of the Eucharistic Prayer, the account of the Last Supper is recited" (IOM, 119). Now the priest pronounces the essential words—"This is my Body," "This is my Blood"—over the essential elements of bread and wine. It is "by means of the words and actions of Christ, that the Sacrifice is effected which Christ himself instituted during the Last Supper" (GIRM, 79d). St. John Paul II explains the sacramental mystery that occurs at this moment: "The priest says these words, or rather *he puts his voice at the disposal of the One who spoke these words in the Upper*

19. Yarnold, *The Awe Inspiring Rites*, 92.

Room" (EE, 5). This conversion is brought about by "the power of the words and the action of Christ, and the power of the Holy Spirit" (CCC, 1353). "Eucharistic spirituality and theological reflection are enriched if we contemplate in the anaphora the profound unity between the invocation of the Holy Spirit and the institution narrative whereby 'the sacrifice is carried out which Christ himself instituted at the Last Supper'" (SacCar 48).

The classic definition of this transformation was formulated at the Council of Trent in 1551: "by the consecration of the bread and wine there takes place a change of the whole substance of the bread into the substance of the body of Christ our Lord and of the whole substance of the wine into the substance of his blood. This change the holy Catholic Church has fittingly and properly called transubstantiation" (CCC, 1376). Christ's substantial presence under the appearances of bread and wine "endures as long as the Eucharistic species subsist" (CCC, 1377). Furthermore, "Christ is present whole and entire in each of species and whole and entire in each of their parts, in such a way that the breaking of the bread does not divide Christ" (CCC, 1377).

Pope Benedict XVI, then Cardinal Ratzinger, describes the ineffable power of the Consecration:

> The moment when the Lord comes down and transforms the bread and wine to become the Body and Blood cannot fail to stun, to the very core of their being, those who participate in the Eucharist by faith and prayer. When this happens, we cannot do other than fall to our knees and greet him. . . . For a moment the world is silent, everything is silent, and in that silence we touch the eternal—for one beat of the heart we step out of time into God's being-with-us.[20]

Our liturgical response is the Memorial Acclamation, which is another instance of the dialogic nature of the liturgy. The priest begins by proclaiming, "The mystery of faith," and the people respond with one of three options: "We proclaim your Death, O Lord" (from 1 Cor 11:26); "When we eat this Bread and drink this Cup . . . "; and "Save us, Savior of the world . . . " (Jn 4:42). This acclamation "has become the 'spark' for a special activity of the people, which, with its acclamation, also expresses an essential aspect of the Eucharist."[21] It is a liturgical

20. Ratzinger, *Spirit,* 212.

21. Johannes H. Emminghaus, *The Eucharist: Essence, Form, Celebration,* trans. Linda M. Maloney, rev. and ed. Theodor Mass-Ewerd (Collegeville, MN: The Liturgical Press, 1997), 184.

remembrance of saving events that "become in a certain way present and real" (CCC, 1363). This acclamation proclaims "the dynamic presence of Christ now working salvation."[22]

The Anamnesis-Offertory/Oblation-Doxology

Immediately following the Memorial Acclamation is the Anamnesis, Offertory, and Doxology, which we described in chapter 1. The anamnesis is "a living re-presentation before God of the saving deeds that he has accomplished in Christ, so that their fullness and power may be effective here and now" (IOM, 121). Now the Church, but particularly "those here and now assembled," offers to the Father "the one sacrifice of praise and thanksgiving, a sacramental offering of the sacrifice made 'once for all' by Christ, the 'holy and living sacrifice' that 'brings salvation to all the world'" (IOM, 121).

Listen to the words from Eucharistic Prayer II:

> Therefore, as we celebrate
> the memorial of his Death and Resurrection [anamnesis],
> we offer you, Lord,
> the Bread of life and the Chalice of salvation
> [offertory/oblation],
> giving thanks that you have held us worthy
> to be in your presence and minister to you [doxology].
> (RM, Order of Mass, 105)

The words "we offer you, Lord," intimately involve the assembly, for they offer not only Christ but also themselves, as the Second Vatican Council taught. "Taking part in the Eucharistic Sacrifice, which is the source and summit of the whole Christian life, they offer the divine victim to God, and offer themselves along with it" (LG, 11). This offering of self along with Christ enables the faithful "day by day to be brought, through the mediation of Christ, into unity with God and with each other, so that God may at last be all in all" (GIRM, 79f). This is a moment of intense, interior participation by all present.

22. Michael Kunzler, *The Church's Liturgy,* trans. Placed Murray, OSB, Henry O'Shea, OSB, and Cilian Ó Sé, OSB (London: Continuum, 2001), 228.

The Communion Epiclesis

In the Consecratory Epiclesis the Holy Spirit is invoked to transform the bread and wine into the Body and Blood of Christ. Now, after the Consecration, the Holy Spirit is petitioned to transform the assembly "so that those who take part in the Eucharist may be one body and one spirit" (CCC, 1353).

The Communion Epiclesis from Eucharistic Prayer III asks the Father to "grant that we, who are nourished by the Body and Blood of your Son and filled with his Holy Spirit, may become one body, one spirit in Christ" (RM, Order of Mass, 113). Note especially the Trinitarian character of this petition: the Father nourishes us with the Body and Blood of his Son and fills us with the Holy Spirit so that we may be transformed "into the image of Christ, by concern for the Church's unity, and by taking part in her mission through the witness and service of charity" (CCC, 1109). The Eucharist is the work of the Trinity to bring us more deeply into Trinitarian life, love, and mission.

The Intercessions

The Church, having offered the sacrificial Victim to the Father in the Holy Spirit and herself as well, "now prays that the fruits of this sacrifice may be experienced throughout the Church and the world" (IOM, 122). These intercessions are yet another expression "that the Eucharist is celebrated in communion with the whole Church, of both heaven and earth" (GIRM, 79g), with specific mention of the Blessed Virgin Mary, St. Joseph (in Eucharistic Prayers I–IV), "and all the Saints who have pleased you throughout the ages" (EP II), and acknowledging that "we rely for unfailing help" on their "constant intercession in your presence" (EP III).

The intercessions are both specific and cosmic. In every Eucharistic Prayer mention is made of the pope and the local bishop. Intercession is also offered for the Church, "spread throughout the world" (EP II), to be confirmed "in faith and charity" (EP III), for "all those who, holding to the truth, hand on the catholic and apostolic faith" (EP I), "and all who seek you with a sincere heart" (EP IV). Even more, the Church has care for the whole world, praying that "this Sacrifice . . . [might] advance the peace and salvation of all the world" (EP III). In times of tragedy such as terrorist attacks and school shootings this petition has particular resonance and poignancy. We are daily reminded of the need to ask our merciful Father to gather to himself all his "children scattered throughout the world" (EP III).

The intercessions are also offered for the dead, and here again the Church's care and concern is wide. Petition is made for "our departed brothers and sisters" (EP III), "all who have died in your mercy" (EP II), "and all the dead, whose faith you alone have known" (EP IV). The desire of Christ's Body on earth is that they would be granted "kind admittance to your kingdom" (EP III), "a place of refreshment, light and peace" (EP I), and welcomed "into the light of your face" (EP II). St. Cyril of Jerusalem described the efficacy of the Church's prayer for the dead: "By offering to God our supplications for those who have fallen asleep, if they have sinned, we . . . offer Christ sacrificed for the sins of all, and so render favorable, for them and for us, the God who loves man" (CCC, 1371).

The intercessions reveal another facet of the Church's union with her head, for Christ "lives forever to make intercession" (Heb 7:25), a permanent exercise of his priesthood (CCC, 662), in which we participate through Baptism. All the members of Christ's body, "living and dead . . . are called to participate in the redemption and salvation purchased by the Body and Blood of Christ" (GIRM, 79g). The intercessions, offered in union with Christ's unceasing prayer, express our union with and care for the Church triumphant, militant, and being purified, for the world and all of creation.

The Doxology

The Eucharistic Prayer concludes with the doxology. The priest raises the chalice and paten and gives "all glory and honor" to "God, almighty Father," through, with and in Christ, "in the unity of the Holy Spirit . . . for ever and ever (RM, EP I, 98)." The gesture accompanying these words "vividly expresses the true nature of the Eucharistic sacrifice as the offering of the Church through Christ the High Priest; with Christ, who is really present in the Church; and in Christ, who has incorporated his people into himself by the action of the Holy Spirit" (IOM, 124). The early Church Fathers emphasized that the people's "Amen" is a "confirmation of all that has been proclaimed on their behalf by the priest" (IOM, 123). The importance of their assent is better signified when it is "sung or spoken vigorously" or prolonged or repeated in musical settings (IOM, 124). In this assent, "the People of God look in faith and hope towards the eschatological end, when Christ 'will deliver the kingdom to God the Father . . . so that God may be everything to everyone' (1 Cor 15:24, 28)" (DD, 42).

The Communion Rite

We now come to the Communion Rite, the Paschal Banquet. It begins with the Lord's Prayer, which has been part of the Mass since the late fourth century.[23] The Church Fathers interpreted the petition for "our daily bread" as a reference to the Eucharist. The word translated "daily" —*epiousios* in Greek—"refers directly to the Bread of Life, the Body of Christ . . . without which we have no life within us" (CCC, 2837). St. Ambrose described it as "'super substantial' . . . not bread that passes into the body. It is, rather, the 'bread of eternal life' (see Jn 6:35–58), which supports the substance of our soul. . . . Take daily what will help you daily. And live so that you deserve to receive it daily."[24]

The petition for the forgiveness of sins has also been given special emphasis in the context of the Mass. St. Augustine explained its placement just before the reception of communion: "Why is it spoken before the reception of Christ's Body and Blood? For the following reason: If perchance, in consequence of human frailty, our thought seized on something indecent, if our tongue spoke something unjust, if our eye was turned to something unseemly, if our ear listened complacently to something unnecessary . . . it is blotted out by the Lord's Prayer in the passage: Forgive us our debts, so that we may approach in peace and so that we may not eat or drink what we receive unto judgment."[25] This petition highlights the importance of coming to the sacrament in a state of grace and receiving the Eucharist with the right disposition so that "what is holy may in truth be given to the holy" (GIRM, 81). The Rite of Peace continues the assembly's preparation for the communion. The priest—now addressing Christ rather than the Father—recounts Christ's gift of peace to his disciples on the night of his betrayal: "Peace I leave you, my peace I give you" (RM, Order of Mass, 126; from Jn 14:27). He then asks Christ to grant his Church "peace and unity in accordance with your

23. Emminghaus, *The Eucharist*, 192.

24. Scott Hahn and Mike Aquilina, *Living the Mysteries: A Guide for Unfinished Christians* (Huntington, IN: Our Sunday Visitor, 2003), 161.

25. Jungmann, *The Mass*, vol. 2, 283–284.

will" (RM, Order of Mass, 126). This is followed by another dialogue between the priest and the assembly in which the priest invokes the peace of the Lord upon them and they reply, "And with your spirit."

The priest (or deacon) invites the people to offer each other a sign of peace, which the early Church "described as a 'seal' placed on prayer" (IOM, 127). Peace in the biblical sense "includes total well-being, a life in harmony with God and with ourselves, with our neighbors, and with the whole of creation. Such peace can only be the pure gift of God. It is won for us by the risen Christ present in the midst of those gathered, and so it is the peace of Christ that is exchanged" (IOM, 128). It is also an acknowledgement that Christ is present in each person present and that communion with Christ cannot be separated from communion with our neighbors. "The rite of peace is not an expression merely of human solidarity or good will; it is, rather, an opening of ourselves and our neighbors to a challenge and a gift from beyond ourselves. Like the 'Amen' at Communion, the exchange of peace is the acceptance of a challenge: a gesture expressing the belief that we are members, one with another, in the body of Christ" (IOM, 129).

The final action before Communion is the Fraction Rite, during which the priest breaks the Eucharistic bread. This characteristic action of Christ at the feeding of the multitude, at the Last Supper, and at his meals with the disciples after his resurrection in the days of the Apostles gave its name to the entire celebration of the Eucharist" (IOM, 130). What may appear to be merely a functional action is in reality a "most powerful symbol" in which "the *natural, the practical, the symbolic, and the spiritual* are all inextricably linked. . . . Just as many grains of wheat are ground, kneaded, and baked together to become one loaf, which is then broken and shared out among many to bring them into one table-fellowship, so those gathered are made one body in the one bread of life that is Christ (see 1 Cor 10:17)" (IOM, 130, italics added).

As part of the Fraction Rite the priest breaks off a small piece of the host and places it in the chalice while saying, "May this mingling of the Body and Blood of our Lord Jesus Christ bring eternal life to us who receive it" (RM, Order of Mass, 129). The words and actions together "signify the unity of the Body and Blood of the Lord in the work of salvation, namely, the Body of Jesus Christ, living and glorious" (GIRM, 83). The Fraction Rite is accompanied by the *Agnus Dei* (*Lamb of God*), a prayer addressed to Christ—now substantially present on the altar—for mercy and peace. The words are taken from John the Baptist's identification of Jesus as the Lamb of God (Jn 1:29) combined with Revelation 5:6 and 13:8. It "may be repeated as many times as necessary until the rite has been completed" (GIRM, 83).

Activity

Explain the different aspects of the Fraction Rite:

1. Natural
2. Practical
3. Symbolic
4. Spiritual

Communion

The priest prepares himself to receive the Body and Blood of Christ by quietly reciting one of two prayers "so that he may fruitfully receive the Body and Blood of Christ. The faithful do the same, praying silently" (GIRM, 84). The priest genuflects then shows the faithful the Body of Christ, holding it over the chalice or paten, "and invites them to the banquet of Christ" (GIRM, 84). The people "respond with the humility of the centurion (see Mt 8:9)" (IOM, 133), confessing their unworthiness and Christ's power to "only say the word" and heal their soul (RM, Order of Mass, 132). "The saving efficacy of the sacrifice is fully realized when the Lord's body and blood are received in communion. The Eucharistic Sacrifice is intrinsically directed to the inward union of the faithful with Christ through communion; we receive the very One who offered himself for us, we receive his body which he gave up for us on the Cross and his blood which he 'poured out for many for the forgiveness of sins' (Mt 26:28)" (EE, 16).

While the priest is receiving Communion the Communion Chant is begun. This is an important liturgical sign, for it expresses "the spiritual union of the communicants by means of the unity of their voices, to show gladness of heart, and to bring out more clearly the 'communitarian' character of the procession to receive the Eucharist" (GIRM, 86).

Although not required, nor always possible, the Communion procession "should be the normal arrangement for both practical and symbolic reasons. It expresses the humble patience of the poor moving forward to be fed, the alert expectancy of God's people sharing the paschal meal in readiness for their journey, the joyful confidence of God's people on the march toward the promised land" (IOM, 135). When permitted, it is desirable for the faithful to receive both the Body and the Blood, since "this clearer form of the sacramental sign offers a particular opportunity for understanding more deeply the mystery in which the faithful participate" (GIRM, 14; cf. SC, 55). Receiving the Blood of Christ is a sharing in the sign of the new covenant (see Lk 22:20), a foretaste of the heavenly banquet (see Mt 26:29), a sign of participation in the suffering Christ (see Mk 10:38–39)" (IOM, 134).

The reception of Communion is a moment of encounter with Jesus. St. Francis of Assisi described this sacramental encounter thus: "That the Lord of the universe, God and Son of God, so humbles Himself that for our salvation He hides Himself under the little form of bread! Look, brothers, at the humility of God and pour out your hearts before Him! . . . Therefore, hold back nothing of yourselves so that He Who gives Himself totally to you may receive you totally."[26] St. Catherine of Siena recorded these words spoken to her by the Lord: "You could receive no greater gift than that I should give you myself, wholly God and wholly human, as your food."[27] Since Communion is an encounter with the living Christ, those distributing the Eucharist should "make every effort to ensure that this simple act preserves its importance as a personal encounter with the Lord Jesus in the sacrament" (SacCar, 50).

The "Amen" is said by the communicant as an expression of faith and action. "Not without reason do you say 'Amen,'" wrote St. Ambrose, "for you acknowledge in your heart that you are receiving the body of Christ. When you present yourself, the priest says to you, 'The body of Christ,' and you reply 'Amen,' that is, 'It is so.' Let the heart persevere in what the tongue confesses."[28] St. Augustine described the "Amen" as our affidavit: "If you are the body and members of

---

26. *Francis and Clare: The Complete Works*, trans. Regis J. Armstrong, OFM CAP, and Ignatius C. Brady, OFM (New York: Paulist, 1982), 50.

27. Catherine of Siena, *The Dialogue*, trans. Suzanne Noffke, OP (Mahwah, NJ: Paulist Press, 1980), 216.

28. Cabié, *The Eucharist*, 118.

Christ, then what is laid on the Lord's table is the sacrament (*mysterium*) of what you yourselves are, and it is the sacrament of what you are that you receive. It is to what you yourselves are that you answer 'Amen,' and this answer is your affidavit. Be a member of Christ's body, so that your 'Amen' may be authentic."[29] We see in this rite a beautiful example of the harmony of liturgical signs—word, movement, song, and gesture—together manifesting the mystery of our union with the Trinity through the Body and Blood of Christ.

This encounter with the Eucharistic Christ imparts to us the power of the risen Lord. St. John Chrysostom expressed this power in striking language and imagery. "This blood, if rightly taken, drives away devils, and keeps them afar off from us, while it calls to us Angels and the Lord of Angels. For wherever they see the Lord's blood, devils flee, and Angels run together."[30] On another occasion he said, "If you show the evil one your tongue moistened with the precious Blood, he will not be able to resist it; if you show him your mouth tinged with red, he will shun you like a frightened beast. Do you want to know the power of this Blood? Then just see where it came from and where its source was—the cross and the Lord's side."[31] He concludes, "Let us then return from that table like lions breathing fire, having become terrible to the devil; thinking on our Head, and on the love which He has shown for us."[32] Receiving the Lord in Communion is an encounter of immense tenderness and profound power.

When the distribution of Communion has been completed, all may "pray quietly for some time" (GIRM, 88). Silence is a necessary part of the Mass and is especially necessary after Communion, for here especially "we need a time of silence . . . in which we converse quite personally with the Lord, who is with us."[33] Silence can be uncomfortable, and so we may need to "learn anew . . . the silent time at one with the Lord, abandoning ourselves to him."[34] Then the priest says the final presidential prayer, "the Prayer after Communion, in which he

29. Cabié, *The Eucharist*, 118.

30. John Chrysostom, *Homily 46 on the Gospel of John,* http://www.newadvent.org/fathers/240146.htm.

31. Cantalamessa, *Eucharist*, 40.

32. John Chrysostom, *Homily 46 on the Gospel of John*.

33. Ratzinger, *God Is Near Us*, 82.

34. Ibid.

prays for the fruits of the mystery just celebrated" (GIRM, 89). This prayer completes "the prayer of the People of God" and concludes the Communion Rite (GIRM, 89).

The Concluding Rites

The celebration closes with a simple rite: announcements, the priest's greeting and blessing, the dismissal (given by the priest or deacon), and the kissing of the altar by the priest and deacon, followed by a profound bow to the altar (or genuflection if the tabernacle is located in the sanctuary) by the priest, deacon, and other ministers. The priest's blessing can be simple or "expanded and expressed by the Prayer over the People or another more solemn formula" (GIRM, 90). The dismissal expresses "the missionary nature of the Church" (SacCar, 51) and sends forth the people of God "so that each may go back to doing good works, praising and blessing God" (GIRM, 90). The purpose of all these concluding rites "is to send the people forth to put into effect in their daily lives the Paschal Mystery and unity in Christ that they have celebrated. They are given a sense of abiding mission that calls them to witness to Christ in the world and to bring the Gospel to the poor" (IOM, 141).

Conclusion

"The celebration of the Eucharist, like the entire liturgy, is carried out by means of perceptible signs by which the faith is nourished, strengthened, and expressed" (GIRM, 20). Signs that express our faith include standing to hear Christ speak to us in the Gospel, sitting to hear his word applied to our lives today, solemnly processing and reverently bowing to receive the Body of Christ, kneeling in prayer, invoking his power through the sign of his cross, and acknowledging his real presence with a fervent "Amen." Signs of the nourishment we receive include the two tables, altar and ambo, the Book of the Gospels, and preeminently bread and wine now transformed into Christ's Body and Blood. Signs of our strengthened faith include a profession of faith that draws us more deeply into the life of the Trinity, a reverent and prayerful silence after sacramental Communion, and standing "at the ready" for the dismissal to be sent on mission into the world. Through these signs we experience the propulsive power of the Mass, from our humble acknowledgement of sin to Christ's proclamation of his Gospel to his substantial presence on the altar and finally to his gift of himself to us in sacramental Communion—through humble and simple signs we enter into and are transformed by "the liturgy's inner dynamism."[35]

Activity

Review how the following ritual elements are opportunities for active participation during the Mass:

1. The silence before the opening prayer
2. Silence between the readings and after the homily
3. The Prayers of the Faithful
4. The procession with the offerings
5. The oblation following the Consecration
6. Prayer after Communion

35. Ratzinger, *Feast of Faith* (San Francisco: Ignatius, 1986), 139.

Chapter 12

The Eucharist: Living the Sacrament

In sacramental Communion we receive the whole Christ, body and blood, soul and divinity, and so "share in the divine nature" (2 Pt 1:4). Pope Benedict XVI comments on St. Augustine's powerful description of this sharing in the divine nature. "Stressing the mysterious nature of this food, Augustine imagines the Lord saying to him: 'I am the food of grown men; grow, and you shall feed upon me; nor shall you change me, like the food of your flesh, into yourself, but you shall be changed into me.' It is not the eucharistic food that is changed into us, but rather we who are mysteriously transformed by it. Christ nourishes us by uniting us to himself; 'he draws us into himself'" (SacCar 70). This transforming union with Christ is the "principal fruit" of Eucharistic Communion (CCC, 1391), and from it flow all of the other effects of this sacrament. It is the most powerful help in our struggle against sin, since "the Eucharist cannot unite us to Christ without at the same time cleansing us from past sins and preserving us from future sins" (CCC, 1393). It is also the principal means for building and strengthening the Church, for union with Christ also means union with his Body, the Church (CCC, 1396). Increasingly conformed to Christ, we increasingly share his care and concern for the poor. We also experience within ourselves his desire that all Christians "may all be one, as you, Father, are in me and I in you" (Jn 17:21). Finally, in receiving the Body and Blood of the risen, ascended and glorified Lord, we receive the pledge of our future glory.

We will now consider each of these effects in detail. Since our approach in this book is "rite-based," in this chapter we will look particularly at two of the presidential prayers, the Prayer over the Offerings, which anticipates the effects of communion with the Body and Blood of Christ, and the Prayer after Communion, a prayer "for the fruits of the mystery just celebrated" (GIRM, 89). In these prayers we hear the Bride (the Church) addressing the Father through her Bridegroom (Christ) in the Holy Spirit.

The Eucharist Augments Our Union with Christ and the Trinity

In his Bread of Life Discourse Jesus told his disciples, "Just as the living Father sent me and I have life because of the Father, so also the one who feeds on me will have life because of me" (Jn 6:57). In his commentary on this verse St. Augustine said, "When Christ is eaten, life is eaten. . . . When he is eaten, he nourishes without diminishing. . . . Let Christ be eaten; when eaten he lives because when slain he rose again."[1] This union with Christ, though, must be understood in its relationship to Baptism. "Incorporation into Christ, which is brought about by Baptism, is constantly renewed and consolidated by sharing in the Eucharistic Sacrifice, especially by that full sharing which takes place in sacramental communion" (EE, 22). The life of grace that we received at Baptism is preserved, increased and renewed through communion "with the flesh of the risen Christ, a flesh 'given life and giving life through the Holy Spirit'" (CCC, 1392). Sacramental Communion is a reciprocal encounter with Christ: "We can say not only that *each of us receives Christ*, but also that *Christ receives each of us*. He enters into friendship with us: 'You are my friends' (Jn 15:14). Indeed, it is because of him that we have life: 'He who eats me will live because of me' (Jn 6:57)" (EE, 22).

The intimate union with Christ brought about by sacramental Communion is at the same time union with the Trinity. In his commentary on John 6:57, St. Hilary of Poitiers asks: "Must not Christ naturally have the Father within himself according to the Spirit since he himself lives through the Father?"[2] St. Maria Faustina Kowalska, whom God called the secretary of his mercy[3], wrote in her diary, "Once after Holy Communion, I heard these words: You are Our dwelling place. At that moment, I felt in my soul the presence of the Holy Trinity, the Father, the Son, and the Holy Spirit. I felt that I was the temple of God. I felt I was a child of the Father."[4] The liturgy itself affirms the Trinitarian dimension of Communion. In the Communion Epiclesis we address the Father and proclaim that we "are nourished by the Body

1. Elowsky, *John 1–10*, 242.

2. Ibid.

3. Maria Faustina Kowalska, *Diary* (Stockbridge, MA; Marian Press, 2012), 965, 1160, 1275, 1605, 1784.

4. Kowalska, *Diary*, 451.

and Blood of your Son and filled with his Holy Spirit" (Eucharistic Prayer III).

The presidential prayers are fervent petitions for this transforming union.

> Grant us, almighty God,
> that we may be refreshed and nourished
> by the Sacrament which we have received,
> so as to be transformed into what we consume.
> Through Christ our Lord.
> (Prayer after Communion for the Twenty-Seventh Sunday in Ordinary Time)

A second example also links the actions of nourishment and transformation, praying that

> we, who by Christ are nourished,
> into Christ may be transformed.
> (Prayer after Communion for the Dedication of an Altar)

Another example alludes to the Incarnation, asking

> grant, we pray, that we may be inwardly transformed
> through him whom we recognize as outwardly like ourselves.
> (Collect for Tuesday after Epiphany)

A final example gives voice to the soul's desire to be always united to her beloved, praying that

> that those to whom you give the joy
> of participating in divine mysteries
> may never be parted from you.
> (Prayer after Communion for the Thirty-Fourth Sunday in Ordinary Time)

The petition to "never be parted from you" echoes a petition from one of the priest's prayers in preparation for Communion:

> keep me always faithful to your commandments,
> and never let me be parted from you.
> (RM, Order of Mass, 131)

Let us conclude by listening to the words of Nicholas Cabasilas a distinguished fifteenth-century writer from the Byzantine tradition who marveled at this mystery.

> What a thing it is for Christ's mind to be mingled with ours, our will to be blended with His, our body with His Body and our blood with His Blood! What is our mind when the divine mind obtains control? What is our will when that blessed will has overcome it? What is our dust when it has been overpowered by His fire?[5]

The Eucharist Strengthens Us in Our Struggle against Sin

In Holy Communion we receive Christ's body which he said was "given up for you" and his blood which he "poured out . . . for the forgiveness of sins" (RM, Order of Mass, 89–90). This union with Christ separates us from sin by "cleansing us from past sins and preserving us from future sins" (CCC, 1393). St. Ambrose asserted his faith in the cleansing and preserving power of Christ's body and blood.

> For as often as we eat this bread and drink the cup, we proclaim the death of the Lord. If we proclaim the Lord's death, we proclaim the forgiveness of sins. If, as often as his blood is poured out, it is poured for the forgiveness of sins, I should always receive it, so that it may always forgive my sins. Because I always sin, I should always have a remedy. (St. Ambrose, *De Sacr.* 4, 6, 28: PL16, 446, in CCC, 1393; cf. 1 Cor 11:26)

In the Mass we express our need to rely on the Lord's mercy as did St. Ambrose.

> We implore your mercy, Lord,
> that this divine sustenance
> may cleanse us of our faults.
> (Prayer after Communion for Wednesday of the first week of Advent)

Forgiveness and cleansing are the gracious gift of God, to which we appeal, asking that

> through the purifying action of your grace,
> we may be cleansed by the very mysteries we serve.
> (Prayer over the Offerings for December 22)

5. Nicholas Cabasilas, *The Life in Christ*, trans. Carmino J. deCatanzaro (Crestwood, NY: St. Vladimir's Seminary Press, 1998), 116.

It is the gift of Christ who, though rich, became poor so that we might become rich (2 Cor 8:9), as we particularly acknowledge at Advent:

> through the purifying action of your grace,
> we may be cleansed by the very mysteries we serve.
> (Collect for Tuesday of the third week of Advent)

Finally, our liturgical prayer recognizes that we need cleansing not only from individual sins but also from sinful habits and patterns of life—"our old ways"—and this is the first step in our transformation:

> We pray, O Lord,
> that the reverent reception of the Sacrament of your Son
> may cleanse us from our old ways
> and transform us into a new creation.
> (Prayer after Communion for Wednesday
> within the Octave of Easter)

St. Bede, in a commentary on Christ's priesthood in the order of Melchizedek (Heb 7:17), draws together Christ's Paschal Mystery, its application in the Sacrament of Baptism, and its re-presentation in the Eucharist.

> Not only did he wash away our sins in his blood when he gave his blood for us on the cross, or when each of us was cleansed in his baptism by the mystery of his most sacred passion. But he also takes away every day the sins of the world and washes us of our daily sins in his blood, when the memory of his blessed passion is reenacted on the altar, when a created thing, bread and wine, is transformed by the ineffable sanctification of the Spirit into the sacrament of his flesh and blood. Thus his body and blood is not poured forth and slain by the hands of the unfaithful to their own ruin, but he is taken by the mouth of the faithful to their salvation.[6]

Christ continues to wash away our venial sins through the memorial of his Paschal sacrifice.

In the same way that food nourishes our physical strength, "the Eucharist strengthens our charity, which tends to be weakened in daily life" (CCC, 1394). This strengthening of charity—"by which we love God above things for his own sake, and our neighbor as ourselves for the love of God" (CCC, 1822)—"*wipes away venial sins* . . . [and] revives

6. Heen and Krey, *Hebrews*, 115.

our love" (CCC, 1394).[7] St. Fulgentius of Ruspe described Christ's gift of love in the Eucharist this way:

> Since Christ died for us out of love, when we celebrate the memorial of his death at the moment of sacrifice we ask that love may be granted to us by the coming of the Holy Spirit. We humbly pray that in the strength of this love by which Christ willed to die for us, we, by receiving the gift of the Holy Spirit, may be able to consider the world as crucified for us, and to be ourselves as crucified to the world. . . . Having received the gift of love, let us die to sin and live for God. (CCC, 1394)

Holy Communion enables us to love with the love with which Christ loved us (Jn 15:9).

The liturgy itself describes the Eucharist as "this bread from the heavenly table . . . the food of charity" (Prayer after Communion for the Twenty-Second Sunday in Ordinary Time). In offering the bread and wine we pray that it "may be an acceptable oblation to you and lead us to grow in charity." (Prayer over the Offerings for the Tenth Sunday in Ordinary Time) This is also a prayer following our reception of the Body and Blood of Christ:

> We have partaken of the gifts of this sacred mystery,
> humbly imploring, O Lord,
> that what your Son commanded us to do
> in memory of him
> may bring us growth in charity.
> (Prayer after Communion for the Thirty-Third Sunday
> in Ordinary Time)

God is love, and through the Eucharist he reorders our disordered love.

Furthermore, receiving the sacrament of Christ's love strengthens us, in the words of St. Fulgentius, to "die to sin and live for God"—in other words, "to break our disordered attachments to creatures and root ourselves in him" (Fulgentius of Ruspe, *Contra Fa.*, 28, 16–19: CCL 19A, 813–814, in CCC, 1394). In the liturgy we pray for freedom from our disordered attachments. In offering the gifts to God we ask that he would "by this holy exchange undo the bonds of our sins" (Prayer over the Offerings for Wednesday of the second week of Lent). In language of humble self-awareness we ask that God would, "even when our wills

---

7. Venial sin is the result of "daily weakness" and a failure to gain "the full freedom of the children of God" (RP, 7)—it wounds but "does not destroy the divine life in the soul" (CCC, glossary).

are defiant, constrain them mercifully to turn to you" (Prayer over the Offerings for Saturday of the fourth week of Lent). The liturgy also acknowledges our inclination to sin (concupiscence), asking that God might "both pardon our offenses and direct our wavering hearts" (Prayer over the Offerings for Tuesday of the fifth week of Lent). We come to Mass aware of our defiant wills and wavering hearts, but confident of God's power and compassion to free us and forgive us.

Finally, the charity that the Eucharist imparts to us also "*preserves us from future mortal sins*" (CCC, 1395, italics in original).[8] This effect is expressed in different ways in the liturgy. We offer God the gifts of bread and wine with faith "that, when consumed by those who believe, they may bring ever greater holiness" (Prayer over the Offerings for the Fifteenth Sunday in Ordinary Time). We present the gifts to Him who always gives abundantly: "May these sacrificial offerings . . . become . . . for us a holy outpouring of your mercy" (Prayer over the Offerings for the Thirty-First Sunday in Ordinary Time). Having received communion, we ask the Lord to "pour into our hearts the strength of this saving food" (Prayer after Communion for Thursday after the Second Sunday of Easter). Another Prayer after Communion speaks of cleansing and strengthening: "May the mysteries we have received . . . bring us heavenly medicine, that they may purge all evil from our heart and strengthen us with eternal protection" (Wednesday of the fifth week of Lent). We pray with confidence in the power of Christ's Body and Blood, asking that "by the power of these holy mysteries, our life may be constantly sustained" (Prayer over the Offerings for December 29). This too is a fruit of Christ's transforming union with us in Communion, for "the more we share the life of Christ and progress in his friendship, the more difficult it is to break away from him by mortal sin" (CCC, 1395).

When we consume Christ and he changes us into himself, he brings about within us a profound moral transformation. "By sharing in the sacrifice of the Cross," says St. John Paul II, "the Christian partakes of Christ's self-giving love and is equipped to live this same charity in all this thoughts and deeds" (VS, 107). This love is accompanied by joy and freedom. Pope Benedict XVI writes, "It is above all else the joy-filled discovery of love at work in the hearts of those who accept the

8. "The Eucharist is not ordered to the forgiveness of mortal sins—that is proper to the sacrament of Reconciliation. The Eucharist is properly the sacrament of those who are in full communion with the Church" (CCC, 1395).

Lord's gift, abandon themselves to him, and thus find true freedom. The moral transformation implicit in the new worship instituted by Christ is a heartfelt yearning to respond to the Lord's love with one's whole being, while remaining ever conscious of one's own weakness" (SacCar, 82). A transformation that equips us to live a life of joyful self-giving is an effect that we pray for at Mass, that "the renewal constantly at work with us may be the cause of our unending joy" (Prayer over the Offerings, Saturday within the Octave Easter).

The Eucharist Makes the Church

Union with Christ in the Eucharist means union with his body, the Church. In the Bread of Life discourse Jesus "proclaimed a mysterious and real communion between his own body and ours: 'He who eats my flesh and drinks my blood abides in me, and I in him' [Jn 6:56]" (CCC, 787). St. Joan of Arc's reply at her trial "sums up the faith of the holy doctors and the good sense of the believer: 'About Jesus Christ and the Church, I simply know they're just one thing, and we shouldn't complicate the matter'" (CCC, 795).

The believer is incorporated into the Church by Baptism, but "communion renews, strengthens, and deepens this incorporation" (CCC, 1396). Baptism and the Eucharist constitute the call and fulfillment to form the one body of Christ, the Church. "In Baptism we have been called to form but one body. The Eucharist fulfills this call: 'The cup of blessing which we bless, is it not a participation in the blood of Christ? the bread which we break, is it not a participation in the body of Christ? Because there is one bread, we who are many are one body, for we all partake of the one bread' [1 Cor 10:16–17]" (CCC, 1396). What the Eucharist brings about

> is the uniting of Christians, bringing them from their state of separation into the unity of the one Bread and the one Body. The Eucharist . . . is the living process through which, time and again, the Church's activity of becoming the Church takes place. The church . . . is not just a people: out of the many peoples of which she consists there is arising *one* people, through the *one* table that the Lord has spread for us all. The Church is . . . united, ever and again, through the *one* Body we all receive.[9]

9. Ratzinger, *God Is Near Us*, 114–115.

The deepening of our membership in the Church through participation in the Body and Blood of Christ is an effect that we pray for at Mass. A Prayer after Communion explicitly makes the connection: "We pray . . . that we may always be counted among the members of Christ, in whose Body and Blood we have communion" (Prayer after Communion for the Fifth Sunday of Lent). Furthermore, this membership is a unity of heart and mind, for which we pray, "Make those you have nourished by this one heavenly Bread one in mind and heart" (Prayer after Communion for the second week of Ordinary Time). St. John Paul II emphasized the power of the Eucharist to bring about unity of heart and mind. "The seeds of disunity, which daily experience shows to be so deeply rooted in humanity as a result of sin, are countered by *the unifying power* of the body of Christ. The Eucharist, precisely by building up the Church, creates human community" (EE, 24; italics original). Only the Lord, through the gift of his Body and Blood, can grant that "by partaking of the sacred mystery, we may be faithfully united in mind and heart" (Prayer over the Offerings for the Twenty-Third Sunday in Ordinary Time). The Church never ceases to ask the Father that "we, who are nourished by the Body and Blood of our Son and filled with his Holy Spirit, may become one body, one spirit in Christ" (EP III).

The Eucharist and the Unity of Christians

Our union with Christ through our participation in his Body and Blood means that we come to love what he loves and to desire what he desires. And one of the things he ardently desires is the unity of all Christians. On the night of his arrest he prayed that his disciples "may all be one, as you, Father, are in me and I in you, that they also may be in us, that the world may believe that you sent me" (Jn 17:21). This unity is a mystery of abiding in the Trinity, as Jesus' prayer makes clear: "I in them and You in me, that they may be brought to perfection as one" (Jn 17:23). On this topic the *Catechism* quotes St. Augustine's description of the Eucharist: *"O sacrament of devotion! O sign of unity! O bond of charity!"* (CCC, 1398). Our experience "of the divisions in the Church which break the common participation in the table of the Lord" lends ever greater urgency to our prayers for unity (CCC, 1398).

The prayers of the liturgy affirm our belief in the power of the Eucharist to bring about the unity of all Christians. In the Prayer after Communion for the Votive Mass of the Most Holy Eucharist we pray:

> sanctify us, Lord, we pray,
> so that through the Body and Blood of Christ
> the whole family of believers may be bound together.

And in the Mass for the Unity of Christians we ask that the Lord, in his kindness, would

> make those who believe in you one in mind and heart
> by the power of this sacrifice.
> (Prayer after Communion, Unity of Christians B)

"Union with Christ," wrote Pope Benedict XVI, "is also union with all those to whom he gives himself. I cannot possess Christ just for myself; I can belong to him only in union with all those who have become, or who will become, his own. Communion draws me out of myself towards him, and thus also towards unity with all Christians. We become 'one body,' completely joined in a single existence" (DCE, 14). Christ's desire for the unity of all believers is also included in the Church's petition to the Father to "gather to yourself all your children scattered throughout the world" (Eucharistic Prayer III).

The Eucharist and the World

Jesus' messianic mission impelled him to go to those who were on the fringes of society. When he was dining at the home of Levi with a large crowd that included tax collectors, the Pharisees "complained to his disciples, saying, 'Why do you eat and drink with tax collectors and sinners?'" (Lk 5:29–30). On another occasion, Jesus himself acknowledged that one of the criticisms leveled at him was that he was "a friend of tax collectors and sinners" (Mt 11:19). In the Bread of Life discourse, he said, "The bread that I will give is my flesh for the life of the world" (Jn 6:51), words that Pope Benedict XVI says "reveal his deep compassion for every man and woman. . . . Each celebration of the Eucharist makes sacramentally present the gift that the crucified Lord made of his life, for us and for the whole world. In the Eucharist Jesus also makes us witnesses of God's compassion toward all our brothers and sisters" (SacCar, 88).

The transforming power of the Eucharist is especially evident in this "service of charity," a service that "consists in the very fact that, in God and with God, I love even the person whom I do not like or even know" (SacCar, 88). How is this possible? It is possible only because of "an intimate encounter with God, an encounter which has become a communion of will, affecting even my feelings. Then I learn to look on this other person not simply with my eyes and my feelings, but from the perspective of Jesus Christ" (DCE, 18). This is the result of "a transfigured existence and a commitment to transforming the world in accordance with the Gospel" (EE, 20). It is the mark of a life that has become "in a certain way completely 'Eucharistic'" (EE, 20). In this sense, the Eucharist becomes "the school of active love for neighbor" (DC, 6) and "a great school of peace, forming men and women who, at various levels of responsibility in social, cultural and political life, can become promoters of dialogue and communion" (MND, 27). So vital is this aspect of the Eucharist that St. John Paul II said that "our concern for those in need . . . will be the criterion by which the authenticity of our Eucharistic celebrations is judged" (MND, 28).

Participation in the Eucharist "increases, rather than lessens, *our sense of responsibility for the world today*" (EE, 20, italics in original). In noting the numerous problems that "darken the horizon of our time," St. John Paul II noted particularly "the urgent need to work for peace, to base relationships between peoples on solid premises of justice and solidarity, and to defend human life from contraception to its natural end" (EE, 20). His successor, Pope Benedict XVI, insisted that "all who partake of the Eucharist must commit themselves to peacemaking in our world scarred by violence and war and, today in particular, by terrorism, economic corruption, and sexual exploitation" (SacCar, 89). In addition, Christ, the bread of life, "spurs us to be mindful of the situations of extreme poverty in which a great part of humanity still lives" (SacCar, 90). The school of the Eucharist "obliges us to do everything possible . . . to end or at least reduce the scandal of hunger and malnutrition" (SacCar, 91). Similarly, the liturgy teaches us "to see the world as God's creation . . . part of God's good plan . . . [and] commits us to working responsibly for the protection of creation" (SacCar, 92). These specific concerns suggest the comprehensive nature of the Church's prayer that the Eucharistic Sacrifice would "advance the peace and salvation of all the world" (EP III, 113).

After we have received the Body and Blood of Christ, we pray that the Eucharist would bear fruit in our lives for the salvation of the world. Jesus, "the face of the Father's mercy,"[10] nourishes us with his Body and Blood so that

> we may draw confidently from the wellsprings of mercy
> and show ourselves ever more compassionate
> towards our brothers and sisters.
> (Prayer after Communion for the Votive Mass
> of the Mercy of God)

After receiving "the food of charity," we pray that

> it may confirm our hearts
> and stir us to serve you in our neighbor.
> (Prayer after Communion for the Twenty-Second Sunday
> in Ordinary Time)

Finally, and quite simply, we ask that we may so "live that, made one in Christ, we may joyfully bear fruit for the salvation of the world" (Prayer after Communion for the Fifth Sunday in Ordinary Time).

The Eucharist Is the Pledge of the Glory to Come

Jesus promised his disciples, "Whoever who eats my flesh and drinks my blood has eternal life, and I will raise him up at the last day" (Jn 6:54). In his commentary on this verse, St. Irenaeus wrote, "For as the bread that is produced from the earth, when it receives the invocation of God, is no longer common bread but the Eucharist, consisting of two realities, earthly and heavenly, so also our bodies when they receive the Eucharist are no longer corruptible, having the hope of the resurrection to eternity."[11] In the Eucharist we receive a pledge of eternal life that "comes from the fact that the flesh of the Son of man, given as food, is his body in its glorious state after the resurrection" (EE, 18). In the Eucharist, it is not the earthly body and blood of Christ that we receive, it is the glorified body and blood of the resurrected Christ in all of its mystery and power.

---

10. Pope Francis, *Misericordiae Vultus,* Bull of Indiction of the Extraordinary Jubilee of Mercy, 1.

11. Elowsky, *John 1–10,* 240.

Our experience of the Eucharist as a pledge of future glory is also a fruit of our abiding in Christ through sacramental communion, for it "*enables us to have a certain foretaste of heaven on earth*" (MND, 19, italics original). This corresponds to the deepest human desire. "Is this not the greatest of human yearnings?" asks St. John Paul II. "God has place in human hearts a 'hunger' for his word (cf. Am 8:11), a hunger which will be satisfied only by full union with him. Eucharistic communion was given so that we might be 'sated' with God here on earth, in expectation of our complete fulfilment in heaven" (MND, 19). For this reason, we pray that those who receive the Body and Blood of Christ "may be filled with every grace and heavenly blessing" (EP I, 94). Although "sated" by the gift of Christ in communion, we are still "straining toward the goal" (EE, 18) and

> There we hope to enjoy for ever the fullness of your glory,
> when you will wipe away every tear from our eyes.
> For seeing you, our God, as you are,
> we shall be like you for all the ages
> and praise you without end. (EP III, Masses for the Dead)

The prayers of the liturgy give voice to the different aspects of the eucharistic pledge of future glory. They tell us that the Eucharist is "our sure pledge of redemption" (Prayer after Communion for the Twelfth Sunday in Ordinary Time) and "the pledge of immortality" (Prayer after Communion for Wednesday of the second week of Lent). But "this pledge of eternal salvation" also implies a responsibility on our part, namely, "that we may set our course so well as to attain the redemption you promise" (Prayer after Communion for Friday of the second week of Lent). This recalls a saying from the Lord that St. Catherine of Siena recorded in *The Dialogue*: "I created you without your help, but I will not save you without your help."[12] This responsibility also brings an awareness of our frailty and weakness, and so we ask the Lord, "May the gifts we have received from your altar . . . kindle in our hearts a longing for the heavenly homeland and cause us to press forward, following in the Savior's footsteps, to the place where for our sake he entered before us" (Prayer after Communion for the Vigil of the Ascension of the Lord). Experience and humility teach us that longing and perseverance too are gifts from the Lord.

---

12. Catherine of Siena, *The Dialogue*, 226.

The liturgy invokes the images of banquet and pasture to express this eschatological aspect of the Eucharist. We know that what we experience in the Eucharist is a foretaste of the Lamb's Supper celebrated eternally in heaven, for we ask that "just as we are renewed by the Supper of your Son in this present age, so we may enjoy his banquet for all eternity" (Prayer after Communion for Holy Thursday, 167). Evoking the image of the Good Shepherd, prophesied in Ezekiel 34 and fulfilled in John 10, we ask the Lord to "be pleased to settle in eternal pastures the sheep you have redeemed by the Precious Blood of your Son" (Prayer after Communion for the Fourth Sunday of Easter, 264). Here is not our home (Phil 3:20), but the Eucharist gives us "a glimpse of heaven appearing on earth" (EE, 19), and this gives us hope that, "by participating in this mystery, we may possess at last the gifts we have awaited and for which our faith bids us hope" (Prayer over the Gifts for December 20).

Conclusion

In the Eucharist we receive the resurrected and glorified Christ, who is inseparable from the Father and the Holy Spirit. To use the language of the Gospel of John, taken up by St. John Paul II and the Church, we abide in him (Jn 6:56), and he, as St. Augustine so beautifully expressed, changes us into himself. In this transforming union we experience his forgiveness and his power to triumph over sin. Abiding in him also means abiding in his Body, the Church, and working with him for the unity of all Christians. We also abide in his care and concern for the poor, the marginalized, and all of creation. Finally, we abide in him who is now seated at the right hand of the Father in glory and who will come again to receive us into eternal glory.

St. John Paul II said that in Communion "we digest, as it were, the 'secret' of the resurrection" (EE, 18). Perhaps we can better appreciate the immensity of this "secret" by listening to Pope Francis' explanation of the power of the Resurrection.

> Christ's resurrection is not an event of the past; it contains a vital power which has permeated this world. . . . It is an irresistible force. Where all seems to be dead, signs of the resurrection suddenly spring up. Often it seems that God does not exist: all around us we see persistent injustice, evil, indifference and cruelty. But it is also true that in the midst of dark-

> ness something new always springs to life and sooner or later produces fruit. On razed land life breaks through, stubbornly yet invincibly. However dark things are, goodness always re-emerges and spreads. Each day in our world beauty is born anew, it rises transformed through the storms of history. . . . Such is the power of the resurrection. (EG, 276)

The "secret" of the Resurrection which we digest in the Eucharist is this "vital power" and "irresistible force" through which goodness and beauty re-appear in our lives, and through us, in the world.

A third image—to complement the images of "abiding" and the "secret" of the Resurrection—can help us appreciate the profound power of the Eucharist. Pope Benedict XVI describes the Eucharist as a kind of nuclear fission, as he explains:

> The substantial conversion of bread and wine into his body and blood introduces within creation the principle of a radical change, a sort of "nuclear fission," to use an image familiar to us today, which penetrates to the heart of all being, a change meant to set off a process which transforms reality, a process leading ultimately to the transfiguration of the entire world, to the point where God will be all in all (cf. 1 Cor 15:28). (SacCar, 11)

In the Eucharist we abide in Christ, we digest the "secret" of the Resurrection, and we participate in a spiritual "nuclear fission" that transforms all of reality.

Let us conclude with words of "Eucharistic amazement" (EE, 6):

> But when Christ dwell in us, what else is needed, or what benefit escapes us? When we dwell in Christ, what else will we desire? He dwells in us, and He is our dwelling place. How blessed are we by reason of this dwelling place, how blessed are we that we have become a dwelling for such a one as He! What good thing is lacking for those who are in such a state? What have they to do with wickedness who have entered into such brightness? What evil can withstand so great an abundance of good? What evil thing can continue to be present or enter from without when Christ is so evidently with us and completely penetrates and surrounds us? . . . The soul and the body and all their faculties forthwith become spiritual, for our souls, and our bodies and blood, are united with His. . . . O how great are the Mysteries![13]

13. Cabasilas, *The Life in Christ*, 115–116.

Conclusion

The three sacraments of initiation—Baptism, Confirmation, and the Eucharist— "form a single saving event—called 'Christian initiation'—in which we are inserted into Jesus Christ, who died and rose, and become new creatures and members of the Church."[1] Our participation in the divine life of the Trinity effected by the sacraments "bears a certain likeness to the origin, development, and nourishing of natural life. Born anew by Baptism, the faithful are strengthened by the Sacrament of Confirmation and finally are sustained by the food of eternal life in the Eucharist" (DCN). In the third century, Tertullian described this spiritual birth and maturation in terms that are still true today: "The flesh is washed, that the soul may be cleansed; the flesh is anointed, that the soul may be consecrated; the flesh is signed, that the soul too may be fortified; the flesh is overshadowed by the laying on of hands, that the soul too may be enlightened by the Spirit; the flesh is fed on the Body and Blood of Christ, that the soul too may be richly nourished by God" (DCN). Through the sacraments of initiation the Lord cleanses us, consecrates us, strengthens us, enlightens us, and nourishes us so that we may share more fully in the life of the Trinity and experience the fullness of joy that Christ promises us (Jn 15:11).

Let us now look briefly at how Baptism, Confirmation, and Eucharist together form one saving event. Baptism, the gateway to the sacraments, transforms us and sets us on the path to full union with the Trinity. Confirmation perfects this baptismal grace, which the Eucharist then "preserves, increases and renews . . . This growth in Christian life needs the nourishment of Eucharistic Communion, the bread for our pilgrimage until the moment of death, when it will be given to us as viaticum" (CCC, 1392). The unity of these three sacraments is manifested in several distinct ways. In Baptism we become God's adopted children, new creatures. Confirmation then configures us more fully to Christ through the sacramental seal or character and the seven gifts of the Holy Spirit. Eucharist deepens this union with Christ, for "the

1. Francis, General Audience, January 29, 2014, accessed May 27, 2015, http://m.vatican.va/content/francescomobile/en/audiences/2014/documents/papa-francesco_20140129_udienza-generale.html.

principle fruit of receiving the Eucharist in Holy Communion is an intimate union with Christ Jesus" (CCC, 1391). In a similar way, the sacraments of initiation unite me to Christ's Body, the Church. In Baptism we are incorporated into the Church, to which Confirmation binds us more perfectly. Eucharistic Communion unites us "to all the faithful in one body—the Church", renewing, strengthening and deepening the ecclesial communion "already achieved by Baptism" (CCC, 1396).

The sacraments of initiation also progressively deepen our fellowship with the Holy Spirit. The Holy Spirit is first conferred at Baptism, a relationship that is strengthened when we are sealed with the gift of the Spirit at Confirmation. In Eucharistic Communion we not only receive the Body and Blood of Christ but also his Spirit, as St. Ephrem explains: "He called the bread his living body and he filled it with himself and his Spirit. . . . He who eats it with faith, eats Fire and Spirit . . . Take and eat this, all of you, and eat with it the Holy Spirit" (EE, 17). "Thus," writes St. John Paul II, "by the gift of his body and blood Christ increases within us the gift of his Spirit, already poured out in Baptism and bestowed as a 'seal' in the sacrament of Confirmation" (EE, 17). This gift of the Lord's Body, Blood and Spirit in turn builds up the Church, an effect for which we pray in the Mass: "grant that we, who are nourished by the Body and Blood of your Son and filled with his Holy Spirit, may become one body, one spirit in Christ" (EP III).

Finally, the sacraments of initiation unfold the depths of the Lord's Prayer. "In *Baptism* and *Confirmation*, the handing on . . . of the Lord's Prayer signifies new birth into the divine life. . . . When the Church prays the Lord's Prayer, it is always the people made up of the 'new-born' who pray and obtain mercy" (CCC, 2769). In Baptism it is prayed before the altar to express "the orientation of Baptism to the Eucharist" (CCC, 1244). Its recitation at Confirmation is of "great importance . . . because it is the Spirit who prays in us and in the Spirit the Christian says, 'Abba, Father'" (OC, 13). "In the *Eucharistic liturgy* the Lord's Prayer appears as the prayer of the whole Church and there reveals its full meaning and efficacy" (CCC, 2770). Recited in the Mass after the Eucharistic Prayer and before Eucharistic Communion, it "sums up on the one hand all the petitions and intercessions expressed in the movement of the *epiclesis* [the invocation of the Holy Spirit] and, on the other hand, knocks at the door of the Banquet of the kingdom which sacramental communion anticipates" (CCC, 2770). Furthermore, its recitation in the Mass "also reveals the *eschatological* [the end times] character of its petitions . . . the time of salvation that began with the outpouring of the Holy Spirit and will be fulfilled with the Lord's return," because these petitions are fulfilled in "the mystery of salvation already accomplished, once for all, in Christ crucified and risen," and now present on the altar and received in Eucharistic Communion (CCC, 2771). "The Eucharist and the Lord's Prayer look eagerly for the Lord's return, 'until he comes'" (CCC, 2772).

St. John Paul II beautifully summarizes the sacraments of initiation as one saving event. "In the depths of eucharistic worship," he says, "we find a continual echo of the sacraments of Christian initiation: Baptism and Confirmation" (DC, 7). The echo of Baptism is heard in Eucharistic abiding: "Where better is there expressed the truth that we are not only 'called God's children' but 'that is what we are' [1 Jn 3:1] by virtue of the sacrament of Baptism, if not precisely in the fact that in the Eucharist we become partakers of the body and blood of God's only Son?" (DC, 7). The echo of being Christ's witnesses confirmed at Confirmation likewise resounds in the Eucharist: "And what predisposes us more to be 'true witnesses of Christ' [LG, 11] before the world—as we are enabled to be by the sacrament of Confirmation—than Eucharistic Communion, in which Christ bears witness to us, and we to Him?" (DC, 7). At Baptism we become God's children, at Confirmation we become Christ's witnesses, and in the Eucharist we abide in him and he abides in us.

Let us conclude with prayers of thanksgiving for the sacraments of initiation written by St. Faustina Kowalska, to whom God revealed the depths of the Divine Mercy.

> Thank You, O God, for Holy Baptism
> Which engrafted me into Your family,
> A gift great beyond all thought or expression
> Which transforms my soul.
>
> Thank You, O Holy Spirit, for the Sacrament of Confirmation,
> Which dubs me Your knight
> And gives strength to my soul at each moment,
> Protecting me from evil.

> Thank You, O Jesus, for Holy Communion
> In which You give us Yourself.
> I feel Your Heart beating within my breast
> As You cause Your divine life to unfold within me.[2]

In the sacraments of initiation God lavishes his grace on us (Eph 1:7–8), transforming us, strengthening us, and causing his very life to unfold within us. Like St. Faustina, we too give thanks to God that through Baptism, Confirmation, and Eucharist we "receive in increasing measure the treasures of divine life and advance toward the perfection of charity" (DCN) in order "to bring us the faithful of Christ, to his full stature and to enable us to carry out the mission of the entire people of God in the Church and in the world" (GICI, 2).

2. Kowalska, *Diary*, 1286. Used with permission of the Marian Fathers of the Immaculate Conception of the B.V.M.

Further Reading

Primary Sources

Benedict XVI. *God is Love (Deus Caritas Est)*. Boston: Pauline, 2005.

In part 1 the pope discusses "The Unity of Love in Creation and in Salvation History," focusing on God's love incarnate in Christ and love of God and neighbor. In part 2 he looks at the Church's exercise of charity, the relationship between charity and justice, and different aspects of charitable activity. Of particular relevance to this volume is his discussion of the Eucharist under the headings "Jesus Christ—the incarnate love of God" and "Love of God and love of neighbor."

———. *Sacrament of Charity* (*Sacramentum Caritatis*). Boston: Pauline, 2007.

A rich and comprehensive discussion of the Sacrament of the Eucharist is divided into three main sections: "The Eucharist, A Mystery to be Believed"; "The Eucharist, A Mystery to be Celebrated"; and "The Eucharist, A Mystery to be Lived." The pope also discusses the relationship of the Eucharist to each of the other sacraments and the Trinitarian dimension of the Eucharist.

———. *Verbum Domini* (*The Word of the Lord*). Boston: Pauline, 2010.

This excellent presentation of the Word of God is divided into three sections: "The God Who Speaks"; "The Word of God and the Church"; and "The Church's Mission: To Proclaim the Word of God to the World." Of particular interest in this book is the section entitled "The Liturgy: Privileged Setting for the Word of God."

Bishops' Committee on the Liturgy. *Introduction to the Order of Mass*. Pastoral Liturgy Series, vol.1. Washington, DC: United States Conference of Catholic Bishops, 2003.

This resource is a good introduction to the Eucharist. Especially relevant in this book is the section entitled "The Eucharistic Celebration and its Symbols." It is a useful resource for all catechists.

Flannery, Austin, OP, ed. *Vatican Council II: The Basic Sixteen Documents*. New ed. Collegeville, MN: The Liturgical Press, 2013.

This is the classic collection of the sixteen major documents of the Second Vatican Council.

John Paul II. *Ecclesia de Eucharistia* (*On the Eucharist in Its Relationship to the Church*). Boston: Pauline, 2003.

St. John Paul II's final encyclical in which he reflects on several aspects of the Eucharist: a mystery of faith, the causal principle of the Church, an expression of the Church's apostolicity, its relationship to ecclesial communion, the dignity of the Eucharistic celebration, and Mary as the Woman of the Eucharist.

John Paul II. *Mane Nobiscum Domine* (*Stay with Us, Lord*). in *The Litrugy Documents,* Vol. 4 (Chicago: Liturgy Training Publications, 2004).

In this brief letter introducing the Year of the Eucharist (2004–2005) the Saint discusses the Eucharist as a mystery of light, as the source and manifestation of communion, and as the principle and plan of the Church's mission.

Secondary Sources

Carstens, Christopher, and Douglas Martis. *Mystical Body Mystical Voice: Encountering Christ in the Words of the Mass*. Chicago: Liturgy Training Publications, 2011.

In addition to being an excellent resource on the Mass, part 1 is an excellent, easy-to-read overview of sacramental theology.

Corbon, Jean. *The Wellspring of Worship*. 2nd ed. Translated by Matthew J. O'Connell. San Francisco: Ignatius, 2005.

This is a classic study of the liturgy by one of the principal authors of the section on prayer in the *Catechism of the Catholic Church*. Corbon's emphasis on the role of the Holy Spirit in the liturgy is particularly illuminating.

Daniélou, Jean, SJ. *The Bible and the Liturgy*. Notre Dame, IN: Notre Dame University Press, 1956.

This is an analysis of the liturgical language of the Sacraments of Baptism, Confirmation, and the Eucharist as well as the Sabbath as explained by the Fathers of the Church based on the Sacred Scriptures and sacred Tradition. This is an excellent resource for those interested in further study of mystagogical catechesis.

Haffner, Paul. *The Sacramental Mystery*. Herefordshire: Gracewing, 2007. (Available in the United States from LTP.org)

This is one of the best introductions to sacramental theology—concise, clear, and thorough. It is an excellent reference for all catechists.

McNamara, Denis. *Catholic Church Architecture and the Spirit of the Liturgy*. Chicago: Hillenbrand Books, 2009.

This elegantly written and beautifully illustrated book offers the kind of mystagogy encouraged by Pope Benedict XVI. Part 1 addresses architectural theology, part 2 the scriptural foundations of church architecture, part 3 the classical tradition, part 4 the nature, meaning, and function of sacred images, and part 5 twentieth-century developments in church architecture. This is a fine resource for understanding how the church and its furnishings are "signs and symbols of heavenly realities" (SC, 122) and contribute to our participation in the liturgy.

Ratzinger, Joseph. *The Spirit of the Liturgy.* San Francisco: Ignatius, 2000.

This is a rich biblical, theological, and sacramental study of the liturgy. It includes discussions of the role of the Old Testament in the formation of the liturgy, the importance of sacred buildings and sacred time, sacred images and music, liturgy as rite, and the body and liturgy. This should be in the library of anyone interested in a deeper understanding of the liturgy.

Walsh, Liam G., OP. *Sacraments of Initiation: A Theology of Life, Word, and Rite.* 2nd ed. Chicago: Hillenbrand Books, 2011.

Fr. Walsh presents a scholarly treatment of the sacraments of initiation, addressing both the history and theology of the Baptism, Confirmation, and the Eucharist. This is an excellent resource for catechists.

Yarnold, Edward, SJ. *The Awe-Inspiring Rites of Initiation: The Origins of the RCIA.* 2nd ed. Collegeville, MN: The Liturgical Press, 1994.

This book contains the mystagogical homilies of four early Church Fathers: St. Cyril of Jerusalem, St. Ambrose, St. John Chrysostom, and Theodore of Mopsuestia. These homilies are a treasure trove of images and insights into the early rites and meaning of the sacraments of initiation.

Index